creative ESSENTIALS

FARAH ABUSHWESHA

ROCLIFFE NOTES

A PROFESSIONAL APPROACH FOR SCREENWRITERS & WRITER-DIRECTORS

creative ESSENTIALS

First published in 2014 by Kamera Books,
an imprint of Oldcastle Books
PO Box 394, Harpenden, Herts, AL5 1XJ
kamerabooks.com

Copyright © Farah Abushwesha 2014
Series Editor: Hannah Patterson
Editor: Anne Hudson

978-1-84344-427-5 (Print)
978-1-84344-428-2 (epub)

10

Typeset by Elsa Mathern in DIN and Univers 9 pt
Printed in Great Britain by Severn, Gloucester

ACKNOWLEDGEMENTS

So many people helped with this book with suggestions and encouragement, particularly my wonderful friends who spurred me on. A special thanks for their never-ceasing support over many years to Louisa Hopkins, Antonio Mendez, my sister, Yasmin, my dad, and two amazing women – my mother, Orla Woods, and my grandmother, Aine Woods. Thanks to my diligent researchers and transcribers Hope Kemp, Stephen Casey, Jessica Ostley and Jessica Reid; to Susan Jacobson, Nicola Woods and Stephany Ungless who at various points read or proofread variations of this book; to those who gave great suggestions and leads for contributors: Clare Bateman-King, Mariayah Kaderbhai, Kam Kandola-Flynn, Camille Gatin, Andrea Cornwell, Kristen O'Brien, Kate Kinninmont, Wendy Mitchell and so many receptive agents; my agent, Susan Smith, my commissioning editor, Hannah Patterson, and my editor, Anne Hudson, for making a goal a reality. And lastly the very generous contributors!

CONTENTS

03

04

05

06

07

12

13

14

15

CONTRIBUTORS

This book would not exist without the generosity and patience of these amazing contributors:

ALAN FRIEL: Writer-Director (Commercial Director & Emerging Film-maker)

ALAN MCKENNA: Writer-Producer (*Pressure, Slammer*), Actor (*Belle, Happy Valley, The ABCs of Death 2*)

ALEX COOK: Senior Manager, Talent Development, British Academy of Film and Television Arts

ALEXANDRA ARLANGO: Development Producer, Cowboy Films & Curator of the Brit List (*The Duchess, Cheerful Weather for the Wedding, Severance*)

ALEXANDRA BOYD: Actress (*Mr Holland's Opus, Titanic, Coronation Street*), Writer-Director (*Boxer on the Wilderness, Widow's Walk*)

ALISON MILLAR: Producer-Director (*The Disappeared, The Shame of the Catholic Church, The Father, the Son & the Housekeeper*)

AMANDA BERRY OBE: BAFTA Chief Executive

AMIT KUMAR: Writer-Director (*Monsoon Shootout, The Bypass*)

ANDREA CORNWELL: Producer (*Suite Française, Last Days on Mars, Micro Men*)

ANDREA HUBERT: Writer

ANDREW NEWMAN: Producer & Chief Executive, Objective

ANGELINE BALL: Actor (*Shameless, The General, The Commitments*)

ANNA EMERSON: Writer & Performer (*Mission Improbable* [Series 1 & 2], *Off Their Rockers* [Series 2])

ANNE HOGBEN: Deputy General Secretary of the Writers' Guild of Great Britain

ANNE-MARIE DRAYCOTT: Writer

ARAB NASSER AND TARZAN NASSER: Writer-Directors – Nominated for a Short Film Palme D'Or (Cannes 2013)

ASIF KAPADIA: Writer-Director (*Senna*, *Far North*, *The Warrior*)

BEN STEPHENSON: Controller of Drama Commissioning, BBC (*The Great Train Robbery*, *Top of the Lake*, *Happy Valley*, *The Honourable Woman*)

BERTRAND FAIVRE: Producer (more than 30 films including *Ratcatcher*, *The Warrior*, *Le Week-End*, *A Little Chaos*)

BOB BALABAN: Producer (*Gosford Park*), Director (*Bernard and Doris*, *Parents*), Actor (*Monuments Men*, *Moonrise Kingdom*, *Deconstructing Harry*)

BRONA C TITLEY: Actor & Writer (*Off Their Rockers*, *50 Kisses*, *Narcopolis*, *How To Lose Friends and Alienate People*)

CAMILLE GATIN: Producer (*Shadow Dancer*, *Endeavour*, *Anthony*)

CAT VILLIERS: Producer (*The Narrow Frame of Midnight*, *The Proposition*, *No Man's Land*, *Ivansxtc*)

CATHERINE WILLIS: Casting Director

CHARITY TRIMM: Writer

CHARLES GANT: Film Journalist

CHARLES STEEL: Producer, Cowboy Films (*The Last King of Scotland*, *Marley*, *Top Boy*, *Black Sea*)

CHARLOTTE KNIGHT: Literary Agent

CHRIS SPARLING: Writer (*Buried*, *Sea of Trees*, *ATM*), Director, Screenwriter & Co-Producer (*The Atticus Institute*)

CHRIS SUSSMAN: Commissioning Editor, BBC Comedy (*Bad Education*, *Cuckoo*, *Rev*, *Him & Her*, *People Just Do Nothing*)

CHRISTIAN MANLEY: Writer

CHRISTIANA BROCKBANK: Writer

CHRISTINA PICKWORTH: Literary Agent

CHRISTINE LANGAN: Head of BBC Films & Producer (*The Queen*, *Saving Mr Banks*, *We Need To Talk About Kevin*)

CHRISTOPHER GRANIER-DEFERRE: Producer (*Gone Too Far*, *Dirty Weekend*)

CLAIRE WILSON: Writer (*Partners in Crime*, Agatha Christie adaptation, BBC1)

CLEONE CLARKE: Associate Producer, Trademark Films

CONOR BARRY: Producer (*Pilgrimage*, *You're Ugly Too*, *Love Eternal*, *Savage*)

DAN HUBBARD: Casting Director

DANNY BROCKLEHURST: Writer (*The Driver*, *Exile*, *Shameless*, *Clocking Off*, *Sorted*)

DANNY HUSTON: Actor (*American Horror Story*, *X Men*, *The Proposition*, *21 Grams*)

DAVID CHIKWE: Creative Director, Blacklisted Films & Writer (*Missing*, *Eve*)

DAVID FLYNN: Chief Creative Officer, Endemol UK; Executive Producer (*The Million Pound Drop*, *Pointless*, *The Singer Takes It All*, *The Bank Job*, *Ejector Seat*)

DAVID FREEDMAN: Writer-Director (*Santa's Apprentice 2*, *The Magic Snowflake* [feature], *Rubi Gets It Right* [series]), Series Director (*Groove High*, *King Arthur's Disasters*)

DAVID PARFITT: Producer (*The Wipers Times*, *Parade's End*, *My Week with Marilyn*, *Shakespeare in Love*, *The Madness of King George*)

DAVID SIMPATICO: Writer (*Zombie Hideaway* [episodic video], *Wish Fulfillment* [short film], *The Screams of Kitty Genovese* [music drama], *The Life and Death(s) of Alan Turing* [opera], *Disney's High School Musical* [stage musical])

DESTINY EKARAGHA: Director (*Gone Too Far!*), Writer-Director (*Tight Jeans*, *The Park*)

15

DICTYNNA HOOD: Writer-Director (*Wreckers, The Other Man, Journey Man*)

EDWARD BAKER-DULY: Actor (NBC's *The Blacklist*, USA Network's *Royal Pains, Downton Abbey, Micro Men*)

EMMA NORTON: Head of Development, Element Pictures (*What Richard Did, Frank, Glassland*)

EOIN ROGERS: Writer

GABRIEL SILVER: Development & Executive Producer (*Life on Mars, Spooks, Poirot, Strike Back, DCI Banks*)

GARETH EDWARDS: Producer (*That Mitchell and Webb Look, Spaced, Still Open All Hours, Dead Ringers, The Bleak Old Shop of Stuff*)

GLENN MONTGOMERY: Writer (*Mammal, The Other Side of Sleep*)

GRAINNE HUMPHREYS: Festival Director, Jameson Dublin International Film Festival

GUY HIBBERT: Writer (*One Child, Blood & Oil, Five Minutes of Heaven, Omagh*)

HOPE DICKSON LEACH: Writer-Director (*The Dawn Chorus, Morning Echo, Cavities*)

IVANA MACKINNON: Producer & Script Editor (*The Scouting Book for Boys, War Book, Slumdog Millionaire, The Descent*)

JACK THORNE: Writer (*The Scouting Book for Boys, War Book, This is England '86, '88 & '90, The Fades, Glue*)

JAMES DORMER: Writer-Exec Producer (*Spooks, Wallander, Strike Back, The Holding, Outcast*)

JEAN KITSON: Literary Agent

JIM UHLS: Writer (*Fight Club, Jumper, Semper Fi*)

JOHN MADDEN: Director (*Best Exotic Marigold Hotel, Masters of Sex, The Debt, Shakespeare in Love, Mrs Brown*)

JOHN YORKE: Managing Director, Company Pictures (*Shameless, Life on Mars, Sex Traffic, The Street, Waterloo Road*)

JON CROKER: Writer (*Woman in Black: Angel of Death, Paddington, In Fear, Desert Dancer*)

JONATHAN KINNERSLEY: Literary Agent

JOSH APPIGNANESI: Writer-Director (*Song Of Songs, The Infidel*)

JULIETTE TOWHIDI: Writer (*Calendar Girls, Death Comes to Pemberley, Love Rosie, Testament of Youth*)

JUSTIN TREFGARNE: Writer-Director (*Narcopolis, Black Rabbit Summer, Desire, Leyman's Curse*)

KAHLEEN CRAWFORD: Casting Director

KATE ASHFIELD: Actress-Writer (*Secrets & Lies, Line of Duty, Nymphomaniac: Vol II, Byzantium, Shaun of the Dead*)

KATE LEYS: Script Editor

KATE OGBORN: Producer, Fly Film (*Hockney, The Spirit of '45, The Deep Blue Sea, The Unloved, Under the Skin*)

KATE ROWLAND: Creative Director for New Writing at the BBC

KATIE GOODSON-THOMAS: Director of Production & Acquisition for Fox Searchlight-Ingenious & Producer (*Shadow Dancer, A Single Shot, Millions*)

KATIE WILLIAMS: Literary Agent

KAYLEIGH LLEWELLEYN: Writer (*Stella, Here Be Dragons, The Cariad Show, Half a Cuppa Tea, Bampy*)

KERRY APPLEYARD: Co-Executive Producer (*Orphan Black*), Producer (*Hustle, M.I. High*)

KEVIN CECIL: Writer-Producer (*Veep, Gnomeo & Juliet, Black Books, Hyperdrive, The Great Outdoors*)

KIRSTEN SHERIDAN: Writer-Director (*Disco Pigs, In America, August Rush, Dollhouse*)

LAURIE COOK: Producer (*Hangar 10, Outpost 37, Pressure, Honour*)

LAWRENCE COCHRAN: Former Development Editor for BBC Independent Drama

LEE ARONSOHN: Writer-Producer (*Two and a Half Men, The Big Bang Theory, Cybill, Murphy Brown*)

LEVI DAVID ADDAI: Writer (*Youngers, My Murder, Coming Up*)

LIAM FOLEY: Writer & Former Development Executive at Working Title

LIZZIE BATES: Writer & Performer (*Mission Improbable* [Series 1 & 2], *Off Their Rockers* [Series 2])

LUCY CLARKE: Writer (*News Quiz, Fabulous, Horrible Histories, Never Mind the Buzzcocks*)

MALCOLM CAMPBELL: Writer (*What Richard Did, Skins, Shameless*)

MANJINDER VIRK: Actress (*Britz, The Arbor, History's Future*), Writer-Director (*Forgive, Out of Darkness*)

MARC EVANS: Writer-Director (*Patagonia, My Little Eye, Snowcake*)

MARGOT GAVAN DUFFY: Producer (*This Is Jinsy, Little Crackers, Spy, The Vicar of Dibley, How Do You Want Me?*)

MARNIE DICKENS: Writer (*Ripper Street, The Musketeers, Hollyoaks*)

MASOUD AMRALLA AL ALI: Artistic Director of the Dubai International Film Festival & Director of the Festival in the Gulf

MATTHEW BARRY: Writer (*EastEnders, Death in Paradise, Stella, Casualty, Here Be Dragons*)

MATTHEW BATES: Literary Agent

MATTHEW DENCH: Literary Agent

MIA BAYS: Creative Producer (*Lilting, Ill Manors, Shifty*), Producer (Oscar-winning *Six Shooter*, BAFTA-nominated *Scott Walker: 30 Century Man*)

MICHAEL KUHN: Producer (*Suite Française, The Duchess*), Executive Producer (*Being John Malkovich*), Big Cheese (*Four Weddings and a Funeral*)

MIRANDA BOWEN: Writer-Director (*Gozo, Women in Love, Cast Offs*)

MOIRA BUFFINI: Writer (*Byzantium, Jane Eyre, Tamara Drewe, Handbagged*)

MUSTAPHA KSEIBATI: Writer-Director (*Big Tingz, Skateboards and Spandex, Painkiller, Mohammed*)

NIK POWELL: Producer (*The Crying Game, Little Voice*), Director of the National Film & Television School

NORMAN NORTH: Literary Agent

OL PARKER: Writer (*The Best Exotic Marigold Hotel, The Second Best Exotic Marigold Hotel*), Writer-Director (*Imagine Me and You, Now Is Good*)

PAUL ANDREW WILLIAMS: Writer-Director (*London to Brighton*, *The Cottage*, *Song for Marion*)

PAULA MILNE: Writer (*The Virgin Queen*, *Endgame*, *Small Island*, *White Heat*, *The Politician's Husband*)

PETER HARNESS: Writer (*Doctor Who*, *Jonathan Strange and Mr Norrell*, *Wallander*)

PETER KOSMINSKY: Writer-Director (*The Promise*), Director (*Wolf Hall*, *No Child of Mine*, *White Oleander*)

PHIL ILSON: Festival Programmer, BFI – Shorts; Festival Director, London Short Film Festival

POLLY STOKES: Senior Development Editor, Film4 & Producer (*For Those in Peril*)

REBECCA DALY: Writer-Director (*Mammal*, *The Other Side of Sleep*)

REBECCA O'BRIEN: Producer (*Jimmy's Hall*, *The Spirit of '45*, *The Angel's Share*, *Looking for Eric*, *The Wind That Shakes the Barley*)

RICHARD COOKSON: Head of Development, Lovely Day & Script Editor (*Doctor Who*, *Peaky Blinders*, *Ripper Street*, *The Fades*)

RICHARD EYRE: Director (*The Hollow Crown*, *Notes on a Scandal*, *Iris*)

ROB BROWN: Writer-Director (*Sixteen*)

ROBIN GUTCH: Producer (*'71*, *Kill List*, *Hunger*)

RON SCALPELLO: Writer-Director (*Offender*, *Pressure*)

ROWAN ATHALE: Writer-Director (*The Rise* aka *Wasteland*)

SALLY EL HOSAINI: Writer-Director (*My Brother The Devil*, *Babylon*, *Henna Night*)

SAM WASHINGTON: Writer-Director, Commercials Director

SARAH GAVRON: Director (*Brick Lane*, *Suffragette*)

SASKIA SCHUSTER: Commissioning Editor (*Little Crackers*, *The Kumars*, *Psychobitches*)

SAUL DIBB: Writer-Director (*Suite Française*, *The Duchess*, *Bullet Boy*)

SEAN GASCOINE: Literary Agent

SERENA BOWMAN: Head of Development, Company Pictures (*Wild at Heart*)

SHANE ALLEN: Controller Comedy Commissioning, BBC (*Not Going Out, Mrs Brown's Boys, Miranda*), Head of Comedy, Channel 4 (*Black Mirror, Peep Show, The IT Crowd, Derek*)

SIMON CHINN: Producer (*Man on Wire, Searching for Sugar Man, The Green Prince, Project Nim*)

SIMON HEATH: Producer & Creative Director, World Productions (*Line of Duty, The Great Train Robbery, United, The Fear, Hancock & Joan*)

STEPHEN FINGLETON: Writer-Director (*The Survivalist*)

STEWART THOMSON: Writer (*Parliamo Glasgow*)

SUSAN HOGG: Senior Executive Producer, BBC productions (*The Fades, Five Daughters, The C Word, Lark Rise to Candleford, Waking the Dead*)

SUSAN JACOBSON: Producer-Director (*The Holding, Pulp: A Film About Life, Death & Supermarkets, One Hundredth of a Second*)

SUSIE CONKLIN: Writer & Script Editor (*The Musketeers, Cranford, State of Play, Pride & Prejudice*)

TERENCE GRAY: Founder & Executive Director, New York Television Festival

TINA GHARAVI: Writer-Director-Producer, Bridge + Tunnel Productions (UK/FR) (*Mother/Country, I Am Nasrine, The Good Iranian, From the Plantation to the Penitentiary*)

TONY COOKE: Writer (*The Armstrong & Miller Show, Danger Mouse, Dead Ringers, Once Upon a Crime, The Legend of Dick and Dom*)

TONY GRISONI: Writer-Director (*Fear & Loathing In Las Vegas, In This World, Brothers of the Head, The Red Riding Trilogy, Southcliffe*)

TONY JORDAN: Writer & Managing Director, Red Planet Pictures (*Hustle, Life on Mars*)

WENDY MITCHELL: Editor of Screen International

WHY I LOVE WRITING

When I just write, I lose myself; any feeling of loneliness or isolation dissipates. Writing has always created a safe space for me to be vulnerable or vindicated. What I first choose to commit to paper, or not, becomes a self-centred act, with me deciding what stays and what goes! Writing for me also carries a certain level of guilt because I can and don't enough. My love of writing and storytelling stems from a nightly childhood ritual of bedtime stories with my mother reading *Wind in the Willows*, *Alice in Wonderland* or an Irish folk tale, followed by my father telling me an Arabic myth or one of his short stories like the one about the 'Walkie Talkie Hedgehog', about a prophetic hedgehog who predicted an earthquake. My early school years were spent in Libya, at a bilingual school in Tripoli where the emphasis was on learning through the spoken word using storytelling, games and word competitions in both Arabic and English. Holidays in Ireland in the 1970s would be filled with poetry readings and book launches with my parents and their poet and artist friends.

In the autumn of 1979, my life changed overnight when I was abruptly sent to live in Ireland with my Irish grandparents following my father's house arrest in Libya by the Gadaffi regime. As a bilingual, tanned, parentless seven-year-old, I was, by Irish standards, considered illiterate by my new educators as there was no place for Arabic in my new school. I lacked what they felt were the basic skills of writing in English. Missing my parents terribly, I longed to reach out and write to them but the best I could muster were the letters 'M' for mother, 'D' for Dada and 'F' for Farah. The school, concerned that my lack of literacy skills would slow down the class, wanted to put me back to infants. However, my grandmother, a teacher, convinced them that she would be able to bring my reading and writing to the level of my peers within two months.

Most children went out to play after school but my evenings were spent transcribing large passages of Enid Blyton into my jotter. If I made a mistake I had to start again. My grandmother made me break down words by syllables and showed me how to create the singular and plural of words. The house was wallpapered with posters containing words so that I never stopped learning. I was as determined as she was and my goal was to be able to eventually write a fully formed letter to my parents. I saw writing to them as a way of reaching out, but I couldn't spell or write in English or Arabic. True to her word, however, within two months Granny had my reading and writing up to the required standard.

That first letter to my parents, painstakingly composed, went through three or four drafts until it was perfect, and I still recall the taste of the stamp when it was finally ready to send. Letters became our lifeline, keeping them close to me, and me them. A year would pass before I saw my mother again, when she returned to Ireland without my father, who was unable to get an exit visa from the Libyan authorities. She later told me that, during that year apart, she lived for the mail, and how hard she found it to even look at other people's children. During the subsequent years, fears for my father's safety left me terrified that any careless word might have an adverse effect on his security, so I would read his short stories again and again but never utter a word about the estrangement. We'd write stories – that's how we kept the bond.

It was 30 years before it was safe for me to return to Libya, after the fall of Gadaffi. When the revolution ended in 2011, I returned to Libya after three decades away. I used my writing skills to write about the human side of Libya and what had happened to our family at the hands of the regime in those early years, and it felt truly liberating. The more I wrote, the more the heavy burden of the conspiracy of silence afflicting our family was lifted. Before, I had been afraid to say what had happened, and this had a ripple effect throughout my family – not just for me but for my mother, father and sister.

I have so much to thank my grandmother for, as well as admiration for her patience and tenacity; she gave me a great gift – a love and appreciation of writing and reading. To this day, I try not to send out the first draft of anything for fear of flaws. Those early days made writing my friend, my saviour and my companion, but I also understood its power as I saw what being a writer did to my father and my family structure. Freedom of expression is something to be valued.

The New Writing Forums began as a group of actors and writers getting together to read scripts above a pub in North London. Over time, I invited industry guests to give feedback and they came. Today the forums are run in partnership with BAFTA and are a recognised international platform for new writing. At their heart they remain an opportunity for novice writers to receive informal advice and feedback from industry experts happy to share their humble beginnings and chat over a pint. This remains an integral part of the event, although the 'pub' is now the BAFTA bar.

When I started trying to work in the film industry, I would constantly puzzle about how to break in. It seemed so hard. Was there a big secret? Was forging a career in this industry impossible? It was only by approaching people, as a new filmmaker, and asking them that I discovered I was looking at it in all the wrong ways – it wasn't impossible; in fact, the possibilities were endless if you sought them out. My aim with this book is to demystify the process by tapping into the experiences of those in the know. I didn't want to create a series of case studies, but a variety of perspectives on the same topic that differ and repeat. Ultimately it's up to the reader to decide which perspectives resonate and which don't. The intention is to make the reader feel like they're part of the conversation, or at least eavesdropping on one.

People will help you because most have a passion for the work and want to support those trying to make their way. As Danny Brocklehurst says, 'If someone asks, I don't want to be the lad that pulled the ladder up behind them. Paul Abbott helped me, and you want to help and show encouragement to new talent and to nurture it.'

Since writing the book, several of the contributors have changed jobs. One tragic note is my interview with Simon Chinn, which reflects on Malik Bendjelloul's approach to *Searching for Sugar Man*, and was conducted prior to Malik's untimely death. This industry, whatever role you take, can be all-consuming; you need stamina and to know when to walk away from a project. Interviewing these wonderful writers, directors, producers and industry professionals has been an honour, their patience and generosity truly appreciated. I've aimed for diverse contributors, from Oscar and BAFTA winners to noted emerging talent. I chose to get a cross-section of people from the industry, from those who deal with a script early in its cycle, to contributions from actors, casting directors and decision makers. Some topics will feel more or less relevant to those who are solely writers, as opposed to writer-directors, but I have included as many of the topics as I could that I've been asked about, or heard being asked about, in the forums. The biggest thing that all the contributors share is that they love what they do, are all human (yes, it's true), and that none of them ever stops worrying about the work or wanting to create it.

You only need one person to say yes to you, to believe in you to drive you forward. My grandmother was my champion in my early years, and that's what each contributor to this book is: a champion, a mentor, and a supporter of new talent. We can all write or point a camera at things but, ultimately, it's what we do with it that counts, as well as the fact that you don't need permission to do it to begin with. This industry isn't inaccessible, as this compendium illustrates – it's just that there's no single pathway in.

Farah
x

WHAT IS THE JOB OF A WRITER?

I grew up watching my father be utterly consumed by writing for days on end, without rest, until he would collapse, but he lived to write and create and still does. Being a writer means something different to each of us. So how do you define the job and what do writers feel about what they do?

MOIRA BUFFINI: I love it. I love it. I escape into my work. There are times when it goes wrong and it can be extremely difficult but if you choose who you work with carefully and pick the projects that you are in tune with (which, as you go on, you get more and more opportunity to do), then this is a wonderful job. It's a privilege. You sit with your cup of tea in the morning and three hours pass before you know where you are. You completely immerse yourself in another world and in the experience of other people. That is writing.

LEE ARONSOHN: I hate writing. But writing has turned out to be the one thing I can do which people will pay me to do which doesn't involve anal sex.

OL PARKER: It's brilliant and I recommend it to absolutely everybody. It's a special way to have a life, meet people. How I describe it to people is that I write films, most of which don't happen. One of the weird things about the gig is that so much of what you do is failing upwards. I have friends who are 40 and they've made a living writing screenplays, yet have never had a produced credit or seen their name on the screen. It's an extraordinary thing. I had a seven-year period where I was writing films for Tom Hanks, for Jonathan Demme (who made *Silence of the Lambs*), and it was a heavy, high-powered and exciting time. I was flying to Los Angeles and whatnot, but I had absolutely nothing to show for it. I had money, but nothing was actually being made. It was great fun and completely unsuccessful. It became increasingly embarrassing seeing family and friends and having them ask, 'Anything?' It's a weird part of the job that rejection and failure are built into it.

JAMES DORMER: I make stuff up.

KEVIN CECIL: I am a scriptwriter, a script editor and a producer. As a writer, I work in a partnership with Andy Riley. What we do is quite varied. It might mean creating shows, collaborating with talent on a show for them or being part of a team as we are for *Veep*. We used to work on chat shows and sketch shows but these days almost all of what we do is narrative. Occasionally we still get to write sketches – it's like a treat.

PETER HARNESS: I love it and it's part of me. I have a compulsion and a need to do it. My relation to it changes every day and very often I feel like stopping doing it entirely and going and doing something else. Sometimes I feel it's very easy and I'm on top of the world, though sometimes it feels like the hardest thing that I could ever dream of doing. I've got a mercurial relationship to it. I think storytelling and coming up with stories and providing things to entertain and move people is a very worthwhile thing. It's probably worth all the stress and ups and downs.

KATE ASHFIELD: I would answer this question differently every day. I love it and hate it at the same time. Writing is so creative, just as acting is great when you have a great role. They can be the best jobs and the most fun. They are both also demeaning and humiliating and really hard ways to earn a living!

TINA GHARAVI: Being a writer (or creative person) is like being a monk in a monastery. One works in the shadows and entirely devotes one's life to its pursuits. That's okay, because it's almost Byzantine, the film industry... so perhaps it's all too appropriate. My role is to make sense of the chaos of the world around and give the audience a cathartic experience. To be a mirror of myself and the world. This is the primary reason for writing and creating. For me, much of this is about confronting mortality and the miracle of being alive... and that is something quasi-spiritual – though those words do make me shudder!

GUY HIBBERT: I tell stories.

JACK THORNE: It's the greatest job in the world; I get to imagine things for a living. And the difference between my world and the world of a novelist, say, is that I get to imagine things *with other people* for a living.

JIM UHLS: Making up and telling stories via the behaviour of characters.

LEVI DAVID ADDAI: It's a mad, crazy job. You spend so much time in your head thinking, talking to yourself, talking to your characters, creating their lives and journeys. It's so taxing. And when it comes to production and there are still re-drafts or amendments to deliver, alongside watching castings or daily rushes, by the end of the day my brain is tired. It's a muscle constantly being used and I can't absorb anything else. I have always done it – telling stories and characters. Even as a child I did it with my toys. I still have that youthful fun with it, I reach for the blank page to go on an adventure.

PAULA MILNE: First of all, I love it. I discovered myself through my work. I discovered who I was and what I cared about; I became political through it to a certain extent and I love the process of it. Being a painter before helped because I already had a lot of self-discipline. I started writing after I had children. I've had five children and I've had people asking me 'Do you feel guilty leaving your children to

27

write?' and I say no, I feel guilty leaving the scripts to go back to the children. I've absolutely no guilt about hiring people to look after my children. You can't have your cake and then decide you feel bad about it. When I started writing, I'm not sure I regarded it as the golden age of TV but there was a sense that TV was the theatre of the people, and that was very exciting. It was saying things about the society we live in to people who didn't necessarily have access to this in any other form in terms of literature or theatre, etc. So I regarded it as an art form really, having started out as a painter.

MALCOLM CAMPBELL: I've finally learned to accept it as a real job (sometimes I tell my family what I do and they still don't understand; they say 'So, is it a documentary?'). I suppose I tell stories with pictures and words. I don't do any other kind of writing. It's about telling stories with economy, a bit of flair and moving things along. I try to entertain but also find the truth in everyday life.

MARNIE DICKENS: Being a writer can be incredible. You get to imagine people, imagine what they say, and then hopefully watch ones that come to life. If you are working with people you like and trust then it's the best job in the world.

JON CROKER: I love what I do for a living. I write an idea into a format that can be used by a director, cast and crew to make into a film.

TONY GRISONI: My job is to make films. That's what I'm thinking of when I'm writing. I'm thinking about trying to get a film made that will excite or surprise me.

WHAT IS THE JOB OF DIRECTOR OR WRITER-DIRECTOR?

A (good) few years ago, I tried my hand at directing, but realised it wasn't for me. Perhaps it was a lack of confidence; perhaps if I'd understood or researched more about what it was before I tried, I would have pursued it in a different way. My shorts had a great unifying effect upon my family, one of them having been based on my dad's short story, *A Blind Arab in a London Pub*, which my mother had translated into English. It gave us back a sense of pride and family union we'd lost decades before. In my heart, however, I enjoy writing and producing more – making it happen. My favourite definition of what a director does is by Roland Joffe, director of *The Killing Fields*, who stated that 'being a director is like playing on a multilayered, multidimensional chessboard, except that the chess pieces decide to move themselves.'

SARAH GAVRON: It's not like a job. People do it because they are passionate about film.

STEPHEN FINGLETON: I am a professional fantasist aided and abetted by a merry band of conjurers, magicians, and sleight-of-hand experts. Together we seek to suspend the audience's disbelief and take them to places they want to go to but daren't in their everyday lives.

KIRSTEN SHERIDAN: I describe it as kind of a form of therapy. The more you challenge yourself and dig down deep into your own psyche, the more you realise you are just writing the same story over and over again on some personal level. If you want to then change that, you have to be very self-aware in order to know exactly why you're writing things, what they're about and what they mean to you. I do think art is incredibly important but sometimes I think of people in the world who are actually building things, helping people and

29

making a career, not for monetary gain but for the betterment of society, and I wonder whether my energies would be better spent. In this industry, you can write something and it can just go into the ether and never be realised.

MANJINDER VIRK: Both writing and directing come from a need and deep desire to tell the story. I start with a personal attachment to the writing and the story I'm trying to tell and then move on from that stage into something more detached and researched.

HOPE DICKSON LEACH: At my film school graduation the writer Richard Ford said that being an artist isn't like being a carpenter. No one needs what you make in the way that they need a chair. You, the artist, have to make your work necessary and work out what it is that you are making. I loved that. Generally it's very lonely, very hard, and really only to be done by people who really can't do anything else – i.e. they HAVE to do it. If you think you can do something else, then you're better off doing that.

REBECCA DALY: The biggest elements of my job are communication and filtration. Communicating my ideas, my vision, to everybody I'm working with and obviously the audience. Then filtering ideas is also a big part, which happens at every stage: the writing, shooting, editing, the whole way through. It's a constant filtration process of the ideas in my head, and those of the people I collaborate with, testing what works and what doesn't, what fits the overall shape, etc. I love it. I feel privileged to be able to do it and to make a living out of it. I'm very lucky.

MIRANDA BOWEN: It's a curious job and one that I attempt to justify continually. I feel that the world would probably survive without film and TV but it would definitely be a poorer place for it. Narrative storytelling is something that is endemic to every culture in the world and we learn about ourselves through reflected histories. Quality TV and film allow us to experience cultures, people and situations that we might not ordinarily come into contact with. At its best good TV and film can expand our minds and ignite empathy where none may have previously existed. At its worst it can do exactly the opposite.

ROB BROWN: I'm a bit dubious sometimes about calling what I do a job! I felt more legitimate calling myself a director once I made a feature, but I've lived with people who do sensible jobs and my friends have quite serious jobs outside the film industry as well, so it's sometimes strange telling them what I've been doing on a day-to-day basis. If I compared the amount of time I spend writing emails and having Skype calls to the amount of time that I spend writing and directing it would probably depress me. I never would have guessed when starting out how uncreative this job and industry can be sometimes!

RON SCALPELLO: It's a demanding career but it's so rewarding. If you think you want to do it because it might be either cool or interesting, if you're half-hearted about it, I don't know if you'll be successful. It's one of those careers that will consume you totally, every day of the week. I can't think of anything else I'd rather do and it's so clearly part of who I am as a person, as a man. To live without making films or TV would be quite a realignment of my own identity.

SALLY EL HOSAINI: I'm in a really privileged position, where I'm managing to get people to give me money to make things up. That's what I do. Although what I've discovered is that when you're a writer-director you spend more time writing than directing. Especially when you're generating your own material. It's cyclical, but when you do the maths you realise that more hours go into writing than hours spent on set. But I don't prefer one stage to the other. They are inextricably connected and two parts of one process. I love what I do and feel really blessed to be able to get up each morning and work at what I'm best at.

SAM WASHINGTON: It's the best job in the world. But it isn't easy. If it was, everyone would be doing it.

ROWAN ATHALE: I would describe writing and directing feature films as the greatest job in the world and I am exceptionally fortunate to be doing it. I know that sounds like a beauty-pageant answer, but I find it's accurate. There are professions of far greater importance: medicine, teaching, policing. I don't build houses for people to live in, and I don't work in agriculture, so I don't feed anybody either. Filmmaking doesn't represent a fundamental, basic need of society. It represents an interest, a hobby or, in the case of the cinephile, a passion. Watching films was, and remains, a defining passion of my own life. And I get to make them for a living. So I don't *think*, I *know*, I'm exceptionally fortunate.

JUSTIN TREFGARNE: Outside of family, this job is everything for me. I am very lucky to be in this position where you are asking me to talk about something I love, which also happens to be my career. I first started thinking about how to make films over 30 years ago and here I am with my first feature under my belt. That gives you some idea of how much of my life I have spent devoted to this in one way or another.

JOSH APPIGNANESI: Being a writer and director in theory is having a Stalinist command of every variable, followed by the Palme d'Or. That's in theory. In practice the disadvantages are clearer to me: you're not so straightforwardly a commercial gun-for-hire as a plain writer or plain director, you're not a clear entity that can be brought on as one element amongst several in the 'package' when producers are putting together a commercial film. It's basically twice as hard to get your own original material out there as both writer and director.

MUSTAPHA KSEIBATI: Steven Spielberg put it best when he said he dreams for a living. I also subscribe to the saying, 'Choose a job you love, and you never have to work a day in your life.' Although some would say I work constantly, I see my work as my life, so don't view it like that.

DICTYNNA HOOD: It's 'total'. Very all-consuming, part of life, not separate from it.

WHAT DOES A DIRECTOR DO?

So how does a director formulate a vision for the project? What *is* the job of directing?

SARAH GAVRON: I am still learning. I have to connect with the material on an emotional level. Finding the right people to work with is essential. The old adage about the importance of casting is right... Understanding storytelling is vital... I learn most about storytelling in the edit.

KIRSTEN SHERIDAN: My directing process is quite specific. I work with actors and get to know them really, really well, probably too well for their liking. With every actor I've worked with, I want to work with them again. If an actor continues to work and grow, learning something about themselves and revealing it (which is an incredibly vulnerable and scary human place to be), then they're infinitely fascinating. Actors have the worst job of everyone. Most of the time, their job relies on someone else telling them what they can and can't do.

TINA GHARAVI: As a director, I am interested in finding the truth of that moment on set with the actors and the crew. Yes, the crew have to find it too. They are 'writers' as well. I don't think writing ever stops... and ultimately it's for the editor, the film's final composer, to finish the score.

REBECCA DALY: I feel particularly personal about the work; I've often spent years writing it, I feel I know it very intimately, I feel very personally connected to it. I've never directed something I haven't written. It's not to say that my work is in any way autobiographical, but I feel very strongly about it. It does become necessary at times to step outside of it, though. To be creative, you have to go with your instincts and the flow of the project, yet every once in a while

33

it's useful to step away from that and try to put on an outside pair of eyes. Obviously I have other people to act in this way at every stage too: my editor, producers, DOP and my co-writer... strike a balance there between creativity and at least an attempt at objectivity.

STEPHEN FINGLETON: When directing, I place a big emphasis on preparation and establishing the key values of what we want to make, which allows people to tailor their work in a personal fashion that works into the whole. In post-production I work very closely with my editor, Mark Towns, who will come with a fresh eye to the material and a different sensibility, and we find something that appeals to both of us. We show it to audiences – much like at script stage – and the process reaches full circle.

MIRANDA BOWEN: Directing is finding the best possible visual language to bring the story to life. That means casting well and choosing your crew carefully as well as really trying to get under the skin of the script, working out the subtexts and how they might be visually or aurally iterated. Then, from there on in, every decision you make should somehow work towards emboldening the story and characters sufficiently to make something credible, visceral and vital.

SUSAN JACOBSON: Directing is the externalisation of the world and essentially rewriting it to work on the screen rather than on the page. Directing is such a vast entity. It's wonderful and dynamic and fascinating. You're coming always from the viewpoint of the story and what you are really trying to say with this story. It's important to keep a strong vision in mind, but also to be flexible, as filmmaking is such a variable beast that you have to be able to adapt quickly and make things work.

WHAT DO PRODUCERS DO?

I'd be rich if I had a pound for every time I'm asked this, and it's hard to quantify. When I try to explain to people, I see that familiar glazed look of disappointment when they realise I'm not the one telling the actors what to do. As a producer, I'm constantly learning new skills and adapting to be as good as I can. I've worked with many different kinds of producers and each one has taught me something new.

NIK POWELL: No one producer will describe their job in the same way. It's one of those mysterious things. It's like trying to define what an entrepreneur is. In the simplest of terms, we're the boss. Pulling together everything that is needed to make the picture – money, cast, crew. That said, you do different things on each film. They are never the same but you hope for the same end result – a good film that sells well and fills cinemas.

CAT VILLIERS: A producer's role is very challenging. A good producer has to hold the film together, the whole film, and the construction of that film. By the construction, I mean how we bring all of the elements together – how to develop, finance, make, and complete it, and then find the most appropriate platforms to get it seen. The producer, a good creative producer, has to have many varied skills. Most importantly, we have to find the best people – writers, crew, financiers, sales agents/distributors, festivals – who can support the vision of the film with the director and facilitate its journey through all the different stages, and all the different twists and turns along the way, from the very beginning with the script to the marketing and its ultimate distribution.

ALEXANDRA ARLANGO: As a development producer I source new ideas, books and scripts for potential film projects. Once we have identified one to take forward I suggest possible writing and directing talent to

35

attach to the project, working with them to develop a script to a level that can attract finance and ultimately get green-lit to production.

KATE OGBORN: Often people have the Hollywood image of a person with a cigar, sitting behind a big desk with a chequebook. That's not the experience of independent producers in the UK or Hollywood. The job can be so many different things – taking the initial idea and developing it until it reaches the audience, or helping filmmakers to shape their ideas. It's a creative job that develops people, ideas and stories, hopefully developing audiences out of that. In many ways it's a pragmatic job about putting the money and teams together, managing the resources, expectations and relationships. That's what makes it so exciting, because you're using so many different mental muscles all the time.

ANDREA CORNWELL: I'm a very hands-on, 'in the trenches' style producer. I work on a mixture of projects, some of which I originate and some of which I join at much later stages, but I'm very much one to sit with the director and creative team and see it through.

MICHAEL KUHN: In a sentence, it's the person who makes things happen. There are line producers who make things happen too, but what distinguishes them from producers proper is that they don't have the risk of coming to the table with an idea or commissioning a script which might fail; of putting together a package which may or may not get financed; of having to see it through without knowing whether it will work or not. All those elements are what a producer does.

BERTRAND FAIVRE: I'm a specific type of producer, in that I produce directors before producing films. Generally, I don't read unsolicited scripts without a director attached. I am the right-hand man of talent and director. When you have a boxer in the ring, I'm like the trainer in the corner. I am someone they can always refer to and I help them between rounds.

CONOR BARRY: I come to producing from the point of view of being a punter, wanting to see things on screen. In a material fashion, a producer for me is somebody who allows talent to get out there so that other people can see their work. On a very practical level, a producer is someone who supports a director in trying to achieve the aims of the project, by achieving funding and support.

MARGOT GAVAN DUFFY: I work closely with writers throughout the process. Some shows come together more easily than others. Some writers are more naturally collaborative than others. Same applies to directors. In production I would expect to work closely with a director from casting and script development through to the final sound mix.

DAVID PARFITT: Producing has been the only job I've done on the production side. It's weird – I have never known particularly whether I do it right. I would say to people that it's a management role. We here at Trademark develop from scratch but also take on outside projects. I like to think I am somebody who can go from the very beginning to the very end of a project, from finding the idea to delivering the film. Inevitably, I do some things better than others, but with producing there's always someone else I can bring in with specialised knowledge. So I see myself as a sort of manager who delegates. Delegation is absolutely key, as well as fast and decisive decision-making. What I've always done, through theatre, film and TV, is find people who know what they are about and surround myself with them.

GARETH EDWARDS: A producer is also a director in radio. Their job is to help realise the vision behind the programme as well as raising the money for it. The role of a producer changes from job to job. What is required might be somebody who feels confident about the job or someone who can invent the whole thing from the ground up. A lot of the job of producing is working out what kind of producing is required. In brief, you have overall creative and financial control of the project.

IVANA MACKINNON: I am a producer, but have come from a development background so am very hands-on in development.

MIA BAYS: I'm a creative producer. I feel strongly that creative producing is an under-recognised skillset. I work in both fiction and theatrical documentary, a balance I love. I'm also useful as a marketing and distribution strategist as I did that for a long time before producing and I also love that aspect of the job. I've also been writing for the last couple of years and just made a short film that I co-wrote and produced which stars Ben Whishaw, who is mind-bogglingly wonderful and great to write for. So I see that as a clear direction – writing and producing.

SIMON CHINN: There are lots of different facets to the job. No two producers are alike. What I want to be is creatively driven, the producer who has the first vision for a project, who sources the material, imagines what it could be, and then ensures everything that follows is in the service of that vision. That's not always the case as I have sometimes jumped onto projects which are other people's visions and helped them realise them. It's always with a creative impetus. I'm not the sort of producer who's interested per se in the process of financing a film. That can be a quite interesting intellectual challenge in many ways. It's like reinventing the wheel every time you do it and like putting a very difficult puzzle together, where the pieces don't ever quite fit. It's about a process of problem-solving and negotiating. It's a means to an end for me: the goal is always to fund a film in such a way that the ambition that I had for it in the first place is realised. Unfortunately that is always a function of having the money and resources as much as everything else. As a producer I'm trying to raise money, but I'm also thinking creatively the whole time. I'm thinking about who I can bring to the project, what talents I can bring together and what the weird alchemy is in terms of the team I form to make it work. I often think it's a black art. That's why producing is sometimes very difficult to define.

OTHER DECISION MAKERS AND WHAT THEY DO

I didn't realise when I began that there were so many other roles and people behind the scenes – talent finders, talent developers, opportunity makers, gatekeepers and the decision makers. There's nothing worse than being introduced to someone and having no idea what they do or what their job title means. Yet it is also really important to know who does what, especially when you are really thinking, 'what do you do and how can you help me?'

SHANE ALLEN: A lot of commissioning is matchmaking. You'll get a talent who will send a showreel or an agent who will send a talent your way. Half the time it's your job to match them up with the right producer. Whether it's a script or an on-screen performer, it's trying to find the right home for them. I did that for *Fonejacker* and Kayvan Novak on Channel 4. That came in through something we used to do called Comedy Labs where entry-level people could send in any idea unsolicited and you would sift through them and find a producer partner for them. The other half of the job is obviously producers and indie companies bringing projects and scripts that they've worked up. You're the filter to help decide what project will sit best on what channel. Does it work, is it different enough, that distinct idea? You're sort of the gatekeeper. I started as a runner, and sent out tons of comedy ideas before I got the gig as a researcher, an AP and then producer. I worked on the BBC New Comedy awards, *Brass Eye*, *Shooting Stars* and eventually became a series producer. From those programmes I developed a relationship with Channel 4 and Andrew Newman and Caroline Leddy. Just from years of making programmes with them you develop a relationship with them. When Iain Morris left to set up his company and write *The Inbetweeners*, Channel 4 asked would I be interested in the job.

KERRY APPLEYARD: I oversee production and development, am the key contact for broadcasters and responsible for bringing new projects to the company. On *Orphan Black* I was co-executive producer, which meant looking after the production from the production company's perspective. I worked very closely with the show-runners and writers on all aspects of the creative and with the broadcasters to deliver the show to a high standard and to budget.

RICHARD COOKSON: My job is to develop new shows and manage our slate of projects. For any given project, that all starts with an idea: either one a writer brings to us or something we come up with ourselves and pitch to a writer. It could be just a vague notion, or a fully fleshed-out pitch, a spec script or a book to adapt. If we like the initial idea, we'll usually get a written pitch from the writer (anywhere between one and five pages) and then take that to an appropriate broadcaster. If they like it enough, they'll either commission a longer treatment or full script. If everyone's happy with the resulting script, this will lead to more script commissions or series outlines – or even a green light to go into production. At each stage, I work with the writer to get the best out of them and move the project forward, usually through meetings and/or notes. It can be a very lengthy process, with the journey from pitch to screen potentially lasting years, so there are writers' schedules to be balanced, commissioners' job changes to be navigated and often, sadly, projects to be shelved. With that process, there are the administrative duties of ensuring that we're timely in our responses, chasing writers to ensure they adhere to deadlines and chasing commissioners for responses to our submissions. Plus, it's important to also be keeping an eye out for new talent – meeting with agents to discuss their client lists, reading spec material, and devouring as much media as possible – whether that's TV, novels, film, theatre or comics.

KATE ROWLAND: My role is sometimes like a matchmaker. The relationship you have with the writer is vital; if you can't work together, you won't bring out the best in each other. It's about finding those partnerships. Thinking about writers and who they'd be perfect with. You know, who will hear them, who will see them and who will take the risk with them. That's really important. I miss producing. Being a producer is very hands-on and you're very involved, through every stage of the script to the final product, whether TV, radio or theatre. You want to shape things and follow things through to the end. There are times when handing over a person or project can be frustrating as you've got so involved. At some point I will get back to the mix.

LIAM FOLEY: I'm part of a close-knit team. There are four people in the development department: the head of film, senior vice president of development, myself as the development executive and the creative executive. We field all of the submissions and maintain relationships we have with agents, we actively track talent, we go out and look for material, we develop the existing projects on the slate. We see them through from soup to nuts really. It's a small team and we're very hands-on. Our work doesn't finish once a film is passed over to production or it starts shooting. We remain very plugged in through the edit. We get a sense of ownership over a project from the very beginning through to the bitter end.

BEN STEPHENSON: I describe the role of controller of drama commissioning at the BBC as being like the conductor of a huge orchestra, made up of many different components. The role is about bringing lots of disparate elements together – hopefully in a way that has both shape and range for the audience – and being someone who can deliver a vision for drama, inside and out of the BBC. The truth is most people in TV drama are passionate about TV drama. They are not passionate about a particular genre or title. I am as happy sitting in the room talking about *EastEnders* as I am sitting in a room talking about Jane Campion's new project. To me, there's no difference. They are telling stories and storytelling is the thing I love. So, for me, great drama, whether it's just there as a piece of entertainment (like *Death in Paradise*) or else has a

41

profound purpose or a particular take on the world (like a *Peaky Blinders*), there's no difference. The job is getting great drama for all audiences.

SERENA BOWMAN: I started out as a receptionist at Company Pictures, and then became PA to the managing directors and then an assistant script editor. As head of development I oversee Company Pictures' development slate and so I take projects and move them forward from development into production.

KATIE GOODSON-THOMAS: There are many parts to my job. I work across development, production and acquisitions. I constantly have all three hats on.

SIMON HEATH: I head up the company and oversee all the shows we develop and produce. We try to work with the best writers to identify, develop and sell new ideas that will make great TV drama.

KATE LEYS: I'm a script editor, also sometimes called a story editor. I work almost entirely in feature films, though occasionally also in TV comedy. I might work with a writer on an outline, to the very end, when I might be brought in to fine-tune (or firefight) during pre-production.

DAVID FREEDMAN: Due to my dubious superpower of being able to read material as a complete moron, I'm often hired as a script doctor. I am then someone else's fresh pair of fresh eyes with my red pen at the ready. I actually have a bucket of them! I don't scribble 'criticisms', I tend to scribble questions (because I'm a complete moron, remember?) such as 'How did he get here?' and 'Where did she go?' and 'How can he know that information yet?' and 'Is this information important?' It's not just about continuity – although that's important too; it tends to be about flow of information, logic of that information, and me, as a fresh-eyed moron, 'getting it'. Then I go back to the client with a diagnosis of what I think is wrong, and where and how I think it can be fixed. I can't stand when you go to a barber and they say, 'Ugh, who cut your hair?!' Hey, maybe it just grew out this way! Same for writing. I never blame anyone for what I just read, least of all the previous writer! Because I have been – and will be again – that person who gets rewritten. As a script doctor I assume things got to this state with all the best intentions. Nobody sits down and says, 'OK, let's make a boring film where the characters talk too much and the plot makes no sense.' It just lost its way, or got lost from some poor notes that seemed sensible at the time, or it's simply a matter of being written way too fast, or it just grew out that way.

DAVID FLYNN: I started in Endemol 14 years ago as a creative intern, coming up with ideas. It was my breakthrough – an entry-level job working on the coal face. As CCO my role now is essentially looking creatively over all the companies that are part of Endemol. The companies span across the entire industry, from comedy to entertainment formats to factual to drama. My key role is ensuring that, creatively, we have the next generation of big ideas coming through. We work with the key creators in the company to make that happen by pitching to broadcasters.

KNOW THYSELF CREATIVELY

Creatively, we need to know our strengths and weaknesses. Much of writing is about skill rather than talent – the skill of being able to identify where our talents lie, as well as our vulnerabilities. By this I mean knowing what you write best, an awareness of what you like to write, what aspects can be written better, or ways of improving your writing to the point where the quality is good. We need to know ourselves so that, every so often, we can appraise our writing and assess where we are as a writer.

GUY HIBBERT: When I first started out, I was put up for doing a series. I went to a couple of meetings for a cop series. I always got incredibly irritated by the process and decided I would rather do painting and decorating than that kind of work. I never write for series.

TONY JORDAN: My strength is that I can write without blocking out first on postcards or notes; I can keep an entire narrative structure in my head. My weakness is writing emails and sharpening pencils when I should be writing.

TINA GHARAVI: My weakness is deadlines and my strengths are collaborating and listening to other 'voices'.

HOPE DICKSON LEACH: I want to know how it's all going to work before I start. I get distracted by theme and meaning rather than character and plot. My brain gets in the way of my heart. But my strength is that I'm happy to discard things if they aren't working. I enjoy writing. I love coming up with new ideas.

TONY GRISONI: You know the light-bulb jokes? How many producers does it take to change a light bulb? *Does it have to be a light bulb?* How many directors does it take to change a light bulb? *I don't know, how many do you think?* How many screenwriters does it take to change a light bulb? *You want to change the light bulb?!* Because you're starting with the idea, it's just you. If it's to become a film, you have to engage with other people and open the doors so that process can happen, which I really enjoy, but there's a little moment just before it all begins where I know I've got to give it up and I want to hold on to it. I'm always aware of that. Once I've done it, I'm fine and really enjoy the whole process. Without giving it up, nothing happens, so it's a foolish reaction, a weakness.

DESTINY EKARAGHA: I guess my strength is I never give up if I truly believe in a project. I've often come close but I keep going. This is a hard industry to get into; if you give up at the first hurdle you'll never make it. That's why I try to keep going! My weakness as a writer is getting started. Sometimes I just stare at the laptop. I have friends who have threatened to literally kick me up the arse if I don't get something done. That warning often works.

CLAIRE WILSON: Characters and dialogue come easily to me. I always have problems with endings and I can't spell for shit.

KIRSTEN SHERIDAN: You have to know what you're trying to say. Don't write about stuff that you think is the next version of *Love/Hate* or *Pulp Fiction*. Don't do something just for that. Find something that makes your blood boil, makes you laugh out loud or makes you cry. Do something that does that.

MARC EVANS: What you need is the right level of commitment, patience and robustness against disappointment. You also need a sort of optimism in the middle of all that to get through it. You've got to know yourself quite well in order to survive the film industry and be prepared to find your place in it. If filmmaking is what really makes you happy, then self-knowledge is the thing that underpins that. Know yourself, keep a sense of who you are.

OL PARKER: I always think of projects in terms of the finished film. If I don't want to see it, it's an easy pass. If I'd rather see it than have done it, it's a pass. And if the fact that someone else has done it will upset me, I'll go up for the job. And then not get it anyway.

JAMES DORMER: I'd say to any writer asked about their weaknesses, don't answer. Never admit to your weaknesses because it's very difficult for producers, once they've heard it come out of your mouth, not to think about it every time they look at your work. Doesn't mean *you* shouldn't know them, though.

PAULA MILNE: I was asked to write *Endgame*, a project based on minutes of those 23 meetings between the ANC and Afrikaans guys. As you would expect with minutes of meetings they were very dry, pretty incomprehensible and referred to all sorts of things I'd never heard of. So that took a mammoth amount of research to decide what to cull because it wasn't relevant to the narrative. The most important things to focus on were the freedom of political prisoners, including Mandela, the unbanning of proscribed organisations like the ANC, etc., and of course majority rule. I had to distil it down to those key areas. I felt creatively scared because it was so daunting, but I did it and now I know it's good to be scared. I thought, if you can do this then you'll be a better writer at the end of it. I went out to South Africa and I met all the key players. I went into the townships and met the Afrikaans and so forth. I went back and wrote it and tried to imbue it with emotion – to give it a beating heart so it wasn't a dry version of events. It was a very female way of looking at things, if you like, where you took the heart of the scene and the emotional tenor of a scene and put that in the foreground. I focused on the distrust between the two sides and their ambivalence about each other and played that against the issues all the time, until in the end they built a fragile mutual trust. So in that process I discovered my strengths and I discovered that I could write something like that, which previously I didn't realise I could do. When I was in America I was asked to write a movie based on an army base, so I went to the army base and met all the GIs; they were all going off to Bosnia and I spent the time researching. The script was pretty much a disaster. I should have never written that movie; it was an alien culture and I was out of my depth, frankly. None of it called on any strengths; it was nuts. But I learned something from that, if only what my weaknesses were as a writer.

ASIF KAPADIA: I went to film school to learn about the history of films, study film theory and primarily to get my hands on equipment, money and crew to continue making them. I kept practising, practising, practising and eventually I had something good enough to show. I wanted to have something to say, to work out my style, to find out what set me apart from other people. I studied film for four years, at Newport Film School, as well as a degree at the University of Westminster. I worked as a director for TV for a while but I quit to do a postgraduate course at the Royal College of Art. There I discovered exactly what I wanted to do – very visual, cinematic films, with very little dialogue. At the RCA I made three short films – *The Waiting Room*, which was eight minutes with no dialogue; a one-minute Western called *Wild West* which was very stylised with a designed set, horses, costumes, etc. and no dialogue; and, finally, my graduate film, *The Sheep Thief*, which was 25 minutes long. With that one I pushed the boat out; we raised money and took a crew to India and made it with street kids and non-professional actors. Those three films created my style, which led on to my first feature, *The Warrior.*

....

ROCLIFFE NOTES on...
WORKING OUT YOUR CREATIVE DNA

Too much self-reflection and self-criticism can be our greatest repressor. It's about balance, however, because it's only by asking ourselves certain questions that we can truly move forward. It's not enough to book a flight to Los Angeles, thinking you are going to be swamped with offers and that's going to get you closer to winning an Oscar. You need to write something that's going to blow the socks off the industry – something that no one else can write – that is unique to you, that only you could have written. By exploring, you can find out more about the boundaries within that need pushing. Start by asking yourself the following questions:

- What is your greatest strength as a writer?
- Which mediums do you like working in – film, TV, etc.?
- Which mediums have you not written for?
- Have you tried or considered them?
- What gives you the most trouble when writing?
- What subjects or themes interest you the most?
- What types of stories do you like or dislike telling?

- Do you finish every script you start and, if not, what do you do with the ones you don't?

- Where do you write best and what time of day?

- How much do you write every day or week?

- Do you carve out time to write every week?

- In the last six months, how many calls for scripts have you responded to? How many competitions have you entered? How many submissions have you made? How many meetings have you requested?

- How do you keep track of opportunities?

- What can you do to better your chances?

- What areas of the craft could you improve by seeking feedback?

- Are there any courses you could go on that would help hone your craft?

- If you had to give yourself one piece of advice what would it be, and what can you do to achieve it?

- Do you write for fun or do you want to write as a career? Dabbling is fine as long as you know that's why you do it.

....

A WRITER NEEDS TO WRITE

Often writers tell me they want to write but simply don't have time – to write you need more than desire. Desire alone is talk with no substance. There has to be the action of writing. Behind any production on stage or screen is a terrible first draft. So don't aim to get it right first time round – just get it written! Don't confuse passion with desperation. Don't talk about an idea for something you don't have time to do. Richard Curtis at a BAFTA Screenwriting Lecture compared the difference between having a good idea for a film and the finished film as 'the same as seeing a pretty girl at a party and being there when your wife delivers the third baby. It's an incredibly long journey, and a good idea is only the tiny little spark at the beginning of this immense process.' A writer must commit to the process.

There are writers on both sides of my family – Libyan and Irish. My father wrote for days on end, solidly through the night before he would stop, sigh in a satisfied way, and then collapse into a deep sleep. When it became too dangerous for him to write under the Gadaffi regime in the 1990s, he took to painting, because he said they (the regime) were 'too stupid to politicise art'. He found a way to create. There's an intensity to his creativity that fascinates me and he is as profilic with the pen as he is with the brush. My uncle, Irish poet Macdara Woods, used to make the house vibrate with his Woodstock typewriter, which he used until 1989. I envied both of them their ability to sit and write. During the Arab Spring of 2011, my proudest moment was when the *Irish Times* published my piece on returning to Libya after three decades away because I finally got to tell my family's story. Nothing is lost when writing. Scripts, stories, articles, blogs, books can do that too – they tell a story, your story, your characters' stories – what use are they in your head?

OL PARKER: I see in a lot of newer writers a lack of desire to rewrite. It's a paradox that desperation to break into the world doesn't always equate with a willingness to do the grunt work to get there.

DAVID SIMPATICO: I write every day, waking at 4 am. Some days I am inspired and clear, some days not so much. But one thing I do know: procrastination is a form of preparation. I like to walk away from a problem so I can think about it without thinking about it; long walks with my dog help a lot.

SASKIA SCHUSTER: All writing, in all forms, is good experience. The various formats require different skills which can be brought to future writing projects. Writing for different formats will also generate a wide range of contacts and exposure for a writer's work.

ROWAN ATHALE: There are thousands of excuses not to write but there are very few that are valid. It's unlikely you are going to make the progress you want to by writing for two hours every other Sunday. Make the time, and force your own hand. No one is waiting for your script. You're the only one that can motivate you.

MOIRA BUFFINI: If you want to be a writer, you have to write. Keep writing. Make it a discipline. Write every day. It took me ten years doing waitressing jobs, acting jobs, temping jobs, other things, but I wrote consistently during that time. There's no way you will not improve if you keep writing. Nothing you ever write is wasted. You come back to things years later and raid them for gems – scenes, speeches, characters, things you thought you'd never use again.

LIAM FOLEY: Start at the beginning, get through to the end and just don't be dissuaded. Don't stop. Whether it's a TV single or feature-length film screenplay, get to the end of it, get it down on paper. Just be very aware that, when you're starting out, it's not impossible but it's very unlikely that the first script you write is going to knock it out of the park and be your gateway to a life of riches and luxury. That first thing, that second thing, that fifth thing that you write, you may have to admit to yourself on reading it back that it's not very good, or just not good enough. But in the writing of it, in the completing of it, you will be finding your voice and learning your craft. You will be learning through your mistakes. You've got to keep at it. Finish, move on, keep moving.

DANNY HUSTON: DO IT! Don't wait for permission. There are no red lights.

ROCLIFFE NOTES on...

GETTING STARTED

- Find a reason to write – for pleasure, work, or to explore a truth. You need to write with purpose. Start by writing an outline – a beginning, middle and end – and then fill it in.

- Stop daydreaming and start scribbling. Buy a notebook. Write down your ideas. Anything that makes you laugh or cry, write it down. You will forget it otherwise.

- Get screenwriting software. If it's a script it must look like a script, not a cheap imitation.

- Think quantity not quality. Don't self-edit. Instead, throw everything into your first attempt.

- Read your script in one sitting. Rewrite what you have written as new ideas or better ways of saying what you are trying to say occur to you. You may, for example, think of better ways to set things up.

- No one needs to know this is your twelfth draft – they just need to see your best work.

- Get someone to read it and ask them to mark an X where they get bored or confused (a tip from Julian Fellowes).

- Set a time each day to write. Put on the alarm clock an hour before you usually do. Use that time to write. If you can't work within the time frame of an hour, set goals of page count, scene count or word count. Don't let yourself walk away until you have achieved your goal.

- What's your writing DNA? Ask yourself when you write best – morning, afternoon or evening? Do you write well to deadlines? What environment makes you the most prolific? Cake helps me!

- Think of it as spending time with someone you love: if you hate writing or what you are writing, why would you spend time doing it?

- Should you find yourself struggling to write, go back and edit the work you have written. Check that what you have changed now works within the framework of your story or plot.

- Take a storyline or even a news article and play 'what if' with it, then integrate what you've come up with into the story. Be as crazily creative as you want – it will free up the story and refresh you.

- Build eye breaks into your writing schedule. Allow yourself time to go to the toilet, surf the internet, tweet or Facebook, but restrict your time on social media. Less guilt is involved when it's part of the schedule – five minutes, say, at the end of each hour.

- Allow yourself to take story or script problems for a walk, sleep or meditate on them.

- Don't tell people that you've started as you'll have them asking how it's going or when they can see what you've written. It can feel like the writing is a sentence rather than a creative opportunity.

- If you have a day job, take a vacation on a writer's retreat, sign up for a writing course or join a writing group. All of this will stimulate you and you will look forward to the time when you write.

••

02

WHAT'S YOUR WRITING PROCESS?

Self-discipline is one of the hardest things for me. At school, I used to envy the girls who were able to sit down and get on with their homework. In my head, I never lost the stigma of arriving in Ireland unable to read and write at the level of my peers, or the intensity of how I learned to read and write. After that school felt tedious – I would tell my doting mother the holidays had begun early in order to avoid going. Of course, I was always found out when we'd drive past and there would be children in the playground. These days, I don't write to a timetable but I *do* have a writing plan. That said it always surprises me when I get to the end of anything I've written. Writing for these contributors, however, is a full-time profession. So how do they do it?

MOIRA BUFFINI: I don't know if I have a process. I don't have a method. I don't approach every story in the same way. Each project is different. Most of my film work has been adaptations, which I approach in a dissimilar way to my theatre work. In original work, I always begin by writing scenes really early because that is how I find my characters. Until I find my characters I don't know what they will do. If you map everything out too early you miss your best turns of plot. My characters often surprise me, which allows me to think of more interesting twists and turns.

PETER HARNESS: I think it's developed over time. What I tend to do, in the actual writing of it, is to write what excites me to begin with. I don't write in a straight line; I write different scenes and different characters and try to feel my way into it. I write an organic first draft, which I try to then shape into the right pieces, and move a lot of things around. I don't tend to plan very exactly before I do that; I've got a pretty good idea of where it's going and what the key scenes and characters are. I don't plan it beat for beat as I find that the magic gets lost in doing that and it's very boring.

JAMES DORMER: It varies depending on what I'm working on. If it's something of my own, it just starts with an idea and I work around it until I feel that I really have something to say. If it's for a TV show, it centres around becoming familiar with that TV show and pitching a story and working around that. I tend to try to think of a hook and then work out a story. Sometimes I can take the lead character out and change it to another character, to see what that does for the story.

REBECCA DALY: I spend a lot of time trying to hit on an idea that is going to keep my interest for a long time. I read newspapers, etc. You can get stories from everywhere, stories friends have told you, etc. I'm always interested in a new story. I start with that, then if I'm working with Glenn, my writing partner, the two of us discuss ideas from shortlists we each have. We work out the one we like the most and put a treatment together which establishes the first-draft structure and tone. Either Glenn or I will write the first draft, then we flip between us for the next drafts.

LUCY CLARKE: Gag writing is very disciplined – it has to be as you usually have a tight deadline to work to. For *The News Quiz* I always write what are to me the obvious gags first, then approach the wider themes of the story and relate them to other things that are going on in the news. Then I drill down into the facts looking for good quotes, other angles. And I try to keep my gags as short as possible. Sitcom is very different; it's all about getting to know the characters. I write pages and pages of character biogs, then discuss them with my producer to work out what each character wants, what they lack, who they think they are, what everyone else thinks about them. Then I write long episode outlines to work out plotting. And then when I find that I'm writing huge chunks of dialogue as part of my episode outlines, that's usually a good indication that it's time to start writing an actual episode. By that point, I know the characters' voices so well that it's fairly easy to get the first draft written – it's getting it down to time that's the hard part!

TINA GHARAVI: I'm glad you don't need to be a great writer to be a screenwriter. My process involves a lot of 'percolation'. I spend vast amounts of time thinking about the story. Carrying it like fragile eggs for years. I watch a film and I turn the egg, I read something and turn the egg... I find a moment of life... and, again, the egg gets it. Once I can't hold on to it any longer, I spew it out. First in little confetti-like fragments, then starting to weave the pieces together... and finally the colouring in. Mostly, the depth of this comes from improvisation and finding the truth of the story in the real world and in the depths of the actors. I'm a psychologist to my actors and they have to be prepared to turn themselves inside out.

OL PARKER: I take the kids to school, come back and make a cup of tea, then sit down at the computer and, before starting work, try to read the entire internet. That's my process. Procrastination wouldn't even begin to cover it.

JACK THORNE: Arduous. I just sit and hope most days.

PAULA MILNE: I started writing before computers, so I still write by hand and type it up on the computer afterwards – probably at the end of the day or every other day. I have a slightly wanky theory about this. When I was a painter I carried a sketchbook around with me. When you're handwriting, it's a private struggle to try to get the very best out of a scene that you're writing. With writing software like Final Draft, it goes directly onto the screen and it starts to look like a polished script, so you're then just finessing the finished product. It seems to me you lose something in the process. On the screen it can look persuasively neat, underwritten, sparse and clever; somewhere in that neatness the humanity can get lost. For me the humanity lies in the private raw scrawls prior to that.

CLAIRE WILSON: If I start as soon as I leap out of bed I have a fighting chance of getting a day's work done. If I go on the internet or read anything at all it's a battle to keep my attention on side from there on. Other than that, key elements are coffee and quiet. Physically I put pen to paper, fingertips to keyboard, and write. Mentally I drag a comb through my memory capturing every emotion, every character, and doing my best to turn them into narrative. I really enjoy what I do. I complain about the deadlines, and I hate to fail, but I truly love the process and I hope that shows.

TONY JORDAN: I try to write three days a week in my writing 'shed' in my garden at home, then the rest of my time is spent at Red Planet.

TONY GRISONI: I'll start jotting down events, images, and sometimes a character will start speaking in a monologue to teach me about themselves. Out of that will emerge the very beginnings of a story. Then I'll knock it together into some sort of shape, which means a couple of pages maybe. Then I go and speak to a couple of people who can maybe commission me, the idea being that I get paid while I write. It's a proper job, not an unpaid hobby. If I'm lucky and I get someone to commission me and give me the freedom that I need and room to make mistakes, I will sit down every day, six days a week. I will start about 8 am and play with the story and see what happens. I'll do that for most of the day. In the afternoon, I might go to a library and look up something in the story and research. I make notes and then go back the next day and continue. I just try to keep going until I get to the end, not worrying about how uneven it is, even if the character changes sex or something like that. I continue writing, trying to find an energy for the narrative through to the end, without going back to edit or polish. So I finish with a whole bunch of notes and I go back over it. Then someone has to wrestle it off of me; otherwise I'd never give it to anyone. I could go on forever with the process of writing.

SALLY EL HOSAINI: I tend to do a lot of research. I tend to write in spurts. I'm not somebody who sits down and writes every single day in a disciplined way. I have to wait. An idea is a gathering cloud in my head. I become a bit of a magpie, collecting little shiny bits of information from everywhere... pieces of dialogue, images, moments I've seen or imagined, etc. I write it all down in my notebooks. In fact, each of my films has its own notebook dedicated to it, and everything to do with that film or idea goes into it. I carry my little notebooks around with me because you never know when you might need to add to them. Then, when I sit down to write, which is usually because of an imposed (or self-imposed) deadline, it all comes out in a cathartic, intense and very focused way. I just run at it and start at the beginning and finish at the end. If I get stuck I flip through my notebook for inspiration. Having the gaps between when I write and when I don't helps me. It means that when I do sit down to write I'm really ready to shut the world out and immerse myself in it.

DANNY BROCKLEHURST: Over the years I've developed a method of finding a way to get the job done. When I am writing, I sit down every day and some days are better than others. If you are story lining and building a story house from nothing it's hard. I go to a café I like, sit in a massive window seat – I find that inspiring for ideas – and jot things down. Force it; you can't faff about with it. Paul Abbott has a sign that says it only takes hard work to make it work.

MARNIE DICKENS: I work best in the morning so I'll take whatever project is in front of me and get cracking.

KEVIN CECIL: There isn't just one writing process. It depends what we are working on. *Veep* was very different to *Gangsta Granny* which was different to *Hyperdrive* which was different to *Gnomeo & Juliet*. Perhaps what everything has in common is idea creation. You need a good amount of material to pick from when you are putting together your story so we will spend a lot of time on ideas. Then we will pick out the things that work and write them on index cards. We'll arrange those on the wall until we have a story. Then, when we write the script, we will always rewrite it before we show it to anyone. You work and you rework. Rewrite, rewrite, rewrite. Then you show it to someone, get feedback and start again.

MIRANDA BOWEN: Hmmm – a lot of procrastination. It takes a long time for me to become convinced of an idea sufficiently to commit to it. I have countless notebooks full of one-liners for ideas for films, TV series and one-off TV dramas but I usually find that I need an outside factor (a producer or respected friend) to endorse the project (or put me in a position where I am forced to work on it) in order to embrace it completely. And then it's a joy. Once I've dived in I find the details of the world and then try to shape all the elements that interest me into some sort of narrative sense. Coming from a visual arts background I find that it's usually the imagery that excites me first, and then I find the context to make that imagery plausible within a narrative structure.

MALCOLM CAMPBELL: I don't do an awful lot of actual writing. I often have a pencil in my hand, so I create the illusion of writing, but not a lot gets committed to paper. I'll always do a beat sheet and character biographies on paper, then if I'm happy with what's in my notepad that'll go onto the screen. I will do the honing and drafting and self-editing on screen. That's when I can take a step back and look at it and see if it makes sense. Ultimately, I don't spend that much time writing – most of it's spent reading, researching, and thinking. Then eventually writing longhand and typing up. I can go for an entire week without picking up a pencil. I'll still be working, doing the same hours; I just won't have written anything.

HOPE DICKSON LEACH: It changes all the time. At the moment I'm in love with treatments – long outlines that give me the comfort of knowing where I'm going, knowing what fits where, so that when I write the scene itself I can relax and inhabit the space without panicking that I don't know what I'm doing there (dramatically).

KIRSTEN SHERIDAN: I have a very specific process for writing. That would be, researching for months and letting it bubble under the surface for months and months and telling people the story as it grows, without writing anything. I make copious amounts of notes and when I actually write the scenes, I go into a room and kind of lock myself away and it's very intensive. I probably write about ten pages a day. But, really, the work is done before that. That's my writing process.

LEE ARONSOHN: I procrastinate to the point of pathology, then let guilt, panic, and fear hold the pencil.

PETER KOSMINSKY: I love the development process with the writer (or the writing itself, if I am writing). I love the research. I enjoy promoting the programme once it's done. And occasionally, very occasionally, I enjoy the actual production process. But, in all honesty, much of it is terrifying and incredibly hard. Each time I swear I'll never do it again. And each time (like a woman almost, but not quite, scared off from having more children by the pain of her last childbirth) I come back for more punishment. Crazy.

GUY HIBBERT: Today I started about half past eight and, aside from having a massage and a 15-minute break for lunch, I have been working continuously and it's 10.30 pm now. That's pretty usual (except for the massage). Depends what I'm doing. If I'm doing something that's based on reality, I do a lot of research on it first. And it depends on whether it has been commissioned. If it's research-based, it's sometimes about six months research and then another three months working out how to write it. The actual writing is quite quick.

LEVI DAVID ADDAI: I don't have a set structure. I usually do a lot of thinking way before I get to the draft, a lot of notes have been written down. I spend a lot of time jotting down details about the character, but in the background there's the process churning with writing down notes. Having time to percolate really helps. Having time to think properly, to assess things from all sides. I can begin looking at the story from 'a' to 'b' to 'c'. How naturally the characters fit into that.

JIM UHLS: Working both inside and outside the script – i.e. scenes with characters that won't be in the script and character interviews; notes that are a free-flowing, internal question and answer session with myself; notes that are more organised as an outline – all this continues while I work on the script itself.

JON CROKER: Get up. Think. Write. Think a bit more. Write. Read. Watch. Write again. I hold off writing the actual script for as long as possible. Prior to that, I research, tell and re-tell the story to myself over and over again – as a page-long synopsis, as a series of ideas, as a 30-second description, as a list of moments, then as a long prose document. Only when I'm tired of that do I start formatting the story as a script.

JUSTIN TREFGARNE: I have been lucky enough to shoot a lot of the scripts I've written and there's no better way to learn. A lot of it is about application – putting in the hours and building up a rhythm. Getting into the zone quickly and efficiently is very important for me – creating an environment where you can really dig deep and explore imaginatively. The hardest part of writing is believing in the story. I take a long time really committing to something as it often feels wrong or too much like something else. But I am pretty clear these days as to the kinds of films I want to make and that helps power me through. I carry a notebook around and this gets filled up slowly with ideas and scribbles for things.

CHRIS SPARLING: Generally speaking, I write for about six to eight hours a day, Monday through Friday (and occasionally on weekends). Thankfully, I love what I do, so it never really feels like 'work'. As for the actual process I follow, I usually write a synopsis first, followed by a beat sheet, then a scene-by-scene outline, and then I finally start on the first draft of my script. This way, I know exactly where I'm going with my story by the time I write 'Fade in'.

ALAN FRIEL: I've written six features; so far none has been made or produced but I got experience. I'd start with an idea and have a rough idea of where it would go. Usually, I didn't quite have an ending. I thought I'd just work my way up to an ending. Over the years I've realised that just doesn't work. You need to work to an outline. The writing part is easy. The plotting is the hardest bit. Be clear on where it's going to go. Then you can relax. You can change things as you go. As long as you have a map of where it's going, it's easier to change the outline than a script. I've realised that I don't want to overwrite.

ROWAN ATHALE: To begin with I break down the story to its most basic concept. Next I ask myself what the story is really about. Satisfied with my answer (and it can take a while, if you're being honest with yourself, to satisfactorily answer that question), I craft the characters around whom the story will centre. For me this is the most important stage as the characters are everything. That doesn't mean that I write chamber piece dramas entirely driven by dialogue – I love narrative complexity, genre structure, action. My point is that all of it must emanate from the decisions and emotional machinations of the characters that you place in the centre of the frame. If you know who your characters are, and have them drive the narrative, you will be better able to take the audience on the journey of your narrative as they will be compelled to follow along by the people at the centre of it. The next stage is to plot the main beats of the story. Not all the beats; a huge amount of screenwriting is about the generation of ideas, and you are going to have a lot more ideas over the 12 weeks it takes you to write the first draft than the week it takes to write a beat sheet. But I find you need to know where you are going before you start, or you can find yourself getting lost. Then I start writing.

IDEAS ARE IN THE ETHER: USE THEM OR LOSE THEM

Ideas are in the ether. Use them or they'll move on to someone who will! Often newer writers are concerned that people might steal their ideas, but I have never experienced this when it comes to scripts. When we are coming up, we hear many horror stories that can be very intimidating for someone who isn't in the know. At drama school, I was told I looked like Minnie Driver (not at all!!) so, when looking for an agent, I steadfastly avoided presenting myself to her agency under the foolish delusion that they would sign me up purely in order to stop me taking her work! We get many scripts during a BAFTA Rocliffe call that explore similar ideas, themes and issues, but it's the telling that makes a story unique, not the idea or concept. So should writers worry about their work being stolen or is it a myth?

TONY GRISONI: New writers are often very scared that their big ideas are going to be stolen by someone. I always tell them that they have to realise that they have an unlimited supply of ideas. They will not run out. They have to realise that they are their ideas; they are not like anyone else's. If someone is, say, writing a film set in the world of boxing, and they hear about another film set in the same world, it's not going to be the same. It's going to be their version of it. They shouldn't worry about that; it leads to a meanness and a closedness that will not help them creatively. They have to understand that they will never run out of stories. They are in the world. They are surrounded by stories.

SARAH GAVRON: You can't worry about it – it's impossible to protect yourself against. There are moments when certain ideas are in the zeitgeist and sometimes one project rules out another, but you have to assume that won't happen. So many factors have to come together for a film to get made.

JULIETTE TOWHIDI: You worry less and less about this one, as you realise one idea can play out in a multitude of ways depending on who is handling it. Generally, with hindsight, I can observe that one tends to be much more precious when one is starting out, and that goes hand in hand with being less self-confident. With experience, you relax about these things, you learn to let go, and that's ultimately a more creative outlook. You learn that the well of ideas is bottomless. It's not about other people stealing them, it's about your own state of mind.

JOSH APPIGNANESI: All I know is if you're working on a good idea, somebody else is working on a similar good idea, and they're almost certainly further along with it than you are.

TONY JORDAN: I've never stolen an idea in my life, I don't know any successful writer who has, and I don't personally know any writer who's had an idea stolen. My head of drama believes that the 'idea' is only five per cent; the execution of that idea is 95 per cent. I'm not sure I agree with her figures, but she has a point.

DESTINY EKARAGHA: There's no such thing as an original idea – *The Island* and *Never Let Me Go* are the same idea but couldn't be more different. Starting out, you have this fear that someone is going to steal your work but often it's a fear that exists only in your head. When I finish writing my scripts, I send them out because that's part of the job, and I stop worrying once I do.

MALCOLM CAMPBELL: I've been on panels where I hear new writers worrying about their ideas being stolen, but I have never heard of it. When you have conversations with development people, either they have heard that pitch before but are interested in your take on it, or it's so distinctive they just want to work with you, because there's only you who can write what's in your head. Don't be afraid. When I started I was putting 'copyright' on everything without knowing what it was and shoving scripts in an envelope, posting them to myself because I'd been told that's what to do. We moved house recently

63

and I found some unopened envelopes and realised they were old spec scripts. It was lovely to have them for reference, but I squirmed at how many stage directions there were on the first few pages!

LEE ARONSOHN: Don't waste time worrying about your ideas. Ideas are a dime a dozen. What makes something valuable is execution.

MUSTAPHA KSEIBATI: The fear of getting your ideas stolen comes from inexperience. Only you can write the story in your way. If someone steals your idea they can never imitate what you would've/have done with it and what got others so excited in the first place by it. Also, most producers would rather work with you as the creator of that idea to get the best out of it. Seems like a long-winded waste of time to steal it and get someone else to write it when they can just get you to do so. Most people are lazy.

LEVI DAVID ADDAI: I do worry about the idea where I have a twist at the end, which is really important. I've tried to protect that because that is how I am going to sell it and keep the interest without revealing the twist. I worry if they don't take up the idea, what if they talk to other people and reveal it before I have had the chance to sell it? I haven't really come across anyone stealing an idea, though. Although, on reflection, there's one show on telly I have a sneaking suspicion I inspired a producer to develop... but I'll leave it there.

MARNIE DICKENS: I don't think there's any greater risk of idea theft when you are starting out than when you are a seasoned writer. There's always a risk but if you love your own ideas and are honest in your own dealings that will see you right.

ROWAN ATHALE: If you are starting out in your career, for the most part, if someone likes your ideas enough to steal them, they won't bother: they'll just ask you for them and pay you a nominal fee, or no fee. Most new writers would jump through hoops at the idea of their work hitting the screen. Plagiarism will always be a concern for every writer, but put it to the back of your mind. If you can get

64

someone in the industry to read your script, let them read it and let them pass it to as many of their colleagues and friends as possible.

HOPE DICKSON LEACH: Lots of people have the same ideas but it's really whether you have the time, talent and dedication to take it from an idea into a screenplay into a film. I do think your ideas are your currency, that that is why people will want to work with you – but your ideas aren't just loglines, they're how that develops into something else, how you see the world differently from other people. No one can steal that.

WHERE DO YOUR IDEAS COME FROM?

Ideas are all around you. I grew up on Patrick Kavanagh's poetry. I love that Kavanagh's work is all about seeing the extraordinary in the ordinary and mundane. If we open our eyes to ideas, look around, listen to what is going on, we'll see a world filled with ideas. Personally, I'd like to think I'm more than just one idea.

TONY JORDAN: There's no particular 'place' to find ideas or to find inspiration; if you're a writer that inspiration is everywhere. I have a thousand ideas a day.

TINA GHARAVI: Students and new writers often ask me where stories come from or how they can find something to write about. My response is to 'find the pain' – where their great concerns are – and to write from there.

OL PARKER: I get asked, 'Where do your ideas come from?' Now, the paradox of doing all right at this job is that people bring you ideas all the time, which makes life easier.

GUY HIBBERT: I have something in pre-production at the moment, which is set in China. It's about the execution of an innocent person.

I thought about this subject because it's a good idea to keep it in the public consciousness. In a violent world, it's always worth trying to correct the violence by writing about something which has humanity in it. It's the only reason why I write. That's why I don't like doing crime dramas; I don't think they contribute anything worthwhile to society. Of course, the world goes on its own course whatever we write but collectively the arts have a vital role in trying to balance that inhumanity and violence. To celebrate violence – as a lot of film does – is profoundly depressing.

CLAIRE WILSON: If I knew where my ideas came from I would have a lot more of them.

KIRSTEN SHERIDAN: My inspiration comes from real life. If there's a real-life element to the story, they're much easier to get under the skin of. If you keep digging, the story will reveal itself. My favourite book on writing is a Steven King book, *On Writing*; in the second half of that book he talks about how everybody describes writing like building blocks, like architecture. But from his point of view, it's archaeology. The story already exists in the society's DNA and in your own personal DNA. If you can slowly discover what that structure is, and what the bones of the story are, that's your job. I find that quite inspiring.

KEVIN CECIL: Anything you do at any point in your life could turn into inspiration. You never know when you'll be doing something that will turn into an idea. We used to have a big ideas book and we'd write all our ideas in that. We don't do that so much now but we have index cards pinned to the walls of the office. It's easier to get ideas when you're meant to be thinking about something else. Or if you know what the broad subject is or have a bit of a direction. It's a bit like digging for oil or for gold; you hit a moment when you know you've found the right subject and can fill up ten pages with material quickly. That's when you know you're on to something.

LIAM FOLEY: Don't put all your eggs in one basket. If you have one idea that keeps you awake at night and which you keep perfecting, slaving over draft after draft, you might get to a point where you simply have to accept that there's something fundamental in the idea that doesn't excite people in the same way it excites you. You need to be prepared to move on to something else, on to the next thing... Often, newer writers won't let go of something until they've knocked on the very last door to get it made or get it read. They just keep nagging and nagging at an idea. Sometimes that can pay off... but sometimes you need the objectivity to accept that it's either just not good enough, or it's just time to move on to the next thing.

SALLY EL HOSAINI: Most of my ideas and inspiration come from reality and real things. Moments I've seen or experienced, or feelings that keep playing on my mind. From those small sparks, a larger idea just grows. And then characters come in, a world is constructed and it expands from there.

JUSTIN TREFGARNE: The thing that's essential is to keep the 'cupboard' stocked up. So that means seeing, listening, reading as much as possible. Sometimes you don't even finish something before the lightning bolt comes. I love stories and I love great storytelling. As a filmmaker (and writer) you have to be available to that – the rich variety of experiences life has to offer – to be saying 'yes' before you say 'no', at every opportunity. And that opens the doors to inspiration. Great art is everywhere, in every medium, and the struggles of men and women go on. So long as these two things continue to exist there will be stories to tell.

DESTINY EKARAGHA: I usually get inspired by the funny things that people say or by incidents that I see when out and about. Scenarios start to form in my head just from everyday things; before I know it, there's the beginning of a story. I try to make sure that the stories I tell have something to say, something different from what everybody else is saying. That's very important to me. It doesn't have to be serious; it can be funny – in fact, I usually prefer it that way. It just has to be saying something. The great thing about living in south-east London is that people always have something to say. The inspiration is endless and so are the jokes.

DANNY BROCKLEHURST: I don't know where they come from and I have no idea how I keep doing this job, but I keep coming up with new thoughts. I don't like to think about where they come from too much. If I analyse it too much, it might not happen. I'm strangely superstitious. If you have an interest in the world around you, read the paper, ideas will come to you. I lead a normal life – well, as 'normal' as normal can be for someone who spends their days with pretend people.

DICTYNNA HOOD: With a script, it can start from anywhere – an article in a magazine, a memory, a person, a feeling, a landscape, a picture, a family scene, a drama witnessed, a book, a play, or most likely a combination of these things – but the key thing is finding my connection with that material. Some ideas just won't go away.

TONY GRISONI: It changes depending on how the whole project starts. If we're talking about an original screenplay, there will be images or perhaps a character, location or incident which is spinning for a while. It could be sitting there, latent, for months or years – more likely years. There's a whole bunch of these different ideas. One day I'll remember a particular idea and put it together with something else – make connections.

ROCLIFFE NOTES on...

INSPIRATION

- Get a notebook and write down ideas, thoughts, things people say.

- Ellis Freeman, creator of the Writers' Gym, suggests keeping a writing journal where you write about topics by channelling or splurging. To do this set the timer on your watch/phone for ten minutes. Then write about that idea without stopping, correcting, rubbing out or striking through what you have written, or even thinking about it – your pen cannot leave the page.

- This allows you to make discoveries – one idea can lead to another idea and, before you know it, when you read back, you'll have a scenario.

- Pick a moment from what you have written and write a scene based around it.

- Write the scene before it.

- Write the scene after.

- You have begun.

- If you still feel devoid of inspiration, you can develop ideas by playing a game of 'what if?' where you take a newspaper story and list questions about the article.

- Some people suggest writing out the meals that the character has or keeping a diary of what the character does on a daily basis.

- Walk with your characters, describe them. Describe the world you want them to live in.

EVERYONE CAN WRITE, BUT NOT ALWAYS A GOOD SCREENPLAY

The truth is, anyone can write! Stick a whole load of characters together, create a dilemma and a bit of a dialogue – *et voilà*, a screenplay. But the reality is that the results may vary somewhat. Every agent and producer will tell you that ready-to-shoot scripts created around an excellent, fresh, exciting premise are exceptional. There's no magic formula but everyone reading a script knows when they find something good. It's instantly recognisable in the same way that mediocrity speaks for itself. In the interview 'The Writer Speaks' (available on YouTube), William Goldman clarified what was meant by 'No one knows anything'. What he was trying to convey was that no one knows what makes a good script.

TINA GHARAVI: The biggest thing is to avoid writing before you know where the story is going. What I mean is, hold back writing the draft. Too many writers explore when they write and then get lost. Hold back for as long as you can... then keep polishing and deepening until it's a movie in your own head. Only then write it. But this is personal advice and not what might work for everyone, so I say it with some caution.

BOB BALABAN: I don't like scripts that explain too much. With lengthy preambles explaining stuff like the history of knitting and un-actable stage directions that could fill a book. 'He paces anxiously, as a look of absolute terror crosses his furrowed brow.' 'She sits down with a catty yet resolute flicker of determination on her large red lips.' And so on. Nobody could act these descriptions. And nobody wants to read them. I hate scripts with photographs on the cover. Or drawings. Or bindings made of fake crocodile skin. If the script needs that much help to tell its story it's not doing its job. I get turned off by characters who are inconsistent unless they're supposed to be, gaps in logic and scripts that haven't let me know what they're at least sort of up to after ten or fifteen pages. I read a script wanting to believe in it. Please don't make it easy for me to doubt your characters or your premise.

HOPE DICKSON LEACH: I hate scripts that are set in Nowheresville or Anytown. I can't stand scripts that don't give their characters names. It takes a long time to understand what a story is, and when your story starts. Likewise with a scene and dramatic action. These things are hard to know, and the only way you get there is by doing all the bad writing for a long time.

MOIRA BUFFINI: You have to be prepared to put the hard graft in. I am proudest of the things I did first, my really early work. They were the hardest to write and hardest to get on. These were plays I put on in fringe theatres above pubs and small theatres and of course my early screenplays, some of which haven't been made. It took a long time but good work will out.

•••

ROCLIFFE NOTES on...
WRITING A GOOD SCREENPLAY

- The most important thing about a screenplay is that it should have a great story to tell.

- It's a package – a strong idea, a theme, compelling characters who want things and try to get them, and a load of stuff going wrong.

- As the writer you must have a clear idea about where the story is going.

- There's no exact science about what exactly makes for a good script but a reader knows it when they see it. It's easier sometimes to point out what doesn't work.

- Before you start to write, read at least 50 scripts of great films. Start with the films you genuinely admire and then read genres you like. Think about what makes them work for you – break them down and analyse. Then pick films that you saw in the cinema that have surprised you. You'll start to get a feel for what works and what doesn't.

- Another exercise is to think about what you would want to watch at the cinema and write that script! Don't try and rewrite a version of the most successful film of that year – you can't reinvent the wheel unless you can give it a very fresh and dynamic twist. That said, you shouldn't shy away from writing about subject matter with well-trodden ground.

- Practise your skills; develop a trust in your own work. It's not just about writing a script – you need to develop your craft.

....

A PROFESSIONAL APPROACH TO WRITING

What is it that makes some artists great? Is it down to approach? In any creative field, whether writing, directing or acting, it's about developing and harnessing your innate talent. One thing that will make you stand out as serious is to be at all times a positive, professional, generous collaborator. The journey to being a writer, director, producer or actor is a hard one – it takes time, money, effort, obsessiveness, research, rejection and an utter, resolute belief in yourself. Anything is possible if you believe you can do it. You have to have a 'can-do' attitude and not see this as a negative industry that locks new talent out.

ROCLIFFE NOTES on...
A PROFESSIONAL APPROACH

- I read that a good writer is a good reader. Many writers, particularly new writers, don't read scripts. When you are feeling burnt out by your own words, be inspired by others. See how they structure their worlds.

- Passion is important but passion and desperation are two different things. A passionate filmmaker will see that only with failure comes success. A desperate writer is afraid to let go. Move forward, write more and then come back to your original work with fresh eyes.

- Be more than one idea – commit to a career, not just one script.

- The first draft of anything is terrible; don't send out your first draft. Your title page doesn't need to say how many drafts you have written.

- Read your work aloud and cut dialogue – less is always more.

- Just as writers need to write, directors need to direct, so build up a showreel and make a name for yourself using shorts – most people work on them for free. When it comes to features, you should negotiate a small fee. Don't pay anyone to represent you.

- Don't pitch in social situations and, if you do, sum up your idea in one line. I went to a birthday party and a writer-actor I know spent 15 minutes pitching his great idea to me. I hadn't even taken off my coat. He bored me. Had he asked to meet for coffee to discuss his ideas I would have been more receptive. A lot of great people made time for me but I asked first and always said thank you.

- Don't be paranoid that your idea will be stolen, that competitions are stitch-ups and everyone in the industry is a wolf in sheep's clothing – which is why you won't reveal the ending of your script or let anyone read it. It's not the idea that's of value but the telling.

- Fall seven times, stand up eight! Feedback and rejection are part and parcel of a writer, actor, director and producer's life. Not everyone is going to like your project; your work may not be for them. If you write, if you create films, if you perform, accept that it will be read, watched, reviewed.

- Criticism of any nature is hard and painful and being rejected can be humiliating, but you have to develop a thick skin and move on. Some notes can be useful, highlighting an aspect of your work that isn't working – YET!

- Opinions will differ and vary. Take what resonates – don't nitpick with feedback. What use is feedback that tells you what you want to hear? How useful is that to you in terms of progressing your work?

- There's no reason to show your anger at rejection. Share your disappointment with those close to you but leave that industry door open. Those who rejected you the first time round may help you the next. Don't be unpleasant or burn bridges! People will forget that an early script wasn't great when presented with a better one, but they won't forget an unpleasant exchange.

....

NO ONE WAY IN

In my early twenties I lived in Paris. My friend Antonio Mendez was at film school, making shorts, and I would help acting and running. Making shorts was huge fun and a massive learning curve. Even though I had trained as an actress at the Poor School, over time I came to the realisation that it was writing and producing that I really loved. With Kerry Appleyard and Pippa Mitchell, I made my first short, *No Deposit, No Return*, about a desperate woman who breaks into a sperm bank. We raised the money by asking men to donate their sperm and give us the proceeds. I joked that none of them wanted to be known as useless w(a)nk*rs! We raised £60,000 – a mix of financial banking and in-kind sponsorship from Panavision, Lipsync, Panalux and Fuji – and shot it on Super 35. I've never looked back. This is a very collaborative business and people in this industry will help you but you need to find your path.

CLAIRE WILSON: I had a script selected for an early Rocliffe forum in a room above a pub in Angel. It bombed. The industry guest wasn't impressed – I was crushed. But one Rocliffe reader was an agent's assistant and he liked it. I was introduced to the agent and signed shortly after. That, for me, was my break. A few years later, I was selected again with John Madden as the industry guest, and he was much more complimentary. The producers I invited to the event optioned my script later that evening. This ultimately started my career in earnest. That first night, when things went from rejection to hope in such a short space of time, felt like the start of everything.

TONY GRISONI: I have been very fortunate in that there have been projects and films that I've been part of which have really changed things for me. For example, working with Terry Gilliam on *Fear and Loathing in Las Vegas* was a big turning point for me. I was suddenly considered to be a screenwriter by people who, before then, wouldn't have known that I existed. I got a chance to write material which would be filmed on a big scale. Working on *In This World* with Michael Winterbottom was another big turning point for me. It completely challenged everything I thought I knew about screenwriting. It was a totally different way of working. I was engaging in something current, something happening at the time.

JOSH APPIGNANESI: *The Infidel*, my second feature, was a step into commercial cinema that made me visible in a certain way.

LEE ARONSOHN: My breakthrough job was writing for *The Love Boat*. Since I broke in 35 years ago, I understand a few things have changed since then. I think if I were getting started today, I wouldn't wait for someone to discover me; I'd write stuff that I could produce and put online.

LUCY CLARKE: I worked in TV production and quickly gravitated towards comedy entertainment shows. *Never Mind the Buzzcocks* was, I think, the fourth show I ever worked on. I was a researcher, but everyone would pitch in ideas for the puns we used on ID Parade. I was quite good at this and I confided in the producer that I wanted to learn how to write gags. After a couple of series I was taught how to write the skeleton script and how to script-edit on studio days (i.e. frantically scribbling new punch lines onto gags as the writers came up with them, and then frantically rubbing them out again five seconds later when someone thought of something better!), and I slowly learned how gags were constructed. Around this time a friend was producing *The News Quiz* for Radio 4. I asked if I could go in and shadow the writers one day, and I had a go at writing gags for one of the questions. After a whole day I'd managed about five gags, but one went in the script, was read out and got a huge laugh – and I was hooked.

GUY HIBBERT: My breakthrough job was my first TV 'play' in 1989. It was a theatre play – *A Master of the Marionettes*. I spent over two years trying to get it going and failed. Then Hilary Salmon, who had been trying to produce it in the theatre and is now a senior drama executive at the BBC, gave it to Michael Wearing, then the head of BBC Drama at Birmingham. Wearing had produced dramas like *Edge of Darkness* and *Boys from the Blackstuff.* He said, 'If you can turn it into a TV play in a week, we'll do it.' I didn't quite know how to do that because I didn't know what EXTs and INTs were; I had no idea how to lay out a script. He employed Pedr James, a theatre director who had done some TV, to work with me on it and to direct it. It was successful and I have worked on screenplays ever since.

MARNIE DICKENS: I began on *Hollyoaks*.

MALCOLM CAMPBELL: *Ave Mansfield* was an original 2 x 90-minute TV piece, based on a group of kids from my hometown who go on a pilgrimage to Lourdes. When C4 commissioned me they suggested collaborating with the people at World Productions, whom I'd already met. They funded a research trip and I went away with a bunch of 80 teenagers from Chesterfield and Sheffield to France for a week. They got up to no good at night, but during the long days they looked after old and dying people and children with severe learning and physical difficulties. The trip was so life-affirming and Lourdes itself was an amazing crucible for drama. I learned how to write on that job and I was working with some great development people. I was full of ideas, but they taught me how to craft them into a story. I'll forever be indebted to them for that as they were patient and they nurtured me. *Ave* was a great calling card, even though it was never made: it got me noticed, got me other work and I'd learned loads on the job.

JULIETTE TOWHIDI: I started as a script reader then progressed to script editor – it's a great way to learn about writing while also being paid. The trouble with film is there's very little hierarchy and, for people who have to be self-supporting, it can be a terrible strain. There's no shame in working in the business in order to learn your art form. My first training was as a journalist, which teaches you a lot about the art of pithy communication.

KIRSTEN SHERIDAN: *Disco Pigs* was probably my breakthrough job. That came at a very different time to the way the industry is now. I was quite lucky, but besides lucky it was also much easier then to get independent films made. That was 2000. I don't know if it would be quite so easy now.

SHANE ALLEN: I was very lucky basically. My first proper job in comedy was on *The 11 O'Clock Show*. It was brilliant and a life-changing job because of all the talented people I got to know on and off camera. I worked on the *Ali G in Northern Ireland* shoot because I'm from Belfast and got on well with Sacha (Baron Cohen), so I went to work on the US series of *Ali G*. Ricky Gervais was part of *The 11 O'Clock Show* and so I got to know him and years later he did *Derek* with Channel 4. The guys who wrote *The Inbetweeners*, Iain and Damon, were VT producers on that – I had a laugh with them. The other guys who were writers set up a company called Zeppotron. I worked with them a lot – Charlie Brooker being one. Years later I commissioned *Dead Set* and *Black Mirror* as a result of that connection. It was from that little fledgling point in everyone's careers where lots of really strong relationships grew, all from one programme.

DICTYNNA HOOD: My first job in the industry was working on a Channel 4 drama series as a producer's assistant. I got to see all the ins and outs of producer-director-writer relationships... as a result of that job I got my first writing commission.

ALAN FRIEL: I co-directed a short film called *Coal* with my best friend. I was his producer, but I didn't want to do that and he asked me to direct it with him. We shot it on a shoestring and borrowed locations. We wanted to go for commercials. We made *Coal*, which was our graduation film at the Royal College of Art, with the idea of making ourselves attractive to commercials companies; it was short and it looked good. Commercials have kept me in the business, honing my skills, ever since.

DANNY BROCKLEHURST: I'd been trying to get into writing for a long time; I was just on the cusp of being taken on by *EastEnders*. I heard that Red were looking for writers for a second series of *Clocking Off*. I had met Paul Abbott and asked him if I could pitch in an idea and he agreed. I thought to myself, this is an amazing opportunity. So I spent a week writing three stories in quite some detail, with storylines. I sent them off and, to my amazement, they said they wanted to buy two of the three. It was astonishing for me that they were willing to take on such a new writer on such a high-profile show. It was a real leap of faith.

RON SCALPELLO: I came through commercials. You think you are always having breakthroughs, but you're not really. You're just taking small steps all the time. Making the first film was important as a breakthrough, but there were so many small steps that I'd taken to make that first film. If I hadn't had those breakthroughs in going to film school, doing pop videos and promos for the BBC that were well received and won directors' awards, if those little incremental things hadn't happened, I would never have got to the main breakthrough of someone giving me some money and a script and trusting me with a project to visualise and actualise. Never underestimate how much people invest in you as a character, as a director, to take responsibility for stuff. It's always a breakthrough to get any film made.

GLENN MONTGOMERY: It's strange because a lot of people I work with I went to college with so it kind of came from growing up with people. I wanted to write, Rebecca Daly wanted to direct, and it just was a very organic thing. She had read and really liked the play I had written so suggested that we write together. We wrote a short film, *Joyriders*, which got funding. It won a load of awards and we were told to get a script for a feature film together and apply for funding. That's how it started, and we've written together ever since.

TIPS FOR BREAKING IN TODAY FROM EMERGING WRITERS

In 2003, my producing partners and I were some of the first filmmakers to use crowdfunding to raise money for a short. Well, as I've previously mentioned, that's not entirely true: we didn't ask people for money; we asked them to donate their sperm and give us the proceeds. It was novel and it worked. Lee Aronsohn pointed out, when I asked him for advice about breaking into the industry today, he pointed out that he started many years ago. He was right – things change; so with that in mind, I asked emerging writers to share what they found worked for them.

ANNA EMERSON: Consider making a taster tape to sell your idea to producers – they can watch a short video on YouTube while they eat their lunch, whereas it'll take them longer to get around to reading a script. We went to a great session on making a taster tape, and the key messages were: don't try to condense a full show into five minutes; think of it as a teaser to sell the idea and the characters, and leave the viewer wanting to see more. Rough and ready is fine as long as it showcases your idea well. Most importantly, make it funny. At the sitcom session at the Edinburgh International TV Festival, the comedy producers and commissioners on the panel all said they read every script they receive – even if it takes a few weeks to get around to it. They are always looking for exciting new writers, so have confidence in your script, make it your best work and, when it's ready, send it to everyone!

TONY COOKE: When you're thinking which channel your idea would best sit on, don't just look at comedy shows. Look at the full schedule of new shows, including drama, factual and shiny entertainment formats. It seemed a bit irrelevant at first, but actually looking at the whole schedule gave us a great feel for the kind of tone, people and worlds the channels wanted to be known for and cater to. Your show needs to fit in with that vision. Looking at everything from the channel indents to the new series of *Baking on Ice* can help when you're developing and pitching your sitcom.

BRONA C TITLEY: Know your project and how to talk about it. Have one jazzy sentence that sums it up in a clear and punchy way. Then, in case the contact/producer/stranger in the loo wants to know more, have a few more sentences to back it up with. People will ask about your project. If you haven't thought it through, you will waffle on for way too long about how 'it's a bit like this but also has elements of this but don't worry it's not too much like that', etc. Write your one-sentence answer and your three-sentence answer, learn them off by heart, and then you will be prepared.

LIZZIE BATES: I sent an email to a producer requesting a meeting, but didn't hear back. When I plucked up the courage to speak to them at the *Guardian* Edinburgh International TV Festival they were extremely friendly and very open to reading our script. Chances are my email passed them by and, although you want to avoid getting a reputation as a stalker, most things are worth a second try. As a new writer, it's easy to presume producers and others in the industry won't be interested in you approaching them – but they are on the lookout for new talent and original ideas and you could be it.

CHRISTIANA BROCKBANK: It's so easy to let the days, weeks, months pass by without writing a scene heading. You might have a day job, order water when you go to the pub with your friends, or excuse yourself from going out with friends in favour of spending your weekend in front of a laptop, but don't give up. It's worth it. No one's going to come and find you. To be discovered, you have to make the first move. Don't keep a script to yourself; enter competitions, email production companies and do all you can to get it read. I went through a stage where I didn't want to bother important people with a script from an unrepresented writer with no credits. Silly, when you realise people are desperate to discover new talent.

STEWART THOMSON: Keep an open mind to networking and never discount someone less senior as that person might be a great deal hungrier, and you never know where their career may be headed. Always try to have more than one project up your sleeve and ready to go. I try to have at least a few on the go at any one time. Should someone like your work and want to read something else, you're not faffing around trying to throw something down quickly that could ultimately do you more harm than good.

ANDREA HUBERT: If you've worked really hard on a good script, you'll definitely have people interested, although meeting the people who can help you turn it into a show is challenging. To find out about what they do and make connections at industry events, if you're not naturally prone to talking about yourself, is difficult, but it's worth ignoring your instincts to talk only to your trusted writing partner in a corner. Walk up to total strangers, ask questions. We met some really fantastic people interested in some of our projects because of a few conversations.

NEW TALENT IS
THE INDUSTRY'S LIFEBLOOD

Everyone in the film industry is always on the lookout for new talent. It's a myth to think they're not. This is largely because the established writers are busy, but also to keep programming fresh. You are a commodity so don't shy away from putting yourself or your work out there.

RICHARD COOKSON: New writers offer a chance to work with new voices and to bring something exciting to drama audiences – be that via alternative and unique points of view or reassuringly confident and traditional storytellers. From a selfish point of view, collaborating with new talent and seeing their skills nurtured, encouraged and hopefully realised is a great reward in itself.

MIA BAYS: I would say established talent are the backbone and new talent are the fresh blood essential to growth and redevelopment. There's a huge focus on new talent in the UK so there are quite a few opportunities. My top tip is focus on the work and making it as good as possible before you show it. Make sure the ideas feel fresh, be clear on what you want to say and how – anyone can decide to be a filmmaker but the ones who stand out are those who really have something to say and a style and angle to their work who

THEN find the opportunities. So many find the opportunities and THEN do the work.

MARGOT GAVAN DUFFY: No matter how tough it seems, I think good work will normally break through. Producers are all keen to find talented writers and there's not a surfeit of them.

SHANE ALLEN: These days it's really hard, with an established show, to get beyond three series. *Miranda* and *Mrs Brown's Boys* have lasted. There's a lot of money to be made in live work and in film and touring. Writers reach a certain critical mass a lot quicker than they used to, which means you need to find new blood all the time. There used to be a lot of long-running TV series, but now the audience's appetites are for newer things all the time. So it really is important that we find new people and that we bring them through in a protective way. You need to have things like comedy feeds on iPlayer/BBC3, one-off pilots where they start online and go on to TV from there. These are like a pilot season where people can learn the craft, learn how to write a story, and grow in their ability.

GABRIEL SILVER: There's a familiar language to a hit show that captures a genre or mood, which everyone then chases – writers, producers and commissioners. New talent breaks the mould but it has to be very strong talent to do that – like with Lena Dunham's *Girls*, which is undeniably a fresh perspective on familiar characters in a familiar set-up, with an entirely new view and take on it. It proved that a younger generation can be represented and can tell stories to a universal audience. New talent is essential so that we don't get in a rut and watch the same old boring stuff.

IVANA MACKINNON: The industry wants to see people who are active; agents want to take on clients who are already self-generating. The most important thing is to keep producing work, get yourself out there, making connections and collaborating with other people. So it's not enough to make something and then wait for the world to fall into your lap. Talk to everyone. Share the things that make you specific, even if they are tangential to film. We all want to find people with a unique voice.

CHRIS SUSSMAN: If you're always working with the same people then they'll just grow old and die. It's the same in every single industry; you have to keep finding new, interesting people. With comedy, part of what makes you funny and part of what makes you laugh is you hear a joke that you haven't heard before, or discover a stylish humour that you haven't seen before. It's the surprise factor. And if we just had the same small number of writers writing all of the shows, people would quickly become familiar with, and bored of, that style of humour. So you constantly need to be looking for new writers and new performers, etc.

GARETH EDWARDS: You have to be very open to new talent, although that might only really come to fruition five to ten years later. I have been lucky to be in at the early stages of very successful people's careers, because I was the person who said something about their work that they found useful. It's about responding to things. If something makes me laugh, I'm interested in developing it further.

KATE ROWLAND: Some people don't believe that their script is always looked at or read. They think that we don't want to find talent. I say to people, 'We're not social workers – we do this because we believe in it and we find talented people.' Even though we put as much information out as possible on the blog about all the different ways we do things, I don't think people realise that it could be them. The other thing I'd like to emphasise is how much other parts of the BBC work with us. We couldn't do it without them. If the Writersroom was just in a shed in the dark with no connection, it wouldn't work.

SASKIA SCHUSTER: Asking a new writer to deliver a series of six or eight episodes is a huge pressure, and can be a risk. There's a tendency to direct newer writers to team-written comedies, or shorter-form opportunities. Sky have produced a few comedies with newer writers and we ensure that they are supported by a very experienced script editor and producer known to be good editorially, and we allow for the writing process to take longer than usual.

WHAT DO YOU LIKE TO FIND?

I honestly think this has to be the question people in the industry are asked most often after 'Will you read my script?' and I'm not sure anyone can absolutely identify what 'it' is. There's something a bit magical, and sometimes unidentifiable, because it's original. But when we find it, we know it straight away.

GARETH EDWARDS: I get asked a lot: 'what are you looking for?' Which is an agonising and pointless question. People shouldn't write what we are looking for; they should write what they want to write.

ALEXANDRA ARLANGO: Fresh, exciting, well-executed ideas. These will get producers meeting writers, even if the writing is a little rough around the edges, or if they already have something similar on their slate. At the end of the day, new ideas can come out of a meeting, and who knows where they will lead.

CHRIS SUSSMAN: I used to think there would be a lot more quality in the writing and in writers out there. But actually we're desperate for material. It's not like we have loads and loads of brilliant scripts on our desks waiting to be commissioned. The sorts of scripts that are the standard, that the average person would want to watch and find funny, are few and far between. So, actually, yes – there are a lot of people out there writing, but if you're a really good writer, you should be able to find a way to get your script made, as people are desperate for good material.

CHRISTOPHER GRANIER-DEFERRE: Creative England launched this nationwide hunt, open for applications; we do nationwide road shows throughout England. I've written articles for publications. We do a very, very, very wide search. We use social media and the radio; we really go out and find a large network, which is part of the BFI initiative. We have people feeding in from writers' groups, theatres and from other interest areas. We may have people from radio. There's a vast network of people who are on the forefront of developing emerging talent that we rely on and share passions with. That all feeds back into our application process.

MICHAEL KUHN: It's always fantastic when you come across people who are unbelievably talented and unbelievably nice, a joy to work with. I've had a few of those: the Coen Brothers and Spike Jonze in particular come to mind.

RICHARD COOKSON: Returnable series as there's huge appetite for these shows – contemporary family, relationship or workplace dramas in particular. We love ideas that foreground character, but we're not against high concepts either – as long as they're about people first and foremost.

KATE OGBORN: We want to make films which are challenging, exciting, and to work with the best talent in the UK. We want to make great cinema. Increasingly, we're looking at the slate we've got and the kinds of films we're developing to work out if something is complementary, or if it's something we're already doing something similar to. In terms of the filmmakers, it's all about what they've done, what their potential is, how we think we can help them, and what we think they will be like to work with.

LIAM FOLEY: Films that audiences want to see – that's what drives every creative decision. Working Title is a commercial film production company. We want to make films that international audiences want to see, films that a wholly international audience can access and enjoy. That generally means films of a certain scale, but the market is changing and Working Title are responding accordingly. We don't have WT2 anymore as a dedicated low-budget division, but films are being made in different ways now. In the past people might have considered Working Title to be the film company that just made romantic comedies. It's not that that should be considered a bad thing, but certainly people in the industry know that there's more to Working Title than that and there always has been. We have had a tremendous amount of success in the past with romantic comedies and with broader comedies; the relationship with Rowan Atkinson has been very fruitful, the Johnny English films, the Mr Bean films. Yet alongside those there have always been prestige literary adaptations, the historical films that Working Title has made, like *Elizabeth: The Golden Age*, Joe Wright's *Anna Karenina* and *Atonement*. There's a very interesting dynamic that lies at the heart of Working Title, and that's Tim and Eric. They have both got tremendously good taste and instinct, and they complement each other very well.

SIMON HEATH: An ear for dialogue. Surprising but believable characterisation. An ability to structure story. TV drama is driven by great characters, but needs a story engine. I guess World is best known for authentic, 'edgy', contemporary drama, and while much of our output is research and writer-driven, there's a broader range to our shows, from *The Bletchley Circle* to *The Fear*, and from *Line of Duty* to *The Great Train Robbery*.

CONOR BARRY: For my producing partner, John Keville, and me, it's down to a marketable script, a person who has the experience to help us get the project off the ground, and something we think we'll be able to find the finance for. Normally you're working with a natural budget range in terms of the budget you're able to raise. There's loads of elements, but generally it comes down to whether you think the script is really moving or not. The work has to be achievable. The first thing to make sure of is that you're dealing with a project that you know the director can handle and make. We try and support that person as much as possible. Where you think something is indulgent, like somebody indulging in a particular character because they love the idea of it, rather than because they want to share it with an audience, we intervene. The aim is to make the best projects we can that can get out to an audience.

WHERE DO YOU LOOK FOR NEW TALENT?

People want to work with new writers and talent. Caroline Norris, a comedy producer (*Dead Ringers*, *The Armstrong and Miller Show*, *Dead Boss*), told me that most producers are looking for, and want to work with, new writers because all the best ones are busy. I've given a lot of page space to this as I think it's so important to know that people are on the lookout for potential new collaborators.

GARETH EDWARDS: People email out of the blue. I might see a show that I like, get sent a showreel or see something funny online. I met an actor at an audition, and he said he'd done an online sitcom, so I watched it and a project has grown out of that. It was very funny, made me laugh. I've made a few things out of watching things on YouTube and stuff like that.

SHANE ALLEN: I'd say even 10 years ago it was about going up to the Edinburgh Fringe and seeing the Edinburgh shows, but access to producers and broadcasters has got so much more egalitarian from the internet. It's incumbent on producers to go and see live comedy or trawl the internet or speak to agents. All these are sources of good stuff, and you've got to be quite keen and quite hungry to find new voices and new talent. Things have got a lot more competitive amongst broadcasters There's a lot more of a keen ambition to find new people all the time. Also, with things like Rocliffe, there's a lot of really good tangible schemes for new talent to get involved with. The BBC have the New Comedy Awards for stand-ups. The BBC Writersroom is very solicitous; they give people specific goals, because it's really hard if you're a writer and you don't really know what you're gunning for. Radio comedies are another big source of opportunity. Things like *Little Britain*, *The Mighty Boosh*, *Knowing Me*, *Alan Partridge*, *League of Gentlemen* – it's brought through a lot of people and so it's a more protected way to learn the craft than straight to TV.

LAURIE COOK: Officially Bigscope Films doesn't accept unsolicited material. Unofficially, if a writer who has researched Bigscope and knows what kind of films we make contacts me and wants to submit something that is suitable – I'll ask for a logline and synopsis. Then I'll follow up if I think it's right for us, asking to read the full script.

SIMON HEATH: I'd like to think World are supportive of new talent. A lot of successful writers, directors and actors have debuted on our shows. Our door is always open to new ideas. If we like an idea but don't know the writer, we'll ask to read a sample of his or her scriptwriting. We'll commission and develop treatments and research for an idea before we pitch to a broadcaster. There are very few writer-directors in TV, though we've been fortunate enough to work with one of the best – Joe Ahearne, who wrote and directed *Ultraviolet*.

ANDREA CORNWELL: I've seen people who have made really good shorts go straight onto features, and then it doesn't matter how big the budget scale; if the continuity of vision is there they will be backed. It's sometimes easier to take a risk on someone new than someone who has done it before, so a first-time director may even be more likely than an experienced one to get a film made.

SERENA BOWMAN: I've worked with a huge range of writers. Our development team (Elliot Swift and Jess Barnes) are very much always on the lookout for new talent, so they read spec scripts sent by agents, even if the writers don't have any prior experience. We go to the theatre and see about getting involved with things like the BAFTA Rocliffe Forums that help promote new writers. The great thing about Company and why I love it so much is the huge diversity in the programmes we make; from *George Gently* to *Wild at Heart* to *Shameless*, they don't really have a lot in common. There isn't a particular kind of drama that we make apart from the fact that they are hopefully quality productions. I think that we have a very broad range and we want to broaden that more and more. We're getting into developing genre series like horror and sci-fi as well.

CHRIS SUSSMAN: By and large projects get brought to us by indies like Baby Cow, Hat Trick, Big Talk, Tiger Aspect and Rough Cut and the writer who will show us the script. There are times when we directly look for stuff ourselves – like at the Edinburgh Festival we go and have a look at all the new comics performing so we know about them when the indies talk about them. But, really, our job isn't going out and unearthing new talent; our job is enabling the indies to find those new talents and get them on telly through us.

DAVID PARFITT: We work with agents, contacts or recommendations. Generally direct contacts. We try to read things quickly but it varies. If we're not in production we will turn things around a bit quicker, but if we are in production it can take up to six months to get something read. The one thing we often say to newer writers when we see scripts that may not be for us, or scripts that aren't quite cooked, is 'go away and write more'. Write as much as you can. It's important to keep writing. Also, things definitely rise to the top depending on who they are from. There's a hierarchy. We would prefer not to receive hard-copy scripts – email is best – but we do scan if we have to.

ALEXANDRA ARLANGO: Cowboy Films don't take unsolicited scripts. The sad reality is that there's already so much to read, we simply don't have the time to take a punt on scripts by very green writers. Of course there's always a need for new writers. It would be a very stale industry if we only relied on an unchanging pool of writers to go to with projects.

CONOR BARRY: I don't think that it's about wanting to work with new people or a new director; it's just that you might get a script that you fall in love with and really like, which could be by someone

91

you've never encountered before. It's rare to find someone that goes straight to Hollywood. Generally people start off by working for someone for nothing; they get some experience and create networks. Then they get to make their own stuff with their networks and they evolve and grow with a group of people. They're growing and learning the whole time. It's a very natural thing that happens. As these people are growing, you encounter them in your spheres, on your shoots, in the media or at film festivals. It's a very natural, organic way that you get to hear about people. You know they've worked hard, they're serious, they've got a great attitude. That all comes from looking at their track record.

KATE ROWLAND: The BBC Writersroom finds them through them finding us. At the moment, the industry is still phenomenally white in terms of writers, particularly in TV. I've been to speak to groups in Tottenham and all over the UK, and people were really frustrated, thinking that as an organisation we don't want to hear from them or see their work. That couldn't be further from the truth. But sometimes you have to be really proactive, and go and run sessions in different places and see work. We really target different approaches to finding the talent and show that we do actually want this, our audience is missing this. But change is coming. The other thing is realising that there are a lot of talented individuals who would rather work in theatre or film because it allows them to work in a different, more authored way. TV is incredibly collaborative; it's a very demanding medium in a different form. You've got to be out and about – you can't wait for things to come to you. I absolutely believe that.

KATE OGBORN: We're a small company and we do have a development producer, who is aware of where people might be coming through. For us as a company now, and as a producer now, it's important to strike the perfect balance between working with new talent, and also working with experienced filmmakers like Ken Loach and Terence Davies. We won't be able to sustain our careers and the filmmakers' careers if we're just producing first-time features. We can't be putting all of our energies into new talent; we will look for it and we will support it when we can, but we have to be quite tough on those decisions. We do have a number of first features on our slate, so at this precise moment we're not looking for any more.

RICHARD COOKSON: New projects can have a number of origins: ideas we develop between ourselves (which might come from a news story, or a friend's anecdote, or a life experience, or even a dream – anything that has the germ of a drama idea); ideas brought to us by writers; or theatre, books and comics. In terms of finding writers to work with, there are people we've previously worked with who we'd love to work with again, or people we've always wanted to work with, or people who come onto our radar from either recommendations from their agents or recommendations from industry friends. We regularly meet with writers without specific projects in mind simply to get a feel for their work and personality and then keep them in mind for the future. In terms of how we receive new ideas, they tend to either be sent over on email by an agent, or brought to a meeting by a writer. In terms of how they are literally presented, to an extent every writer – and every project – is different, and they should be presented in a way that's tailored to the project. However, in general (and practical) terms, new ideas tend to start as verbal or written pitches that summarise the lead characters, setting, the main thrust of the plot or set-up and an indication of the tone. A sense of audience and broadcaster is useful but not essential. Written pitches tend to be between one and five pages long. Sometimes we receive entire spec scripts that 'click' straight away and manage to sell the idea as a complete package.

LIAM FOLEY: We don't take unsolicited material. There are legal and business affairs reasons why we can't. On a practical level, this is a four-person department and we don't have the human resources to open the door in that way. We physically wouldn't be able to sift through that level of material here. It would be lovely to open the door, but there has to be some filtering mechanism in place. If someone is determined and has a passion to write and share their work, they will find a way. Talent will out. If someone is good and persistent, they will find themselves an agent and a way to come full circle for Working Title and other production companies to be reading their material. We can never afford to be complacent so we will be scouring theatre, books, TV, emerging talent, etc. One of the key things that has led to Working Title being what it is today is that so many ideas have been generated internally, and often through discussion with writers or directors who we already have a relationship with. As well as being reactive to projects and talent and material that comes through the door, we're equally proactive at developing our own ideas.

BEN STEPHENSON: Dominic Mitchell, with *In the Flesh*, had never written anything for the BBC before, and nor had Julie Geary who wrote *Prisoners' Wives* – so there are always exceptions. The truth is, it's hard to become a great TV writer. But that's because it's an incredibly competitive environment and you've got to be brilliant. I don't think anything worth doing should be easy. At the same time, every single writer at the BBC has started with nothing and no one. They've all started writing the script in their room. What you've got to have isn't just talent; you've got to have absolute belief, passion and the ability to push it forward yourself. Although people are looking for great writers, no one is going to find you if you don't put yourself forward, really push and present your best work. The truth is, I've turned down more things by high-profile writers than I have by newer writers. For me, the name on the cover doesn't really matter – it's how good the script is. If I read a script by a really famous writer and it's not good, it's not good or right. Ditto with a new writer. Writers are the key to everything in drama. Ultimately, I'm not the person developing the shows. Those are the people that really find the writers. But when I was a script editor, you looked anywhere and you read anything. Whether it's a radio play, a stage play or a pilot script, it doesn't really matter. There's a feeding frenzy over great scripts. When you find one, not necessarily one you'll make, but one where you think the voice is really interesting, it's what every script editor/producer/executive producer is desperate for. Everyone wants to read a script and go, 'Oh my God, this is brilliant. I want to make this or make something else with the writer.'

HOW DO PROJECTS GET DEVELOPED AND COMMISSIONED?

When I first learned how producing and commissioning worked, I was surprised by two aspects. The first was that not everything happened in-house, and the second that the pitch never stops – with the ultimate judge of whether the decision to back the project was right or wrong being the audience. This is the bit that the newer writers and writer-directors I encounter seem to know the least about.

BEN STEPHENSON: Essentially, what will happen is that a writer will have a brilliant idea and talk to a producer, either an in-house or another producer. If everyone likes it, that project will then be commissioned into development. I don't sign off development at the BBC, I let my individual commissioning editors or in-house team do that. They are very close to me and know what our strategy is, so they'll know that it's not something totally ridiculous for the BBC or not something that's already in development. Then I really believe it's up to them to wave the flag for projects that they are totally passionate about. When they're ready for it, they'll bring it to me. One of three things will happen: I'll say 'Yes, let's make it', or I'll say 'I have concerns about it objectively', or I'll say 'It's interesting, but I think I'm missing something here'.

KERRY APPLEYARD: As a production company we pitch to broadcasters and work closely with them on projects in development, which then hopefully leads to a production order. Commissioners offer creative guidance to ensure the programme will work for their channel, yet hopefully will trust you and the vision enough to give the creative freedom needed. When the relationship works, it's hugely supportive and empowering, and produces a successful show everyone is happy with. And another season!

SERENA BOWMAN: If I read a script by a writer and I think the writer is really talented, I'll meet them and have a general chat and see what ideas they've got. Then if there's one that I think is particularly sellable, I'll ask them to send me a page and look at it with the rest of the development team. If they like it I'll share it with my director, and if he likes it we'll condition a treatment and take that to broadcasters.

ALEXANDRA ARLANGO: There are certainly similarities between a development person and a commissioner, although very generally speaking, commissioners are usually overseeing a very big slate of projects. Development departments in independent production companies (companies without a deal with a studio), if they are lucky enough to have a dedicated development person, tend to be one or two people at most. With very small production companies, the producer will also act as development person. The reason for having a development department is to support the producer (and production company) so as to free them up so that they can get on with the job of physically producing a film and (ideally!) readying up the next project for them to produce once they've wrapped up the one they are working on.

CAMILLE GATIN: Every writer and every director is different, and the producer's role is to understand how to get the best out of their team. I would usually meet with a writer – either one I have worked with previously or one I have recently discovered through an introduction by their agent or another industry professional – discuss their ideas and, if one hits a chord with me, I will find some development finance to enable them to take their idea to the next level. It's a fine balance between giving support to the writer to deliver the best script possible, and bearing in mind who the target audience is – and, as a result, where the production financing might be coming from. It's usually about finding a balance between creativity, budget and financing.

RICHARD COOKSON: When developing ideas, I try not to second-guess commissioners and broadcasters: any steers they give in terms of wants and needs are useful, but a brilliant script can overturn a proclamation or sidestep a shopping list. As a script editor (and still to some extent as a head of development), the first thing to do upon receiving a script, pitch or treatment is to acknowledge receipt and estimate a time frame for a more detailed response. I advocate sending the writer the headline thoughts (couched in a celebration of everything that's working) and then ideally bringing them into the office for a face-to-face discussion where we can cover the headlines and specifics. It's important not to be too negative. I've some experience writing myself, and understanding how much thought, effort and passion a writer has poured into a project – even one that isn't working – is massively important in terms of reinforcing the idea that we're all still invested in the idea and the writer's approach. It's often useful to look at intentions when discussing problems. Looking at what it is hoped can be achieved offers a more positive approach than looking at what hasn't worked (even if the two are obviously the different ends of the same problem).

POLLY STOKES: Before we bring something onto the slate at Film4 we will have a conversation, or a number of conversations, about what that film is, and why we want to make it. This is really an opportunity for us to ask a lot of questions so that we can all know what the film is and be sure that we want to make the same film. Also we truly believe that through talking in a group we can find the best version of a film. These conversations are with the writer and the producer, and possibly with the director too. Then we will put together a development budget, which in a way becomes a schedule for how we're going to develop that piece of work. We will meet at every delivery stage. A treatment will be developed, we'll read it and we'll think about it and meet. We'll usually send some notes either before or after the meeting that give our reflections on the best approach or direction to get to the next draft. Most developments are fairly conventional – they go from treatments to first drafts, to first-draft revisions, to second drafts, to second-draft revisions, to polish. We're open to other ways of working though, through workshops for example.

DAVID PARFITT: You always have a lot of confidence in projects that you're putting out to the market and that confidence can be undermined very quickly by the market response. We always feel that we are prepared to adjust when necessary. I often hear stock responses from commissioning executives, something like 'There's no market for period drama', and it's never true, so we ignore that. It's always easier for executives to say 'no'. I never take those things terribly seriously.

SASKIA SCHUSTER: Ideas need to be submitted to Sky through a production company, and so the development process usually starts through a conversation with a producer. Quite often the writer will be present at that initial meeting. During the development period we either have meetings to discuss notes with the producer and the writer, or send notes to the producer to feed back to the writer. Once we are in production, feedback is usually given by email or phone call to the producer.

PERSONAL VS PROFESSIONAL TASTE

I wrote a treatment for a film, based on a true story, about an Irish priest who had a secret family with his housekeeper. The response from one particular reader was more about their personal sense of outrage at the subject matter than the viability of the project. By contrast, an experienced producer read it and the feedback was more about how I needed to work on developing the conflict and narrative to make it more interesting because much of it took place behind closed doors. It was a lesson in only showing your work to experienced industry professionals who know how to be objective, or else paying a professional to look at it for you.

KATE ROWLAND: We talk a lot to our readers about professional and personal taste. You have to be able to understand what is good and what it is that emotionally engages you individually. You've got to be able to separate those two. We were judging the Northern Ireland Film and TV Awards recently and there was a very instinctive storyteller, who wasn't my cup of tea, but they were still in the room because they were phenomenally talented. You can recognise talent, you can see it and you know the audience will want it, but it might not be your taste. With my job, it's so important to think about the mix.

ANDREA CORNWELL: It really depends on whether it's a project that I've originated as a producer or not, where you've come up with an idea and you're looking for a writer to work with to bring it to life. That's always a very difficult and delicate process, as you will have a very strong vision of it yourself and you have to learn to partly let go. The best thing you can do is to try and be the ultimate audience member. Try as much as you can to get away from your own personal views about small details. If it's someone else's own work that they are invested in, you are just trying to offer an outside perspective and it's a very different process.

SHANE ALLEN: Much of it is instinct, and I've grown up loving comedy from when I was very tiny. I used to read comics and the jokes pages. I got obsessed with that and all the way through school I devoured all sorts of comedy. I do think I've got quite a broad appreciation of comedy so maybe that helps see what appeals to different sorts of audiences. But at the end of the day it's quite subjective.

RICHARD COOKSON: You can't let personal taste colour your approach to any project – we'd be in real trouble if we only made TV for ourselves. It's important to understand why shows are successful and find audiences, even if you're not naturally part of that audience – and then seek to deliver entertaining and stimulating dramas to those audiences. My personal taste tends towards finding new ways to approach things: fresh takes and different spins. I prefer to avoid repetition of past successes and reliance on nostalgia. However, I recognise that nostalgia and familiarity can be great comforts for huge swathes of the audience and can be handled smartly with a lack of self-indulgence. Additionally, I'm a complete geek about science fiction, fantasy and comic books – which is obviously quite niche in UK TV drama, but explains my absolute love of *Misfits*, *The Fades* and *Doctor Who*.

BEN STEPHENSON: I could never, ever make it about my own personal taste. In truth, if it was about what I would individually want to watch, I wouldn't be able to make 450 hours a year. Our individual tastes are very specific. What I use as my professional taste is very different to personal taste. Personal taste is what you're in the mood for when you're in the mood for something. It can change from minute to minute. Like when you're on your iPod, you'll listen to classical music one day walking into work, then the next you'll listen to pop music. That's personal taste. Professional taste is having objectivity and looking at the overall picture of what BBC drama could offer audiences. The bit that taste comes into in that, is whether it's good or bad. Inevitably, there's an element of personality involved in that, but there is in any job. I love that ability of one minute commissioning *Sherlock*, the next minute talking about *Holby City*. For me, there's no difference.

SENDING OUT SAMPLES OF YOUR WORK

You have to get your work read. The sample of your work that you send out has to be a must-read – if there's a better extract, send that instead. You must make the reader want to read more. The power of sample work is extraordinary – even if a producer doesn't think the idea is commissionable, if they feel that the writing has something they will want to work with you. It may get you into a meeting that could get you work.

PAULA MILNE: Maximise your chances. Have six ideas out at a time doing the rounds. One of them will land. Just keep going.

BOB BALABAN: I try to follow my own advice. When I'm sending out my own material I always look for a friendly conduit if I don't already know the recipient. It just works better. And faster. It's one of the benefits of being a multi-tasker. I cast a wider net than your average character actor.

KATE OGBORN: People do need to do their research and want to work with you. There's a clear difference between the people who take a scattergun approach and send things that neither Lisa Marie nor I have produced anything like in our careers, and the people who've looked at what we've done and seen a connection.

TONY JORDAN: In my first five years as a writer, every job I got came from the same 'calling card script'. It never got made but it showed what kind of writer I was perfectly.

RICHARD COOKSON: A spec script is first and foremost an example of your writing – it's not the end of the world if we don't like the main idea. Proving you can handle characterisation, dialogue and plotting is more important than nailing the perfect idea for a TV show on your first go.

JAMES DORMER: The key for me to get into the industry was writing a really good spec script. I wrote a feature script. Whatever you show people first, it should be something that you're happy with, as people will just want you to write the same thing over and over again for a bit. Make it something you want to do. If you want to write crime, write crime. Don't worry if something's a film script, it can still open doors for you in TV. In fact, it might even help you more. A lot of people in TV would like to work in film, so they feel they're getting a film writer, even though they're not really.

SASKIA SCHUSTER: In all my time working for indies, I've developed only one spec script. It was picked up by a broadcaster and went through several drafts but wasn't green-lit. Despite this, spec scripts are a really useful way to get to know a writer's voice and sense of humour, and in my experience have often been instrumental in helping form relationships with new writers. While I've been at Sky, I commissioned a script from a writer whose spec script I had read years previously and had really liked and always remembered. The spec script itself wasn't commercial enough to develop, but I liked the characters, tone and comedy of the piece. So when a producer brought me an idea by that writer, I was confident that the script would deliver. And it did.

GABRIEL SILVER: A spec script is how we judge a writer – be it for an episode of *EastEnders* or any show. I would say if you haven't got a spec script you are not a writer. I am speaking as an ex-script editor and development producer who has occasionally considered writing himself. And I've thought, no, I'd have done it by now if I were going to. So I must admit I'm not convinced by someone turning to it in their fifties, because it should have been in your blood in one form or other long before. A spec script or three is a good start.

DAVID PARFITT: A writer producing a spec script is absolutely as valid as any other route. We read spec scripts that come through agents. Good agents also don't put stuff through that isn't worth a read.

When you read a script you can usually tell whether it's going to work when you are about 20 pages in. The one thing we often say to newer writers when we see scripts that may not be for us or scripts that aren't quite cooked is 'go away and write more'. Write as much as you can. It's important to keep writing.

IVANA MACKINNON: There's a great value if you get it right – and if you don't, hopefully you have a good sample. There are few spec scripts in this industry so, when there's a good one, people go mad for it. *Eden Lake* was a spec script that James Watkins wrote in order to make sure he was attached as director, and often when writers are moving into directing the only way to do that is with a hot spec.

SIMON HEATH: If a new writer has a good idea but no track record, it may be necessary to write the script on spec. It will open more doors.

ANDREA CORNWELL: It's simply about writing 'that' spec script, getting it to the right people and learning how you develop a project to make it come to life. The key thing is to somehow tap into busy people and inspire them enough that they will sit down for two hours and read your script, even if they don't know you at all. That's definitely possible, even without an agent. You just have to approach people in the appropriate way.

READ MY SCRIPT – THAT IS THE QUESTION

Feedback and advice are essential if we want to grow as writers and filmmakers. Half this book will tell you to reach out to people and the other half will tell you to expect to hear 'no'. In these interviews people expressed a genuine desire to support new talent but found it hard to find the time to read new work and make notes. Saying 'yes' to something can mean saying 'no' to yourself.

BOB BALABAN: I like reading scripts by unknown writers. They haven't been around long enough to become trite. Or obvious. Maybe. What I don't like is reading scripts by total strangers. It's scary. I don't like getting sued. Or stalked. Sometimes in a blue moon I will make an exception but not unless the writer signs a 'release' first. Maybe the person says something that makes me want to read their script. Maybe I'm just feeling lucky. I once optioned a movie handed to me by someone in the accounting office at Showtime and the movie was made about five seconds later. It doesn't usually happen that way. I'll read anything with cast attached I'd like to work with. I'll read the scripts of friends and relatives. And their offspring... and their offspring's offspring. I'll read the scripts of people I've worked with.

MARGOT GAVAN DUFFY: Always happy to read work from new writers. If they have a good idea I would usually encourage them to get on and write it. Development money is in short supply and they'll have a much better chance of making headway if they have a good script to show around.

LUCY CLARKE: I generally only read friends' work as I'm short of time and aware that it would just feed into my procrastination problem.

SARAH GAVRON: I'm interested in other people's work and enjoy reading it and giving useful feedback on a script I've had to immerse myself in. Much easier to give feedback on a rough cut as you can see the decisions.

LEE ARONSOHN: I dread it, because I feel obligated to give an honest opinion and I don't even like my stuff that much.

MOIRA BUFFINI: I don't read many because I don't want to give false hope and feedback that isn't useful. Also, it's incredibly time-consuming. I have two kids, I'm caring for my mother and I've got more work than I can shake a stick at. I take on very little in the way of teaching. I know later in my life I will do more. I want to teach more and encourage the next generation when I'm not in the throes of the bringing-up-kids years. Every minute I'm not writing, I want to be with my family.

CONOR BARRY: 'Will you read my script?' Often I say 'I can't read your script' or 'I will, but it'll be a while before I get back'. It depends on whether I know a bit about the project beforehand; we can only work on certain budgets, in certain countries, genres, etc., so straight away I know whether it's possible or not.

JACK THORNE: Part of the reason why I refuse to read new writers' scripts is because I'm petrified I'll inadvertently steal something.

KEVIN CECIL: I take it on a case-by-case basis. It's a time thing. I have no power anyway. I can't commission scripts. It's not my job to do that. Those people work in the development departments of production companies. I attend Q&As at scriptwriting events and I support initiatives like Rocliffe.

JON CROKER: Thanks for asking me this question. I'd really love to answer it but unfortunately, as you correctly guessed, I'm just too busy at the moment. (Be prepared to hear this a lot. But keep trying to get lots of different people to read it.)

OL PARKER: I get asked a lot about reading people's scripts. I always say yes as I'm too embarrassed not to. As a result, I literally have at the moment 17 scripts that I haven't yet read and feel like a dick for not having done so. And the people that sent them now hate me too. Which I totally get. You've done a thing, you've put your heart on a page, you want to know someone's opinion on it. It's harder when they're not that great; I'm never going to be Simon Cowell and say that they shouldn't try to do this for a living, I don't have anywhere near that level of self-confidence (or cruelty). But it's hard when you read a script and you don't personally see any merit in it.

TINA GHARAVI: Most of this is unpaid but recently I counted the number of things I did in a week (aside from my students) and realised I probably needed to cap this a bit. However, I still remember how much people have helped me along the way so I remain faithful to the idea that it's important that filmmakers, indeed all artists, help those who are coming along behind them. It is, after all, reciprocal. And karmic and all that.

DAVID SIMPATICO: I always try to read a script, if someone asks me first, realising I may not have time, or time to get to it any time soon. I was lucky enough to get support and encouragement when I was starting out, so I like to offer advice and help when I can. I love teaching young writers.

TONY GRISONI: To read someone's full-length screenplay, you have to give yourself to it for a long period of time, and consider it very, very seriously. It's a big ask. I remember wanting people to read stuff I'd written and the reason I was doing it was I desperately wanted to get into the business any way I could. The idea of having someone you feel is established in some way reading this material and talking to you feels like it helps draw you into the game. I'm fortunate in that I can sit down with my friends, and if I'm worried about something I'm writing I can say 'Look, I've got this man and he was married, but I've got something I want to show about him and his ex-wife. I don't want it to be a flashback. Do you think it would work if I did this or this?' Playing with an idea. Someone can leap in there and say 'I saw this film which did this' or 'I read this book, which dealt with it in this way'. You're just chatting around an idea and that can be very liberating. Because they aren't aware of the rest of the tale, the prison of the plot or whatever. They share something with you which you can go away with and try to work into your tale. It's freer, more of a conversation and less humourless than 'Read my script and give me notes'.

WHAT MAKES THE FIRST READ THE LAST?

As a champion of new talent, I want something that excites me or elicits an emotional response. Common notes from my panels are that the ideas are brilliant but the writers aren't pushing themselves enough; that the concept is great but the pages are filled with exposition, that the female characters are undeveloped; that a script isn't about a specific, identifiable thing. A reader is your first audience – make them want to know what is going to happen next from scene to scene.

GARETH EDWARDS: William Goldman talks about the screen executive who goes home for the weekend with a pile of 50 scripts. Every script he picks up he thinks, 'Maybe this is the one.' It's that spirit of openness that a producer owes it to a writer to have. Nobody is looking for a professional layout or a list of reasons it will work, they are looking for a good script. If it's comedy they want to be made to laugh. I hate it when people send me a dry, dull or formulaic treatment, boring and too formal. If a comedy treatment isn't funny, why on earth would I want to read the script? I want to see the way characters talk to each other, not mood boards or graphs. I want to know if the writer is funny or not. Everything else follows on from that. Selling me comedy? Be funny!

DANNY HUSTON: Don't show me a cut and paste job that has been patched together. A collage of ideas is fascinating, but when it feels patched it can be really distracting and unattractive. Too much camera description feels very amateurish. I have read good scripts that have 'pan to' or 'fade in' or 'fade out', but when the writer is describing the camera movements you're not seeing the images – you're being told them. If I read 'the retina of an eye' I know to get out a micro lens. If it says 'the Amalfi coast' I know it's a grand shot. How you present things creates the shot. Don't tell me *how* it will be shot.

KATE ROWLAND: Tony Grounds always says, 'Don't think about the first draft, think about the first read.' What's the impact that your script is going to have? Are they going to commission the first draft? What he calls his first draft, it's actually his tenth, but it's the first draft that he would give to people. Writers need to put that work in. Sometimes writers are so excited and relieved that they've finished something, they just send it off.

ALEXANDRA ARLANGO: Generic plots and no clear idea of the audience their film is aimed at.

SERENA BOWMAN: Not proofreading scripts and sending them in with mistakes and grammatical errors. If there are mistakes it shows you really don't care. If you don't take the time to proof it then I won't take the time to read it.

CATHERINE WILLIS: Don't send stuff that's not ready, an early draft that isn't complete. Send something that's ready – it needs to be working on paper. If you know you're going to change something don't send the unchanged one with a cover letter. There's nothing worse than sending in a script and then letting the agent know a week later that there's a new draft of it. You will only get read once, and that's it, that's your shot.

BERTRAND FAIVRE: A lack of distinctiveness. I see people trying to join the flock, telling me it's a cross between Mike Leigh and Ken Loach. Don't try to be someone else. Be yourself and be accessible in your own manner. If you're not special, do another job.

POLLY STOKES: A lack of scale and ambition in the ideas. Projects that have a kind of 'smallness' to them. A lack of evenness over a range of characters – because it can be really hard for inexperienced writers to find truthfulness outside of direct personal experience. A personal bugbear is writing that doesn't let scenes play out properly, when you end up with a kind of montage effect, rather than a chance for the scene to breathe and find depth.

IVANA MACKINNON: On one end, stories which are hugely personal and internalised and where there's no access for the audience; on the other stories that feel like cardboard copies of big US movies without understanding the huge amount of work on character, action and plot that actually goes into those movies.

JOHN YORKE: Bad structure, derivative story, weak exposition.

LAWRENCE COCHRAN: My pet hate in all scripts is chatting. A scene with two people having a cup of tea. If it's inconsequential in terms of the larger picture, then it just makes my head hurt at how boring it is because it doesn't move the story. I love terrible exposition. It's a mean thing to poke fun at, but when done badly it's one of the joys of reading a lot of scripts. I had one set in Nazi Germany where someone was basically talking about what Hitler was doing in a really crass way. If you set something in Nazi Germany, you don't need to announce certain things. Also, too many stage directions or too few stage directions where I won't have any clue who anyone is or what is going on. Too many characters is quite a common thing.

•••

ROCLIFFE NOTES on...
HOW TO HELP YOURSELF
AND SCRIPT HOUSEKEEPING

- The title page is so important. Personally, I hate a long list of 'writing credits', i.e. story by, written by, originated by, by the same person. The TITLE by WRITER'S NAME is sufficient – similarly, endless film credits for the same person say 'big ego' to me, especially on short films. I also loathe a clichéd title or one I need to look up in a dictionary.

- Don't use camera or edit directions in a script – i.e. CUT TO, PAN UP, CLOSE UP, FADE IN. The writer is unaware of how film works. Your craft is to tell the story, not tell the cinematographer or editor what they do. Why limit what they bring to the project? Everything you want to convey should be possible through images.

- There's no excuse for poor presentation, dodgy punctuation, spelling mistakes and incorrect formatting. You can get free software to check these things for you.

- Don't use 'ing' in action verbs such as 'is walking' instead of 'walks' – go back through your script and, if you've used 'ing', change it.

- Overly long paragraphs of description are a massive turn-off.

- Avoid overusing the word 'feels'. How does the character *show* how they feel? What emotional action will demonstrate this? Give the actors something to do.

- Avoid overusing the word 'looks'. What kind of look? Is it a glance, a stare, a glare or are they peering?

- Excessive swearing indicates amateur writing – actors will add swear words if it feels natural. It doesn't make the character harder or edgier, nor does it add realism. Occasional use is fine but be aware of watersheds and the need to obtain PG ratings.

- Run the script in your head – that's what a reader will be doing. Your script must read like a movie, so describe it like a film. Discard anything that doesn't work.

- Make sure your script doesn't take too long to get started. Would you sit in a cinema waiting for a film to get going?

- Take the time to make it the best it can be. Everyone reading scripts is rooting for it to be good so they can say they discovered you. You have one chance with each reader.

• •

LESS IS MORE — IDEAL LENGTH

I use paper copy for breaking down a script for production (for budgets and schedules), but nothing kills my back more than lugging around a weighty script!

DAVID PARFITT: With heavy stage directions, I skim through on the first read, sticking to the dialogue. On a first read, you get a general view: has the story grabbed you, the shape of it, and the quality of the dialogue? Can I distinguish between the characters without looking at the names? Surprisingly often, that isn't the case. You get to the end of a dialogue exchange and you think 'I have no idea who's been talking', and you go back and read it again. You should be able to read it and know. Please, no more three-hour movies! It's a relief when something arrives and it's 90 pages, not 200, but I can cope with up to 120. Length is an issue.

ANDREA CORNWELL: There's no ideal length, but few films are better longer than shorter. Long films are expensive and hard to sustain and get right. People would prefer to make films of around 100 minutes, which equates to about 100 pages, not 140 to 150 pages.

BERTRAND FAIVRE: It's like when you are reading a book, turning the pages and you are almost sad that it has finished.

CHARLES GANT: A script should be the length that the story dictates. While Martin Scorsese can make *The Wolf of Wall Street* at three hours, audiences may be less tolerant of such epic duration with a newer filmmaker. I'm sorry to say that some of my peers arrive at screenings with two questions: will there be any catering, and how long is the film? In many cases, 90–120 minutes is the sweet spot, and it's a rare comedy that goes longer. However, if your story needs longer in which to breathe, so be it.

OL PARKER: I see a lot of overwriting. That's a basic of screenwriting: go in late, get out early. Poor structure is another one.

CLEONE CLARKE: I have to say my heart sinks when I get a script of 130 pages or more! Of course, the Scorseses of this world can deliver a script at any length.

REBECCA O'BRIEN: Hanging on to every scene and making things too long. That's a big error. Not letting go of stuff is a major problem.

MASOUD AMRALLA AL ALI: Many films are over two hours and into two and a half hours, which is very long. A festival programmer may not watch longer films or just part of them. When you have 3,000 submissions and one is three hours long, you might only watch half of the film or ten minutes of it. The filmmakers need to chop as much as they can. A reasonable length for a feature film is 90 minutes, unless it really is interesting enough to go to two hours. The same applies to scripts. Film length can prohibit a festival selecting it.

COMEDY WRITING

Comedy is extremely subjective but, given the voracious appetite for it, I really do feel it's a very accessible door into the industry for new talent. In no other medium have I seen content go from script to screen in such a relatively short space of time. Sharon Horgan advised at a BAFTA Rocliffe event to get as many gags on the page in a pilot as possible.

ANDREW NEWMAN: The rules for comedy writing are that there shouldn't be any rules, but I'd say be original, funny, brave, persistent, positive, creative and friendly. And also it seems that growing a beard helps (unless you're a girl).

SASKIA SCHUSTER: Jokes are a good thing to have in a comedy. I'm not being facetious – you'd be surprised at the number of scripts that seem to forget that. As well as jokes, for me it's all about character. Plot stemming from character. Finding that little kernel of recognisable truth, and then having fun with it. A good cast is obviously a bonus, as is a talented director, but everything starts with the script.

KAYLEIGH LLEWELLEYN & MATTHEW BARRY: Brevity. Generally, the shorter the joke, the funnier it is. Don't cram your script with long, rambling stage directions – especially on the first page. When you think of something funny, write it down EXACTLY as it occurred to you. Resist the urge to edit or replace words. It made you laugh for a reason. Put a clock on your characters. It's not just important they make it to dinner, it's important they make it to dinner by 8 pm. A ticking clock adds jeopardy and raises the stakes. Silly doesn't always mean funny.

SHANE ALLEN: In very broad sweeps it would be: you want lovable characters on some level; a really accessible world, or a relatable world that you can digest and understand, nothing too obscure that feels alienating; and really good, smartly written, crisply written jokes – if it's a comedy it's got to make you laugh.

LEE ARONSOHN: Don't overwrite; know where the jokes are.

KEVIN CECIL: Great characters are what make a good sitcom. I like a funny, clever plot as well. Characters and story are the two things. A lot of writers I know have a natural spark to them. You have to really want to be a comedy writer. In the early years, there isn't any pay or recognition; you must really want to do it. I don't think there's much point unless you have a burning desire to write comedy. If you are someone who does have that burning desire, it's probably an inherent ability. To get started, you need to have raw talent to get noticed when no one's paying you. There's always hope.

TONY COOKE: Simpler and focused is always better; cutting that extra joke, dropping that spare character, jumping over that detour, wrapping your exposition into a joke. Also, time spent on structure can set you free at the scripting stage. Having a detailed plan of beats each scene needs to hit lets your brain be more spontaneous, not less. My golden rule of what doesn't work would be 'No montages'. I love writing a comedy montage, but they never survive, and the alternatives are (almost) always more satisfying.

MARGOT GAVAN DUFFY: Fresh and surprising characters and dialogue. Finding a new way to spin a familiar situation.

DAVID FREEDMAN: Thanks to the internet I've learned that a puppy fetching a lit firework is funnier than anything anyone can or will ever write… so our work is more challenging than ever. If it's funny it flies. If it's funny and helps the story, bonus. If it's funny but pointless (you know what I'm talking about) and, by cutting it, something else just got funnier, then cut it. Lastly, farts may always be funny, but not when used randomly. Fart jokes need to 'earn their place'.

LUCY CLARKE: Make it shorter. This advice came initially from the world of gag writing, but it's good advice in sitcoms too. You love your characters so much it's easy for scenes to become overblown as they chat away amusingly to each other – and it's hilarious to you – but you've got to keep the plot motoring on otherwise everyone else is going to get bored. It also means when something important or meaningful does happen you can slow everything down and it has real poignancy.

CHRIS SUSSMAN: With new writers they often think they need to come up with a really brilliant, stand-out, original idea. And actually it's not about the idea at all, it's about the writing. So you can come up with an original sitcom about a group of aliens living on Mars, which no one has ever done before, but that doesn't mean it's going to be really funny. And if you come up with a really boring story set in a stationery cupboard in an office in Slough, that doesn't mean it's going to be really boring. It could be brilliant. It's all about the writing and the characters.

ANNA EMERSON: A big risk as a comedy writer is that, in trying to pack a script with gags, you can lose sight of what makes each character individually funny and they can end up simply becoming vehicles for your jokes. Let the comedy come from who they are, what they say and how they respond to people and situations. Shoehorning in a joke or keeping a joke you love when it no longer fits is always tempting, but do what's best for the script as a whole, deleting stuff when it's not working.

LIZZIE BATES: Also, comedy allows for all sorts of bizarre and surreal set-ups, but no matter how wacky a premise, the characters and how they respond to problems thrown at them still need to seem true and logical within that world.

GARETH EDWARDS: It's deeply personal and what someone looks for in a script, if it's comedy, is something that they personally find funny. I don't think there's any point going out to look for what the market wants at the moment. A privilege of how the BBC works is that we have long lead times. We can follow our instincts as far as developing shows goes. If you are trying to second guess what people want, you almost always fail. You have to look for what you want.

KEY THINGS YOU WANT TO FIND IN A FILM SCRIPT

This is an industry and people want to connect to the work. Those who are reading it, with a view to making it, know it's an investment of time and money, so what are the key elements needed?

JOSH APPIGNANESI: Strong premise, clarity about what the rising story is, a character with an actual arc... and an ending that suits the beginning. I feel like I can help improve on detail if the idea is strong and follows through.

MICHAEL KUHN: With most genre films they follow a pattern and the bits that work, work for a good reason. You'd be a fool to ignore the reasons why those work. The thing I'm always looking for is something that turns it slightly in the light, so that you don't recognise it so much as a genre film or see the rules of genre working. It feels fresh and different. The example I often give is when you think of Jaws. Actually, Jaws is an old 'cabin in the woods' movie – 'Don't go in there, look behind you, the creaking door' – but you don't recognise that, because it's all on a beach in the sun, not at all in a cabin in the woods.

BOB BALABAN: Well-written scripts don't always make wonderful movies but it's a start. As someone once put it: 'If it ain't on the page, it ain't on the stage.' The quality of the writing is the first thing I notice. If there's something original about the script. Or if it expresses something incredibly mundane in an original way. I'll generally consider a great story told in a mediocre way. I try to separate the writing from the story. I've seen some great movies made from inelegant but well-plotted scripts. And vice-versa. Often I'll pick up a script I loved years after I originally read it and wonder what I saw in it. Sometimes it's all in the timing. You've been thinking about reincarnation and someone sends you *Ghost* that day. Or you had a dream about a shark and Peter Benchley walks in.

CAMILLE GATIN: Primarily, I would say there are two obvious factors – one is scale and the other one is confidence. Newer writers have a tendency to write scripts which they consider to read cheap (three guys in a cottage) because they'll be cheaper to make. It takes an experienced writer to make three guys in a cottage interesting for 90 minutes. An excellent example of 'guys in a cottage' done well, and a great idea for a first-time, low-budget film is *Tzameti 13*: a penniless young man follows instructions to a remote cottage knowing only that great wealth awaits; little does he know that rich men bet on poor men's lives in an illegal Russian roulette tournament, of which he becomes one of the participants. The other factor is confidence.

ANDREA CALDERWOOD: What connects every time is an original voice – scripts that are derivative or trying to bend into a genre are much less interesting; also a sense of immediacy – having the drama happening in the present, not relying on lengthy backstory and exposition. Scripts need a genuinely dramatic idea that can play out over the duration of the film.

JON CROKER: Many scripts waste a lot of valuable time talking about what happened before. What happened in the past of your characters is only important if it moves things forward in the film's present. Even if the film is driven by the characters and not the plot, we should still be eager to know what they are going to do next. This is vital not only from scene to scene, but for every line of scene description and dialogue.

CHARLES STEEL: When reading scripts by newer writers for the BAFTA Rocliffe New Writing Forum for Film, on quite a few occasions I found myself getting confused by the one-page outline or treatment. Having to re-read paragraphs a few times to make sure I understand the set-up of the story is frustrating. It doesn't make for a good start, especially when one is reading one pitch after another. The extra time spent making it easy for someone to get into the writer's story can only be of benefit (try it out on a friend to see if it's as clear as you think it is).

SEAN GASCOINE: I'm always a little surprised at the number of writers who want to write for film or TV who don't really bother watching them. That's why I still read so many scripts that are supposed to be feature scripts that read like something you'd watch on a Sunday evening on BBC2. Film especially needs to be international, otherwise it's almost impossible to finance. My other big tip is relax and stop trying to impress people with your intellect. I read so many scripts filled with knowledge that the writer has picked up and feels compelled to share with us.

MANJINDER VIRK: Find the stories you want to tell, not the stories you think will sell or get made. You really have to nurture your own voice. Sometimes an excess of ambition and heavy, plot-driven ideas can get in the way, making the script less accessible. That shouldn't be confused with being bold and brave with ideas, but you always need to maintain a truth. If you truly believe it, the reader will believe it.

AMIT KUMAR: When I read a good script, I get physically excited. I can't sit still and read it. I am moving around and wondering what is going to happen next. When I am reading and I find something interesting I think, 'Why wouldn't anyone else living in the same world as me find this interesting?' For me personally, the thing that fascinates me most is humans and their capability for extreme violence, despite supposedly being civilised beings. When I think of a project which touches upon this aspect of human behaviour I get quite excited.

CREATE A WEB SERIES

With the advent of Netflix and online digital content, it has never been so important to understand what a web series is. Many writers and writer-directors could do with knowing more. People think it's simply a case of transferring a terrestrial show to a web channel. Many are let down by not following the rules of webisodes and by shoddy production values which don't cut it. There's also the unfair perception in the UK and Ireland that web series are of low quality, lowbrow and badly performed when compared to Web-TV on major channels such as Netflix, BBC iPlayer, etc., which it must be said have massive budgets behind them. It's like comparing a low-budget feature to a blockbuster.

One of the key developments of the digital age is that producers, directors and commissioners are becoming more and more inclined to click on viral you've made, rather than read a sample of your work. It can also be a great self-promotional tool – if done in the right way. According to comScore, an online engagement and use accessor, we watch 32.2 videos a month and there are more than 100 million internet users. That's one hell of a market to get noticed by.

By following the mini-web series format, writers, directors and performers can create an amazing showcase as long as they understand that web series are a medium in and of themselves. They are not short films cut down into half a dozen two-minute segments. There's absolutely no reason why they shouldn't be the great showcases they can be. There's no need to compromise on quality in terms of script, sound, grade, and especially not performance.

The optimum two-minute length is founded on research. A few minutes seems to be the longest you can go to. The Video Brewery cited statistics (at time of writing) from various studies which showed:

- Desktop users click away after two minutes or less
- Mobile phone users have a longer attention span
- iPhone users watch for about 2.4 minutes
- Android users do three minutes
- Symbian users stick around for just over four minutes
- Tablet and iPad users watch an average of five minutes of viral content

In the US, many TV stations, web channels and search engines are creating their own online outlets for home-generated series. The prize in MSN's annual competition at the New York TV Festival is a $75,000, six-part, two-minute series for their channel, based on a two-minute pilot you've created.

••

ROCLIFFE NOTES on...

WRITING AND CREATING A WEB SERIES

- **Brevity is key. It's important to understand why this is and why it still has to conform to the rules of storytelling.**

- **A web series needs a script and a three-act structure. It needs to be well written, rewritten and written some more like with any script. It has to be compelling but avoid set-up. Each webisode has to have an objective and must be entertaining. They must have a plot and follow a timeline.**

- The first ten seconds must be engaging and compelling. Twenty per cent of people click away after ten seconds, one third after 30 seconds, 45 per cent after one minute, 60 per cent before two minutes is up.

- When and what time of day to upload your series is also important. It's usually at 11.00 and 13.00 that most people get bored and look for online distraction (distraction programming). From 17.30 to 19.00 is the rush home on the buses and people watch on devices. Later in the evening people want to watch fuller shows (appointment TV) so the shorter formats aren't as popular.

- When you consider these figures you don't want to waste your time and money making something only you and your editor are going to watch so cut it back to no less than 30 seconds and no more than two minutes. The reality is, the shorter the webisode, the more likely people are to watch it. Many of these devices will be outdated in a couple of years but the point is, regardless of the technology tomorrow, why would you spend time and money making longer webisodes people won't watch today?

- People like to be uplifted, informed, surprised or impressed so go for something quirky and funny or poignant and intelligent. This is an ideas platform for sketches, sitcoms, drama and historical factoids.

- The ideal cast size is two with no more than five. An audience will connect better with more rounded and developed characters, with dramatic conflict.

- One-word titles work best. Lose the credits; a title is all that is required. Put this in the information or caption below the link or link to a blog page.

- Regarding production values – sound and grade seem to be the biggest area people don't do well in. While a poor grade may diminish the image, few people can forgive inferior sound quality.

- Prior to launch, cut a trailer and post it on social media sites. It's a great advertiser. Build up hype about when it's going online.

Releasing a webisode once a week may not keep your audience tuned in, but releasing a webisode at the same time every day will. Continuity builds strength, a following and momentum. Newton said an object in motion stays in motion, so with your show's story arcs you can build traction! Make sure your series is easy to find. Six episodes over six days!

- When writing it, think of your series strategy. Wait a month to see what the views are like and then start again with the second series, developing it and rewriting it and making it better than series one.

....

WRITING FOR THEATRE

Writing for theatre is no less challenging as a craft production-wise but it's an easier medium in which to get your work on its feet quickly, primarily because it's cheaper than film and TV.

BOB BALABAN: A play I produced and directed called *The Exonerated*, about the lives of five men and one woman who were wrongfully convicted of murder and spent a combined total of nearly 75 years on death row, is the work I am proudest of. We did it in New York and all over the US, in the UK and on TV. It's a docu-play, which means every word of it was taken directly from testimony, court records, letters and depositions. It helped change some hearts and a few minds, and gave a voice to a mostly invisible segment of the population. The entire experience was a great life lesson for me.

MOIRA BUFFINI: What the UK has is a thriving fringe theatre network with a thriving new writing scene. That isn't only creative but brilliant fun. Through my theatre work I acquired knowledge of plot, narrative, structure and a sense of character, which I carry with me. I didn't have to start at the bottom in film. I had an agent for my theatre work who helped me to cross over. My reputation as a playwright helped to make the transition easier because of what I knew about the craft. I would say if you cannot get a screenplay made, write a play. Get it on, even if ultimately you want to work in film. It will get you noticed and you will learn so much. As a writer the journey of seeing your work produced is so important. Whether it's film or play. A play will happen earlier in your career as it's cheaper to produce.

IVANA MACKINNON: Everyone has a different career path. Jack Thorne always quotes Paul Abbott telling him that a writer will write anything they are commissioned to write, even a menu. You learn something from everything and different disciplines like radio are very useful. Getting things made is important – until there's an audience reacting to your work, how can you truly know how it comes across? That's why writers who come out of the theatre often move faster through the world of film – they know how their work is received, and they know where their line in the sand is.

LEVI DAVID ADDAI: I decided to write my first play as my dissertation at university. I had no idea how to go about this so researched online and found the Royal Court Theatre was doing a special, free Young Writers Programme course for black and ethnic minorities. I joined and developed my play. It was later staged in the Theatre Downstairs.

JACK THORNE: My break came from a reading at the Young Vic, and then a play at the Bush. Jamie Brittain came to see it and told Bryan Elsley to come. Bryan then offered me a job on the spot on *Skins*. At the same time I'd made a short film with Dan Outram called *A Supermarket Love Song* – we got into Sundance. Ivana MacKinnon watched it and hired me on Celador's First Film scheme and that script became *The Scouting Book for Boys* (I liked long titles then), my first film.

DAVID SIMPATICO: Disney Theatricals hired me to adapt the cable movie *High School Musical* for a live stage show. They had seen a workshop of my play *Bad Blood*, about a Puerto Rican transsexual agoraphobic psychic, and thought I would be an interesting choice to adapt the teen movie. They looked beyond the context of the play, and saw the potential of my talent, and took a chance.

TV WRITING

If you want to make TV programmes, you need to compare what you are writing to what is on TV. A comment frequently heard at the BAFTA Rocliffe industry panel on the work of newer writers is that things need to play out and not be solved too neatly. This refers to the fact that, often, the issue or problem or conflict occurs and is then resolved too conveniently and quickly to ever satisfy a reader, and ultimately the audience, who will switch over if they get bored.

KERRY APPLEYARD: Create and invest in long and complex arcs for characters who can undergo incredible change as they move through the world of the TV show they are in. *Breaking Bad* broke the mould and is the current touchstone for character-focused writing. I want to be engaged by, and therefore invested in, the characters and their story. That means strong, intelligent writing with nuance and subtext that feels real or completely of the world the writer has created, being impacted by relatable characters on an emotional and dramatic level, and storylines that are driven through character. I love being surprised by reveals or actions in a script that feel original and provocative yet right for that drama. For new dramas and comedies, it has to be an idea that has some originality to its premise, characters and treatment, and generates enough story ideas and arcs to sustain multiple seasons. Believe in a project completely to be able to sell it.

JAMES DORMER: Family. I've read this elsewhere, but it's true; most really good TV shows are about family, whatever genre they are. If you look at *The Sopranos*, *Breaking Bad*, *The Walking Dead*,

The Simpsons, etc., they're all about family. Even when it's not clearly about family, it can be about a group of people who form a family, like *Waking the Dead*. You have the grumpy father, the long-suffering mother and the kids who are mucking about.

SUSAN HOGG: Received TV is dead TV. Stories must have a truth about them. Most importantly your spec script demonstrates your 'voice'. There are many hours of TV drama so there will always be room for an original voice with something to say. You need a narrative, which kicks off right from the start. Get the 'big thing' happening straight away and let your characters run with it. Let your characters surprise you, shock you even. As long as they're working within the boundaries of their truth we will believe in them. This applies as much when you're crafting a relationship drama as it does to a cop show. Research always pays off. What you don't use today will support you in the years to come. When I was a script editor I was told to make sure I applied the rule of the four Fs – a fight or a fuck in the first five minutes. It's a bit crude and not to be taken literally but I've never forgotten it!

MALCOLM CAMPBELL: Working on long-running series has been very good for me, in terms of learning the craft and how to write on other people's shows. It's also crudely where the money and work is. I'm always trying to develop my own stuff and generally, if you've proven you can work on the more established shows, you will get asked to work up your own.

SUSIE CONKLIN: I'm a peculiar one in the sense that I am American and British – I grew up in America mainly but I was in love with British drama, so I moved to London where I got my training as a script editor and as a writer. I think it's an exciting place to work, but I have friends who work in the US and I've spent a fair bit of time in LA, so it's been fascinating to compare the two. The American writer's room is such a dynamic place, and I do believe the quality of their long-running shows is due to this team-writing approach. But the British system really develops individual authors' voices and has blazed the trail in short-form and serialised drama for years. This is now flourishing in America (from *Homeland* to *Breaking Bad*), but people shouldn't forget that the UK has led the way. From a writer's point of view it's good news – I don't think there's ever been a time when there were so many potential markets for drama or such openness to new ideas.

CLAIRE WILSON: Skills for TV writing – one green light, two near misses, and plenty that died a quick death.

BEN STEPHENSON: TV, ultimately, is all about character, but not without a great story, because an hour's worth of TV is a hell of a lot of time and needs a lot of story. Ultimately, though, great characters are the reason people come back week on week. For me, the process of thinking about whether something is good or not is, firstly, asking myself whether an audience would be excited by the idea. Our lives are busy so it's got to be something where they go, 'That sounds brilliant, I really want to watch that.' Secondly, I ask whether the script is a complete iteration of that idea. Does it feel like it has a total world? Is it confident and does it feel original and surprising? Thirdly, I ask myself whether the team making it have an absolute passion for the project and want to get under the skin of it, exploring that passion.

••

ROCLIFFE NOTES from...
PAULA MILNE

To conclude, here are some observations from Paula Milne, which were tweeted by the audience from an amazing event she did for us at BAFTA Rocliffe on this very subject:

• When you come home from work, grab the remote and scan the channels for a story – a story that's stronger than you.

- Bear the format of your TV programme in mind so you can defend it.

- You have to take the audience into a world they thought they knew and then confound them.

- With TV, the dialogue must underpin the visual, and when writing you must know where you are going or you'll lose the momentum.

- The advantage of screenwriting is that you can invite the audience to share moments alone with a character.

- Ordinary things can appear malignant and benign depending on the POV of the character.

- How does something earn its place narratively and thematically?

- TV is the theatre of the people.

....

ADAPTATION

There are so many books and other works in the public domain, but find out via the publisher if what you're interested in is available *before* embarking on the script. Nothing is more disheartening for a writer than to discover a script will never see the screen because of rights issues.

JOHN MADDEN: You need to try to pull out the essence of the story that you're responding to. It's important, because you're selling a movie on the basis of the story or the novel, that you are true to it. It's not rocket science to understand that that doesn't mean reproducing it exactly. It just means honouring something and finding the most articulate way to express it in cinematic terms. It's very, very difficult; the longer the book, the harder it is. Some of the most successful transfers are from short stories and short fiction because the movie is such an incredibly compressed form. To distil something into a single paragraph, which is essentially what a movie is, is quite tough. You have to pick your projects carefully.

KATE OGBORN: Taking *The Deep Blue Sea* as an example, that's an adaptation of a play, but it feels absolutely authentic to Terence Davies as a filmmaker. It articulates his view of the world, his passions and the emotional landscapes he wants to occupy. It began as somebody else's words, somebody else devised the characters, but reading the screenplay, you know you're absolutely in Terence's world.

CHRISTINE LANGAN: Interrogate the underlying material and decide what makes it compelling. Has it been done before and, if so, how? If it's a classic text, is there room for another interpretation? If it's a contemporary novel, is it well known and loved? These factors have an impact on what kind of adventure you are about to embark on. It's important to know whether your audience has prior knowledge of the work. Audience familiarity could make it a 'hot' project and attract attention but, equally, it might leave you feeling restricted in how you approach an adaptation. We normally develop something from scratch so the conversation would be less about the merits of the novel than about the virtues of adapting it or not. Why this novel? What could it be? Is it something that will lend itself to adaptation? Is it going to be incredibly complex? Are we going to have to change it radically or considerably? What's the point of view; is it a first-person narrative? What are the technical issues involved in adapting it? For me it's more useful to think of it as a mutation than an adaptation. You are taking one form that is expansive and digressive and turning it into something that is much less forgiving. You can break the rules in the form of a novel in a way that you can't in a screenplay. A screenplay, and the resulting film, needs to be impelled in a particular way so as to maintain momentum through the beginning, middle and end, whereas a novel can afford to depart from this requirement. Failing to understand this fully is a risk we run all the time.

JAMES DORMER: I will read the book and start finding a take on it – an angle that allows me to take some ownership of it but which is true to the vision of the original creator. I've adapted a few books into feature scripts – none of which has ever been made. But on the two occasions where the authors were a part of the process they were both very happy, even though some quite radical changes were made to the original stories. That's important to me.

MOIRA BUFFINI: You come to an adaptation to make the thing itself. You're not making it your own; you are making something accessible to a massive audience. You have to set out to make it what it is. If you attempt to make it your own, you diminish that. Naturally, you bring a lot of yourself to the project. There's a lot of me in my version of *Jane Eyre* – but you have to be quite self-effacing. The challenge with *Jane Eyre* was that the novel structurally is never going to work as a film in a satisfying way. I had to change the structure of the novel to make it more filmic while illuminating the heart of the novel. My most difficult experience of adaptation was with *Byzantium*, my own play. That was much harder than working on someone else's work – I had no objectivity and was less reverential. I have recently adapted other novels that exist as scripts but have not yet gone into production. They have all been very different and I had to change significant things in each book. In one, there's a love story between the two central characters that isn't in the book, but it illuminates the themes of the book in a more dramatic way.

RADIO

Radio is another accessible medium for newer writers because productions cost less than TV or film. We had great fun in college writing and performing radio sketches – they were only ever aired on the college campus and were very silly, but they *were* aired nonetheless.

GARETH EDWARDS: Radio is very interesting because you have total control over the revelation of information. It's entirely up to you when you tell people what's happened. Somebody might be dressed as a chicken in a scene but you don't have to reveal that till the end, whereas if it's a TV programme you have to reveal that straight away. That means more work has to be done on the dialogue of the script, but not too much, as people do love it if a joke is told by a sound effect. Essentially you have a much narrower range of ways to tell people things, as it all has to be done with sound. You can also do fewer jokes about the difference between appearance and reality, for obvious reasons. With radio comedy, people won't laugh if they don't understand the situation. You can't rely too heavily on subtle sound effects. The audience might not be listening very carefully; they might be driving a car, for example, so they won't have subtle appreciation of all the different sound effects. You can't assume everyone is going to notice the soundscape – don't hang a joke on a bird tweeting quietly in the background. A lot of people won't have heard it.

KEVIN CECIL: We started writing sketches for *Week Ending*. I was 21 and Andy was 20. We'd make between £11 and £30 a week, which we would split between us. Then we were very lucky and were taken on by the BBC radio comedy department on a trainee writers' scheme. They gave us £6,000 each over the course of one year. They sent a cheque for £500 every month. It was enough to move to London and get off the dole. I have a debt to radio for that.

ANNE HOGBEN: Radio is an incredibly visual and free medium. The production costs are so low; you can make anything happen in a recording studio. It can be set in the past, the future. You can create incredible worlds and what would be expensive locations in the mind of the reader. Radio provides freedom. You don't have to do all the logistical things you have to do when writing for the screen.

DOCUMENTARIES AND UNSCRIPTED — FROM START TO FINISH

Documentaries tell great stories, connecting emotionally in a very different way to fiction films. While the execution may differ, however, the conventional rules of live-action films still apply – a story, a narrative, captivating characters. And there are many other paid work opportunities for writers, be it writing gags, voiceover or commentary, all of which require strong writing skills.

DAVID FLYNN: Writers work slightly differently in unscripted and documentaries. They are needed to a greater or lesser degree, and are employed in a more ad hoc way, depending on the project. For example, on a game show, a particular host may have their own writer who creates their gags, different lines and helps on the script. Similarly, if we are working the script up for a show that has more of a kind of comedy bend, we'll bring in writers at that stage. Quite often the series producer does the writing but there are times when a different tone is needed and, in this case, a writer will be brought in.

SAUL DIBB: For ten years before making feature films, I made documentaries. What I learned most from the approach in documentaries fed into the making of *Bullet Boy*, and the other films as well. I always want them to feel authentic, as if they belong in the real world, shot on location, natural light where possible.

ASIF KAPADIA: My first short at film school was a documentary about a young man, Tarborda, from Brazil, working for his Italian uncle in a pizzeria in Wales, fighting corruption and standing up for what he believes in. It was about not fitting in, dealing with local gangs. I never thought about it until *Senna* but my first film was a documentary with similar themes. I have always been interested in the space between fiction and non-fiction: writing a script, going

131

to India and working with non-professional actors who can't read, casting real people to be themselves and nudging them to tell your scripted story. Using camera, sound, music and other elements to tell the story rather than them telling you the story via dialogue. People incorrectly feel documentaries are less worthy or less important than fiction, or easier, all of which is totally wrong. Emotionally, I have been far more engaged by the great documentaries I've recently seen. Documentary wasn't a huge leap for me. Things come along by chance and you've got to be open to them. With *Senna*, I had the chance to do something completely different to *Far North*, my previous feature shot in the Arctic. I found a style that I wanted to express, very similar to every fiction film I've ever made, and as personal as *The Warrior* and *Far North*. I made the stylistic choice of not wanting to have talking heads, and none of my short films or feature films has long sequences of people talking to camera either. With my documentary I tried to use the same stylistic idea using archive and for me it's a continuation of a personal style.

SIMON CHINN: The director and editor 'write' the film in the cutting room, but it's not like writing a screenplay; it's simply crafting the film from available material. Often directors take writing credits on documentaries; I find this a bit mystifying because, as a documentary maker, I understand what the role of the director is. I expect most directors want to put that authorial stamp on a film by taking a writer's credit, as most people don't understand how documentaries get made. Huge credit must go to documentary editors who share the burden of the writing process with the director – they should probably share the writing credit when that happens.

ALISON MILLAR: When an observational film changes structure (as they often do in the cutting room), and it's decided to make the film 'more personal', then a script is developed. If a filmmaker is too close to the story, it can be difficult for them, and help is required. Rarely is a 'writer' brought in. Usually the editor is brilliantly helpful, or the executive producer, in honing the director's script so that it complements the story and fits naturally and keeps true to the original intention of the film. If done well it can add another layer to the story. While making *The Disappeared* I cast a BBC reporter more as a 'character' in the film – mixing up the genres of current affairs and documentary. Darragh MacIntyre and I worked together on the script and it was very rewarding because he's a naturally gifted writer. It added greatly to the documentary, both on a factual and emotional level.

DAVID FLYNN: In the unscripted, the first stage is identifying the core of the idea, the interesting thing that makes us stop and think this is worth listening to. When pitching to a channel, they give feedback specific to their channel and its needs. At that point, it could be that you pitched something for primetime and the feedback is, 'Our real requirement is for five o'clock.' At which point the process will be about working out how to make it work for that slot, for the money, for that particular audience.

SIMON CHINN: If you find a great story, get access to it and attach a great director – that can be all that's required for the process of developing a documentary. For *Project Nim*, which I made with James Marsh after *Man on Wire*, we were financed on the strength of a very brief outline and a book that I'd optioned. That was it. There are other projects, however, where it isn't a ready-made story; you're constructing a narrative out of nothing and these do take longer to develop. It's sometimes about trying to persuade a financier that there's a film in the material at all. I'm doing such a project with Louis Theroux, which has been about a year in development. That's quite unusual for docs.

ALISON MILLAR: In TV documentary the development process can be painful. Once the paragraphs have been sent to the commissioning editor and development money released you have to have a taster tape or a 'sizzle'. It means we need to jump into a story and a relationship with our key characters faster than we would like to.

But a good taster moves a documentary out of development into commission swiftly. The worst side of development is when the station, or their commissioning editor, isn't certain what they want. So when a good fresh story and strong taster is presented, they can order it to be re-cut and pounded until, often, it's thrown out because of a lack of vision and assertive decision-making from the commissioning editor or channel.

SIMON CHINN: The distinction between TV and theatrical documentaries is very hard to articulate. You know it when you see it. The kinds of films that I've been making are driven relentlessly by something that feels like it could work narratively and aesthetically on the big screen, and draw paying punters to the cinema to see it. That's a really challenging and tough thing to do. Every couple of years there'll be an example of a film that has competed on equal terms with similar scale fiction films. When *Senna* comes along and does three million pounds at the British box office, it gives hope to us all. Nowadays, theatrical documentary is acknowledged and recognised as a genre. There are all these people who have paid to go to the cinema to see a documentary, who have never done so before but hopefully will again. It's getting better but it's still an incredible challenge. What makes *Senna* cinematic or theatrical is its approach to its subject matter, its approach to narrative, its visual approach, its boldness. Often the films that work theatrically are doing something that hasn't been seen before. They push the boundaries of the form.

DAVID FLYNN: With unscripted, what works best isn't dissimilar from scripted. Both need to have a compelling narrative at their heart. You need to ask yourself the question, is there a beginning, middle and end to the story? Who are the key characters? Do I care about them? How does the story move on? Is it just something that could be a magazine article, or does it have enough depth and journey to really create a full hour of TV? Some of the rules for scripted apply to unscripted ideas as well. Ideas that really don't work are the ones where there isn't any form of journey or narrative and the characters aren't interesting enough. You have to always ask yourself, 'Have I managed to deliver that?'

ALISON MILLAR: With TV documentaries we are told that we have to keep the audience from 'flicking channel', so right from the very top of the film we start with a 'menu' of what's coming up (all the best bits). Once I cut a slow, slightly lyrical intro to a TV documentary, only to be told by the commissioning editor that 'it wasn't for a film festival' but for TV. I had to re-cut with a 'pacy' pre-title tease. It depends on the slot or channel. Few slots allow films to be cut with a more intriguing top. Often a TV documentary top can be re-cut many, many, many times. I have less experience in the theatrical documentary world but, from the films I watch, there's a slower paced intro gently seeding the character-story and the story is allowed to unfold.

SIMON CHINN: In documentary, it's easier sometimes to convey really complex emotion in a really economical way than it is to do the same thing in fiction. I'm talking about Jean-Louis' tears in *Man on Wire*, the response of Rodriguez as he steps out on stage in South Africa for the first time, and this moment of his resurrection and being discovered. I've often thought of Jean-Louis' tears in *Man on Wire*. It's very difficult to put your finger on exactly what he's crying about. It's not possible to reduce that moment to a simple explanation. And who wants to? His emotions are incredibly complex, based on 30 years of being defined by this event. Three decades of sadness, joy, bitterness, whatever. How would a screenwriter deal with a moment, a set of emotions, like that? I think with huge difficulty. Maybe it's impossible. At their best, documentaries can deliver emotion in a way that no other form of filmmaking can.

CO-WRITING – HOW DOES THAT WORK?

There's an adage about two heads being better than one, but this does involve a commitment. The ground rules need to be worked out beforehand and it also means half the pay.

REBECCA DALY: We spend a certain amount of time in a room together bashing out ideas and so on and working on the treatment and structure. The actual writing of the first draft is something that either Glenn [Montgomery] or I would do on our own. Maybe it's different when writing for comedy, but typically what we're doing is drama so it's difficult to do that as two people sitting in a room together – you have to get into your own head to write that kind of stuff. It's very collaborative but it's not always in the same room together.

GLENN MONTGOMERY: It's worked very well for me because my collaborating with a director [Rebecca Daly] has, in a lot of ways, meant that my work is getting out there quicker than it might otherwise have done. I couldn't advise people enough to consider the collaboration route because I can't imagine having done it any other way. A director helps get a script off the ground. Another nice thing about collaborating for me personally is that you have someone involved with you throughout the process.

DAVID FREEDMAN: My agent prefers me to write on my own, but I prefer to write as a team because it's more fun. Tennis is more fun with a partner, as is sex – or so I'm told. Having someone to bounce off is far more fun than putting the material to one side and 'sleeping on it' to get perspective. Besides, I love the fast-paced exchange of ideas, which can be like a brilliant volley in a game of tennis. And, like sex, I find that working with a partner means we finish a whole lot faster! Wait, can I rethink that last analogy? It's different every time. As a rule, there are no rules. I've written with the other person pacing in the room and by swapping drafts and notes via email. Mostly I find it's best to block things out together in the same room and then both go to your corners and Skype from time to time. The more you agree at outline, the less you argue over the scripting. In fact, if the outline is really nailed together beat by beat, one of you can get run over by a bus and the other will be fine to finish alone, take all the credit and cash. Physically I only have one rule, and that is you MUST take turns travelling to the other person's house. It's only fair.

BRONA C TITLEY: My partner [Tony Cooke] and I tend to brainstorm for ages, pick out bits of the brainstorm we like and chisel that into a story. Then we brainstorm details of the story, and chisel that into beats, etc. And we take a nice long lunch during which we usually watch a comedy show as it's important to know everything that's being made in the industry.

TONY COOKE: The biggest consideration is when to work together and apart. I've worked in two collaborations, and they've been at opposite ends of the scale. One was essentially writing in parallel, acting as souped-up script editors. With Brona [C Titley], from day one we've improvised and written every line and stage direction together, working at one computer. This method has the benefit of avoiding any nasty surprises for either of us, and saves on electricity bills. We do still go away separately to think, when certain ideas or fiddly bits of script need quiet mulling time.

ANNE-MARIE DRAYCOTT & CHARITY TRIMM: We live 200 miles apart but at the start of any project we come together to brainstorm, draft an outline and maybe write the bare bones of a script or treatment. Then separately we write or rewrite sections, and reconnect via the wonder of Skype. There's countless more rounds of rewriting and reconnecting until we feel it's ready to share.

KAYLEIGH LLEWELLEYN & MATTHEW BARRY: We write everything together. In the same room. From beats, to a scene by scene, to the first draft. We sit side-by-side figuring everything out. Then one of us will do the first pass at a scene, before handing it to the other to amend, and we continue like this. Not every duo works this way of course, but we're strongest when we write together.

CO-WRITING — THE PROS

The thing to know about co-writing is that, as with all working relationships, there are benefits...

KAYLEIGH LLEWELLEYN & MATTHEW BARRY: When writing comedy, you have the instant gratification of knowing whether your material is funny. If you're making each other laugh, chances are it's going to make other people laugh. And, similarly, if you think you've written a little nugget of solid gold, and your writing partner just looks you dead in the eye and says 'You're insane', you know it's a dud that needs to be cut. You can play off each other, bounce ideas around, and everything seems a little less scary when you're sharing the burden.

ANNE-MARIE DRAYCOTT & CHARITY TRIMM: We constantly push each other to write better. Working on your own, you might think, 'That'll do', but working as a pair there's always someone saying, 'Can we make that stronger, better, funnier?' Sometimes the answer is 'no'; but most of the time we encourage each other to rewrite and improve a script before sending it out. Also, when you run out of ideas, the other person usually has something up their sleeve (always a relief!).

LIZZIE BATES: When you write in a pair it can be a bit like having your own little writers' room. If you sit together around the same keyboard to write – in the slightly laborious way we do – then every joke is discussed and scrutinised by both of you as you go along, which helps weed out any really clunky stuff early on. As a result, our first drafts often feel quite rigorously written by the time we've finished them. Another nice thing about being a team is that success, when it comes, is a lovely thing to share.

ANNA EMERSON: Writing together also means you don't always have to write whole jokes! Often, one of us will come up with the structure of a joke, or a promising premise, and the other will fill in the details and help hunt about for a punch line. If you're bouncing off each other well, writing together can just be wonderful fun – it's all about trying to make the other person laugh, and if you've done that then you know a joke probably has legs. And rejection is less painful divided by two as well!

BRONA C TITLEY: Writing by yourself definitely holds a certain pleasure, but it's all too easy to convince yourself that something is awful when it isn't, or indeed that it's fantastic when it's really not. With a partner you have a second brain to 'sanity check' everything you come up with in the moment, so you never go too far down the wrong path. Having said that, sometimes they can be wrong. Like when my partner blocked my amazing space-vampire-musical-thriller idea. Why WOULDN'T it work, huh??

TONY COOKE: The right writing partner will make it feel easy. Or at least slightly less painful. It means having someone funny to laugh with, bounce off, and help provide twice the selection of snacks. It's also far harder to fall back into the soft arms of Facebook with another person across the table, so your brain keeps focused and firing for longer. Then there's the extra momentum a writing team can give you – mutual decisions are much harder to go back on, so having a partner can help you keep the faith when your demons of doubt come knocking.

CO-WRITING – THE CONS

And, as with all relationships, there's a downside too...

ANNE-MARIE DRAYCOTT & CHARITY TRIMM: Sometimes an idea or line you think is utterly hilarious is met with silence – or worse, confusion.

But ultimately that's a good thing – there's always an in-built filter in the system before anyone important sees it!

BRONA C TITLEY: Cons? Cons? Well... I mean... not to be a, you know, big 'ol materialistic, money-grabbing capitalist or anything but... you split the fee. You split the fee. You split the freakin' fee. Also you do have to learn how to pick your battles, compromise and wear clothes to the writing room. Writing in your pyjamas by yourself is cool, with another person not so much. Having said that, onesies are acceptable.

TONY COOKE: One thing I'd say isn't a drawback is halving the cash – if a writing partnership isn't helping make your scripts twice as good, twice as quickly, then something's probably not working. There's certainly a need to compromise, so it helps to be adept at stepping back and judging your own ideas evenly. When there are disagreements, you have to know the right time to really pitch your case. Mostly, though, it's about ignoring who came up with what, and trying to pick the best idea.

KAYLEIGH LLEWELLEYN & MATTHEW BARRY: If you've found the right person, we genuinely believe there are very few (if any) cons. The struggle is finding the right person. If you're not in a position to be honest with one another, it can cause a lot of difficulty. It's important to be able to tell the other person 'That's crap' without there being any hard feelings.

ANNA EMERSON: Scheduling is probably our greatest problem. We have to book in sessions to work together weeks in advance so that our writing time is protected against other commitments. Similarly, organising meetings with people in the industry can become a game of email ping-pong as we try to find dates we can all do.

LIZZIE BATES: It's also worth remembering that, when you do get something commissioned, you'll have to split the fee between the team, so you need to be happy that everyone's putting in equal work.

KAYLEIGH LLEWELLEYN & MATTHEW BARRY: The only thing to be aware of is that, when you feel passionate about your work, it's inevitable that you will have disagreements. Disagreements that sometimes blow up into ridiculous and laughable arguments. We recommend having a cup of tea, then just pretending it never happened.

INDUSTRY MISCONCEPTIONS AND REALITIES

There were so many things I got wrong when I was starting out. The biggest one was not realising that being a freelancer is hard. That the phrase 'hurry up and wait' is true. I had no idea things took so long to happen. This is hard work and it isn't all glamour.

KATE OGBORN: One of the myths is that this industry is very adversarial. I don't think it is; it's hugely collaborative and that's the pleasure of it. The great people I've worked with know that and instinctively behave like that. A good idea is a good idea and it doesn't matter where it comes from. There's too much energy spent on building it up as an industry which is competitive and adversarial, which I don't think is the truth.

BRONA C TITLEY: One scary thing is how GLACIAL it can feel at times. Everything seems to take FOREVER in development and by the time your script gets to TV it'll be 2090 and there won't even BE TVs anymore, as we'll all be watching TVs in our EYEBALLS. The way to overcome that is to have lots of projects on the boil and lots of ideas in the bank. Try and strike a balance between the projects you do for money, the ones you do for your career, and the ones you do for your soul. People think comedy writing is a difficult industry to get into. The truth is it's actually a lot easier to get into than you think. Producers WANT to find great writers – their jobs depend on it. If you can write good stuff, get it to the right people, and follow it

141

up with more good stuff, you'll be laughing. Not necessarily all the way to the bank, but certainly all the way to an envelope under your mattress where you can stick that £300 you just earned.

KATE LEYS: People seem to think there's a special secret that film industry insiders know and that functions as a sort of golden ticket in, and if they can just figure out the thing, or get someone to tell it to them, they'll be sorted. Everyone in the film industry is making everything up as they go along and asking their allies and peers and friends for advice every day. Which is what anyone who wants to work in the film industry needs to do: have allies and peers and friends (people who care about the things you care about and are trying to achieve the same things you are), ask their advice, and then get on and do stuff. There's an awful lot of waiting around to be noticed by someone successful when what people really need to do is get on and do stuff with the people around them. And become successful! It's a real, massively successful industry. This means that a) there's room for everyone, and b) it's not amateur hour.

TONY COOKE: I'd say the industry's very random. The 'sure things' don't come off, while the 'long shots' can suddenly take flight. It's exciting, but the uncertainty can be tough. The best way to deal with it is to not get too buried in one project. Always slightly spread your efforts, keep half an eye looking ahead, plan for things not to happen, and maintain a delicate balance of development and commissioned work. And if anyone knows how to do that, please tell me.

ANNE-MARIE DRAYCOTT & CHARITY TRIMM: There's always the fear that people won't find our work funny or 'get it', but you have to trust that what you're doing will capture someone's imagination and share it anyway. The levels of bureaucracy a script has to go through before anyone decides whether to make it – or not – are unbelievable. We've been told that many stars have to align before a script actually gets made – so maybe during a Mercury Retrograde when Saturn passes Uranus we'll get another commission.

142

KAYLEIGH LLEWELLEYN & MATTHEW BARRY: A writing career isn't a series of rejection emails, it's a series of unanswered emails. The industry's ability to ignore you is both impressive and devastating. Not working is a constant worry. Fear that your scripts will never receive any recognition. Oscillating between crippling self-doubt and dizzy elation. You've got to think you're the best and the worst. This business takes you on an emotional rollercoaster. Our mantra is, 'Throw enough mud at a wall and some of it's bound to stick'. We say this to each other constantly, when one of us needs to be talked down from a bridge. If you work hard and stay motivated, it will pay off eventually.

ANNA EMERSON: The thought of having a sitcom commissioned but losing control of our idea so it turns into something different from what we'd hoped is pretty scary. But you can mitigate against that by trying to work with producers who clearly share your vision for your script and are equally invested in the idea from the outset. It's easy to think you just need one big break but, while in a sense that's true, we've learned that the best way to get noticed and keep people interested is to always have several projects on the go at once – don't just rely on one script or one idea to make your career.

LIZZIE BATES: For a long time we thought that producers were all intimidating and unapproachable, but the truth is they're really keen to uncover new talent and new ideas. If you have a script you've worked hard on and you're happy with, don't be afraid to send it to people to find out what they think. They will read it – although it will probably take them a few weeks. Also, you have to accept that as a writer you can't control everything – it's such a huge collaborative effort to get something made. Lots of other people will have input along the way and they'll usually help to make it much better.

DAVID FREEDMAN: Nobody hands over the 'rich and famous' contract like in *The Muppet Movie*. It's a job. A great job. I get to live in my own imagination for 70 per cent of my day. The other 30 per cent is email, procrastinating on Facebook, and frustrations like any business. I know what frustrates me. But thankfully no terror... yet. I have worked with a few unique people who are notoriously 'terrifying' but, at the end of the day, when they're finished shouting, it's just a job and shouting is just how they talk.

COVER NOTES

I sometimes feel a little taken aback when someone sends me an email with 'READ MY SCRIPT' as the subject line, or else sends me a dense email all about themselves. Make your covering notes short. Another no-no is misspelling the name of the person you are writing to, especially when the name is in the email address. I've had Farrah – Farragh – Farra – Fara, AND THE WORST – FARRITT! Also, don't send a 'review' of your work. Let the reader be the judge of whether it's good or bad.

GARETH EDWARDS: If a script arrives and the cover letter makes me laugh I will read that script. I work in this industry because I like laughing. I will want to read the rest of the script. I had one gutsy email that made me read the script straight away. It said 'Hi, I've written this, it's funny. That's basically my whole pitch.' I read that instantly as it was bold.

CATHERINE WILLIS: Being new in a creative industry isn't an indication of how good or bad you are. Lack of experience isn't necessarily a problem. However, receiving a blanket email where you get the sense that they've probably sent it already to 20 other casting directors, with no indication as to why they think I'm right for the project or what they know of my work, just feels like – 'We have a script. Would you like to pitch for it?' I feel it needs a more personal approach, particularly from the less experienced. You need to be very honest about what your project is. The other thing that people do which always makes me laugh is that they try to sell it as an opportunity for me to hitch my wagon to their rising star. I'll meet with you because I like the sound of the project, not because you're the next big thing, because my career is established. Don't try to make it sound like you're giving me an opportunity.

KATIE WILLIAMS: I look at the covering letter and CV, searching for some sort of indication of an 'engagement with the industry' in whatever form. BAFTA Rocliffe is a good example – those sorts of competitions or bursaries or schemes – or it could be that you've made a short film, had a play on, you've done some radio. Personally, I find that's quite helpful in terms of showing awareness of some part of the industry. You've made some inroads with networking, you have existing relationships, and also there's an element of realism to it. I have had it happen in the past that somebody has sent me all 13 parts of a period adaptation of a novel. Then their covering letter and CV shows they don't have any previous experience, that it's clearly something they've written for their own pleasure. Good for them, but it feels like such a disconnect from the reality of writing that sort of show for TV. I can't do anything with that. Check who you are sending your work to. I went through a phase of people calling me 'dude'. It was really strange. I had, like, three in a week. 'Hey dude, check out my work.' Just no!

FILLING IN THE APPLICATION FORM

From funding applications and courses to festivals and competitions, it seems you're always facing a lot of effort for very little reward. No matter how advanced the electronic systems become, applying for something still takes careful thought and planning and last-minute entries sometimes feel like the only way to get it done – I've seen Rocliffe entries coming in minutes before the deadline. This leaves you open to all sorts of potential stresses – computers breaking down; careless mistakes happening; you might be confused by something on the form but have no time left to ask for clarification. Mind you, even though we all know from experience that leaving things till the last minute can be a major headache, we still do it!

• •

ROCLIFFE NOTES on...
WHAT TO CONSIDER WHEN FILLING IN FORMS

- Read the terms and conditions. Why would you not? You are sending your intellectual property to strangers. What are they going to do with it? Read the small print ALWAYS!

- Check your entry details. A missing digit in a phone number or an incorrect email address can be the difference between your being selected or losing out. If an organisation can't reach you, they will move on to someone they can.

- Avoid being over-communicative – it's nice to make a connection, but be sensible and list all your queries in one email, not a multitude of emails. It comes across as needy.

- Having emails or calls ignored is extremely annoying for an organisation, but what reflects really poorly is bad communication within a team. With BAFTA Rocliffe, if you nominate a lead writer for correspondence then it's up to them to pass on and share the information.

- Don't apply expecting to lose or not gain anything. This is a disservice to your work.

- Send what is requested in the instructions. Nothing more and nothing less. Don't try to bargain or expect them to fill in the gaps.

Someone else will have done it properly. Don't try to negotiate special dispensations – if asked for ten pages, send only ten, not twelve. We often get told by writers that a treatment or synopsis can't be shortened – of course it can! That's editing.

- Don't send requests minutes after you've submitted your application or panicked messages at 1 am on Saturday when we are likely to be asleep. Don't find a number and then call or text message it over and over again. Don't tweet everyone you can find associated with that organisation and their mother – if you haven't heard within a reasonable time frame then, yes, follow up, but allow 24 hours.

- Being rude in communication for whatever reason is unacceptable. While an infrequent occurrence when it happens it's not forgotten – there's a human being picking up that email, not a robot. Keep your dignity and professionalism intact. You will just appear petty and embittered no matter how justified you may feel. There were better scripts than yours – that's how competitions work.

- Once you've sent it, let go and see what comes back. Whatever the outcome, savour the relationship. If it's a rejection, lick your wounds – you are more than one script. You may not be on the winners' list this time but you could be the next. Build on it. Think on this as making a connection.

A SHORT BIOGRAPHY – 100 WORDS

It's hard to write about yourself. How do you sum up so much in so little space? The main thing is to not let your ego (or lack of it) get in the way of telling the reader a little bit about yourself. Think of your bio as a fun way to present yourself. Imagine you're dictating to someone who knows nothing about you how they should think about you as a writer. I think Ralph Waldo Emerson said it best when he observed that great geniuses have the shortest biographies! When it comes to Rocliffe biogs I love to see the writer's personality revealed. Allow us to begin to like you on paper. This can be done in very subtle ways with punch and wit, but, most of all, make it personal to you as opposed to bland and generic.

....

ROCLIFFE NOTES on...

WRITING A SHORT BIOGRAPHY

- Start with your name. At this point, no one knows who you are! You wouldn't believe the number of biographies I've seen with no identifying features. With BAFTA Rocliffe entries, include your application number and contact details.

- Write in the third person and refer to yourself in the third person. My biography begins with: 'Farah Abushwesha is an Irish-Libyan writer and filmmaker'. It states who I am, what I do and where I am from. I wear my dual nationality as a badge of honour and it explains the Irish accent and Arabic name. Irish newspapers often refer to me as 'Dubliner Farah Abushwesha'.

- Make each bio relate to whomever it is you are sending it to. Adapt it accordingly. If you are bored by yourself, then we will be too. Should you be writing it for work purposes, keep it professional and formal.

- For industry-related biographies, don't give an autobiographical account of your life from how your parents met, your birth, etc., but rather focus on the milestones relating to your career.

- What are your writing achievements? List educational qualifications if they are relevant to writing. Include items like whether you have a blog – go straight into what you do, what you are... you are a writer. How many scripts have you written, have any of them been optioned? List any awards or prizes you have won and if you have been shortlisted for any. With your features, are you drawn to a particular genre? Have you done anything with these scripts? Are they being considered by anyone? If they've been optioned, by whom? Do you have any virals online?

- Don't be generic, e.g. 'I've written a wide range of scripts'. Brilliant that you are committed to writing, but what have you done with them and what are they about? Have you written any shorts, and have they featured at any festivals? Put 'I've written several shorts, one of which, *JACK*, was in XYZ festival'.

- With Rocliffe, while we are looking for people with the potential to maintain a career, we are also very excited when we find a complete newbie! If this is your first script then say so. We have featured the work of many first-time writers and we'll be only too thrilled to have given you your break.

- What makes you stand out – only list your achievements if they are relevant.

- Don't tell porky pies or embellish – you'll get caught out. Once a manager in the US contacted me to find out what I thought of a writer they were considering representing. The writer claimed they had won the BAFTA Rocliffe award. Firstly, no such award exists. What we do is make career introductions, help people launch their careers and elevate unknown or newer writers. People will check this out. It's a very small industry. Think of it as a village.

- Don't use exclamation marks, and proofread and spellcheck your work. Always.

....

SPEC SAMPLES OF WORK

Should you be asked to send a sample of your work, it can be a mind mess to know exactly which extract to pick. Some people ask for your first ten pages; if so, make sure they are your BEST ten pages!

LIAM FOLEY: The key is choosing the most dynamic, eventful (or characterful) scene or sequence to include as a sample. A sample that starts right at the beginning can sometimes take too long to get going – start in the middle of a story or sequence, hit the ground running – as long as the reader isn't confused, a sense of pace or incident or intrigue is more likely to hook the reader than flat set-up and exposition. Again, make the sample pages count. The writer should be able to take an overview, look at them and be able to identify what the dramatic function and purpose is of each scene or sequence. Why is this scene here? Is it genuinely propelling the story or building the character effectively? Ideally, it should always be both.

KEVIN CECIL: Your first scene is almost certainly too long. Make it shorter and get the story going more quickly.

SASKIA SCHUSTER: If possible, don't submit an extract from an opening episode: first episodes can all too easily become bogged down by the set-up. A later episode can often showcase the comedy and the characters far better.

TONY JORDAN: Have a script or a piece of film that you think shows WHO you are as a writer or a director, not what you think is prettiest or most commercial. It has to be something that represents your unique voice. Then you can use this piece of work as a calling card.

KERRY APPLEYARD: It's quite rare for inexperienced writers to get their concepts produced into broadcast shows so be realistic with your expectations. Make sure you have strong and relevant samples – always have one original piece that showcases your strengths and tastes well, i.e. a cable piece if that's your ambition, plus write a spec of an existing drama or comedy to show you can write in a different voice and tone.

MARGOT GAVAN DUFFY: I have experience of a spec script being produced. But even if this doesn't happen, they are a good calling card and usually the starting point for a relationship between writer and producer. A producer can't assess a writer's ability to write comedy until it's demonstrated on the page. Treatments aren't much help in this instance.

DAVID CHIKWE: It's completely pointless to get out of bed if you haven't got a spec script. You've got to have a spec. As writers, it's about writing. That's the only thing you care about as a producer: can someone write, do they have good ideas? Everything else is window-dressing. It comes back down to the spec; you've got to have a really good spec. It is the thing that will get you through the door. When someone's written a really good script, dedicated themselves to the craft and to the storytelling, honed their skills for no commission or money, just because they have to tell that story, well, that's the best thing any writer can do. That takes balls. Never stop doing that. If you want to work in film, you should have a film spec. Sometimes I find that there is a reluctance amongst writers to put themselves out there creatively, i.e. I'm going to sit down and write something and have something to present. Sometimes there's that desire to jump ahead and I think the classic thing with any artistic form is that you need to cut your teeth. You need to go through an apprenticeship of learning your craft, whether as an actor, writer or director. There are no shortcuts in that sense.

•••

ROCLIFFE NOTES on...
SPEC SAMPLES

- Pick an extract where something happens and that isn't just chat. Make sure it's dramatically driven and relates to the central question or plot. It must sell the story.

- Don't just use the first few pages: in the horror genre the first few pages are about set-up and atmosphere, but we want to see drama!

- Don't worry that a scene is too visual. Some of the best writing is in the action. Don't be overly descriptive.

- The scenes must match the treatment.

- Entertain the reader. Make it a 'must-read' not 'nice to read'. Allow us to get caught up in the story and ultimately want more.

- Does this sample demonstrate your skills as a filmic storyteller?

- Don't give them more than asked for. If you are asked for ten pages and they don't like them, an extra page will not entice them to read more.

••

IT'S ALL ABOUT CHARACTER, CHARACTER, CHARACTER

Conflict, drama and comedy all come through characterisation. It's intrinsic to the quality of the narrative. Characters must be compelling and can compensate for a weak plot. Consider how similar many genres and films are in terms of theme and setting. What makes them different? It always comes back to the characters! A frequent obversation by the BAFTA Rocliffe panel is that newer writers are not delivering characters that are reflective of the diversity in our society or the female characters are underdeveloped.

JAMES DORMER: Character and emotion. Finding some heart in a character is stuff I like doing. Actors like really chewy stuff that lets them exercise their acting muscles. I've been lucky enough to work with some really great actors. There have been occasions where I've had a script and changed the sex or sexuality of the character. For whatever reason, I find that sometimes it can give an extra level to the character, whether male or female. It can give it an extra freshness.

SUSIE CONKLIN: I keep a little file of interesting characters that just pop into my head. I don't know where they are going to go in any particular story. Sometimes it's just an attribute, something you see someone doing. I write a lot in coffee shops because I get bored of being at home. So I spend a lot of time looking at other people and listening to all sorts of conversations. But I don't have any one way of developing a character when I'm writing. I think about qualities the character has, and where that would take them in a particular story; what they would do. Does it enhance it? Take it in an interesting direction? Once I start writing, it becomes more organic and characters tend to take on a life of their own. Sometimes they are very bossy and push themselves into the story in ways you hadn't expected. For me, it's one of the most mysterious things about the process. A character will leap out of the grey matter of your brain and simply demand attention.

TINA GHARAVI: Find the truth in your own character or that of someone you know very well. Find the character's voice and let them speak. I'm unsure who told me that, or where I read it, but I often think about it when I'm writing. If you can hear them, then it's probably good writing.

BOB BALABAN: I notice characters that leap off the page. Not because they have six heads and webbed feet. But because the writer has been able to capture the essence of their character in a way that makes you shake your head and say, 'I know those people... those characters didn't walk through a door marked "archetypes enter here".' I bring as much of myself as I can. If you look hard enough inside yourself you will find something you can use for any character in the world. A murderer? I can think of a few people I'd like to strangle. Would I really do it? NEVER. Multiply that feeling by a hundred, though, and I've created a credible inner demon.

HOPE DICKSON LEACH: Wants, situations, idiosyncrasies and problems. Sometimes I cast actors in my head; it makes it much easier to write dialogue. I tend to live with characters or places or plots in my head for ages before they become something more than that.

KAHLEEN CRAWFORD: Unless it's essential, use as little in the way of physical description as possible. If there isn't a backstory, we ask the writer/writer-director to tell us what the character used to do. So, for example, if he used to be a surgeon, does it matter whether or not he has red hair? Does he have to be over six foot? If these are not story points, why are they in there? Maybe tell us what accent they have, where they are rooted, where they are from, as it allows the actor to come in prepared. It's good to show key emotional character traits and major points along their journey, especially if we have to send it out to people who don't or won't have access to the full script, e.g. if you know that further on down the line he's going to get divorced, then this information allows the actor to bring more to the casting.

DESTINY EKARAGHA: The characters in all my scripts tend to start with a 'what if' scenario. What if I can turn into a butterfly? Then who would want to be a butterfly, what kind of person is that? That's when a character starts to emerge. I explore the reasons why someone would want to be a butterfly. Maybe it's because they are dealing with things that they wish they could fly away from. My mind works with scenarios after that; I get into the character's head and explore them for a while.

LIAM FOLEY: Every character needs to sound distinct. They should be as identifiable by what they say and how they say it as they are by what they think and what they do.

CREATING A CHARACTER

Characters need a huge amount of thought and work. What a character biography should reveal is the character's appearance, if relevant, their personality, needs and wants, and some insight into their particular traits. They reveal the central conflict within a character and the role they play within the plot. Ben Stephenson has described it as needing to 'walk in the character's shoes'. So what do you need to consider when creating a character backstory?

KAHLEEN CRAWFORD: I worry when people are too prescriptive – when you get a three-page description of who the character is and where they've come from. Often it means you're trying too hard to tick a lot of character boxes when in reality what you end up doing is finding someone to play the role and then working backwards. It's very good to have a strong sense of who these people are, but until you start casting you don't really know who they are. Often a first day of casting is about finding out who the characters are. The characters evolve throughout the process. Obviously if you're offering a role straight to a big-named actor, that's something the director and the actor will explore between them, but when you're doing auditions the character build-up happens between the castings in chats in the audition rooms.

KERRY APPLEYARD: Sometimes there's lack of voice and inconsistency of character – it's always a good idea to go through the draft as one character to make sure you know where they are, what they are doing and why they are doing it at all times, rounding them out in the most interesting way so they feel believable and their dialogue feels rich and colourful.

PAULA MILNE: They have to come side-by-side with the story, with what it is you're trying to say with the scenario. I'm always quite interested in challenging myself in terms of the way you tell a story – the way you begin it. With *White Heat*, for example, beginning in the present and then going back. One aspect of a character in *White Heat* was that she was very unforgiving. In order to make the story work you have to have something in her past that has led her to be so unforgiving. I created something so huge that she couldn't forgive it but also she discovered in herself that she was disconcertingly unforgiving and lacking in compassion – many people are but are never tested in that way. You think about what would make someone harden like that. Some of what you come up with, you might shed as you're writing it, but it somehow becomes absorbed in the substructure of that character. When I describe characters, I say their age as a reference point but I never say that they have dark hair or any physical attributes. I'll say 'He's someone who invades a room rather than just entering it' or 'He's the sort of man who has a whisky when it's your round and half a bitter when it's his'. So you get the kind of essence of a character in a very simple, direct way. I wrote about a character that his emotions lay in a rarely visited place. What you're doing when you write something like that is creating an arena also for the actors to explore. So they look at that and ponder it and then they can talk to the director or myself about it. Then they can bring something to the role.

●●●

ROCLIFFE NOTES on...
CREATING CHARACTERS' BACKSTORY

When I teach, these are the kinds of exercises I ask my students to do when considering a character profile. What are the facts around your characters? Build up a life for them. This is to help you make the character within the script stronger – you build up this backstory and then use how that has formed the character traits in the script. This is research and preparation. No one has to see this except you. Each character must serve a purpose with a solid plot line or they can come across as tokenistic and will seem like a worrying blind-spot in terms of building characters and story. Why are they in the story at all if they only serve to get a character to reveal something?

- **WRITE:** What did each character feel before the script started? How did they relate to life and every day? What was their life about?
- **CREATE:** A short piece of prose about their life prior to the script starting.
- **PHYSICALITY:** This can define them. Are there key physical attributes?
- **PERSONALITY:** What are they like? Do they have a personality trait?
- **NEEDS/DESIRES:** What do they want? What do they need?
- **HOPES/FEARS:** What are their hopes and what are their fears?
- **POINT OF VIEW:** What do they think about the world? Their views and beliefs.
- **CHANGE:** How do they change as a result of their desires or how do they change over the course of the story?
- **ATTITUDE:** How do they react to things? Are they happy or sad? Do they stay or go?
- **STAKE:** What does the character want to gain or fear to lose?
- **RELATIONSHIPS:** How do they relate to other characters? Each supporting character should be different and contrast with the main character.
- **CONFLICT:** Create conflict – we don't really want to see a room full of people agreeing – it doesn't create drama. Each character should have their own standpoint. This can come about when there's a clash in needs and wants.

....

THE TREATMENT

Treatments are notoriously hard to write. They can be frightfully dull but are great at outlining what your story is. Not only do they have to be entertaining and engaging; they also have to reveal the beginning, middle and end of the story within what can feel like a very tight word limit. They are an acquired skill and, as with all skills, practice makes perfect. Think of a treatment as telling your story in a fast-forward sort of way. Use them to show off your descriptive writing skills as a filmic storyteller. It's an opportunity to captivate and entertain, making the reader like a script more!

When a treatment is written in the style of 'and this happened and then that happened' it can be dull and at times confusing. The last thing we want to do is put the reader off before they get to the script. So ENGAGE! Choose words that sell and drive the story. Don't tell us what makes this a great script – beauty is always in the eye of the reader. This is not a review.

JON CROKER: Never write a treatment that doesn't tell the whole story. A treatment or synopsis isn't the same as the blurb on the back of a novel – it's not there to make you want to read the script to find out what happens. Executives and producers don't care about spoilers. They want to know your film has a beginning, middle and end and that you've figured out what happens in each. If it shows that, then they will read the script to see how well you have executed it. But if it ends with something like 'Will Jane be able to save her cat from the burning building or will her own personal demons consume her?' then you haven't ended your script. Tell us which it is – cats or demons.

●●

ROCLIFFE NOTES on…
TREATMENTS

There's no magic ingredient that makes something great to read, but here are some guidelines which may help you to get there:

- Capture the setting, genre, atmosphere and tone of your script/ series.

- Write in prose, third person and present tense. 12 pt font is fine. Don't use dialogue or too detailed action.

- Tell the story in the order of the script. For BAFTA Rocliffe entries, make sure you refer to the action of a script extract you send, even if it's only a brief reference, so the reader knows where the extract comes in the screenplay.

- Don't avoid ending your story but do avoid 'dot dot dot' endings – you need to reveal how you tie up all the loose ends.

- Really identify the conflict between the characters and their motivations, and then show us the resolution. You don't need to name every character, just the main ones. Gradually add detail but don't get bogged down. Concentrate on getting to the end.

- If you are still struggling then perhaps you need to ask yourself how well you know the story you are trying to tell. Have you developed your plot enough? What is at the heart of this tale? What are your characters' reasons for being, their motivations? What do they want or need? Is there enough believable conflict between them and how is it resolved? Only you, the writer and creator of this world, can tell this story and make these decisions – so you have to know your story and what it's about. Sometimes the difficulty with treatments lies not with the treatment writing itself but with being sure of the story you are trying to tell.

- When you have finished writing the treatment, print it out and read it. How does it relate to the extract? If you're not happy with it, change it.

- I read once that the key to writing a good synopsis is to read, reflect, write and revise. So now put it away for a day and revisit with fresh eyes.

- BAFTA Rocliffe calls ask for no more than 500 words or one A4 sheet [NOTE: other initiatives/schemes may ask for more]. The same length of treatment is required for TV series, short film and feature film calls. Use this as an exercise in writing (not torture!). If you are struggling to create a treatment, try breaking it down: 100 words on the beginning or set-up of the world you are creating; 300 on the middle – or muddle if it's a comedy; and 100 on summing it up.

•••

WRITING TV EPISODE GUIDES OR STORYLINES

Writing a storyline is great fun. You are creating characters that you can make do whatever you want. Hanging out with pretend people, in a pretend world, is or should be like child's play, but sometimes it's not. There are a few basic rules to it. When writing an episode for TV, you have to think about the length. An hour on screen has to fill the time with something that drives it and sustains our interest, not just the long-story narrative. Storylines need to be threaded through, and you need to know what structure that will take.

Structure is all about planning. With TV episodes you can't over/under-run, so you need to plan carefully. The first thing to understand is that an hour-long episode on most channels will be around 50 minutes, so a full script will be somewhere between 46 and 50 pages. It's worth noting that some channels have longer ad breaks and that these will dictate the exact length of the script, and you will also need to allow for credits. That's a lot of pages if you are writing a six-episode series. Each episode needs its own structure and story to drive it forward. You need to show you know what those stories or storylines will be, and this is where the guides come in. While the treatment is an overview, the guides give us snippets of insight into how it will work and entertain.

ROCLIFFE NOTES on...

STORYLINES AND EPISODE GUIDES

- These are written in the third person, present tense. No dialogue should appear at any point. I would suggest 50–100 words per episode – less can be more if you can entice us with the story progression.

- Each episode must have vital moments, so describe the essential moments in each episode. Stay true to your story. Be dynamic – in drama, significant things should be a consequence of what has happened before, not coming out of a clear sky. Too often we see superfluous scenes – everything should be part of the bigger story, driving the story forward. When writing episode guides or storylines you are describing the dramatic moments within the script.

- When you have a series arc, which is apparent in a long-running story or a mini-series, this is the backbone of the series and we should see progression of this in each guide. The overall structure of the beginning, middle and end is in the treatment. The episodes must match the treatment.

- Each episode has to draw the audience in, keep them coming back the following week, revealing enough of the main story while still telling single story strands within the episode. There's a complexity to this but it should be clear what your main story arc is.

- When creating a storyline that is contained within a single episode ensure that it has some closure, even if you continue other storylines into future episodes. It's by engaging with these characters that an audience is drawn in, making them come back for more. Show the characters' history, backstory and interrelationships/interactions with the other characters. A great example of this was the series *Cold Feet*, which ran for six series, 32 episodes from 1998 until 2003. The series bind was the ups and downs of three ordinary couples in Manchester. Good times and bad times were followed through the 32 hours, which were finally tied up in the last episode of the sixth series when all the history of the previous years came together.

- While we all follow the maxim 'show not tell', even in guides and storylines, that doesn't mean you replace loads of dialogue with lengthy emotional description and action. Replace it with one line.

- Know the medium – watch and read shows. Assess how they finish stories that are interspersed within the main series narrative. This will give you a greater understanding of the structure of the show as well as a greater appreciation of what your story can be.

- Work out the ending of each episode, right at the start, as this makes it easier to know where you are driving the series rather than rambling along. You can't wing it.

- Stay true to your story. Don't self-sensor at the first draft or second-guess at the spec script stage what our panel or a commissioner will be looking for. Ensure that your characters are believable and by that I mean that they behave the way real people actually do today. Go out and observe the world. Spend time in the world you are creating if you are reflecting a world you don't know.

••

SAY IT IN ONE LINE — THE ELEVATOR PITCH

When we are asked to summarise our story in 25 words it seems impossible, but it's essential if you are going to sell it. You may only get ten seconds to pitch someone, and in those ten seconds you need to entice him or her to want to know more. The first thing to understand is that there's a difference between a logline or tagline and a 25-word synopsis. A tagline is like an advertising slogan –

it's like a slogan for a story. Think of 'Catch Me If You Can – the true story of a real fake'. What does that tell you about the film? Nothing, but it looks great on the poster.

A logline or 25-word synopsis is a brief outline of what is at the heart of your script in terms of conflict and that magical ingredient: how does it end? It shows a development executive or producer exactly what the story is about.

....

ROCLIFFE NOTES on...
THE ONE-LINE SYNOPSIS

- You need to think of your logline as the way to entice someone to want to read your script. You need to bring the same passion and element of excitement to it as you have to your script. The old rule of thumb is – if you are not excited by the story you want to tell, why should anyone else be? This one line should *sell* the story, not tell the story.

- Before writing, you need to know your story – what the beginning, middle and end are. You know what are the key things at stake and what type of story it is. Read Wikipedia for tons of examples of short-film synopses.

- Who is your protagonist, what do they need, what's stopping them, and how are they going to get there?

- Identify your protagonist. You don't necessarily have to name them, but you do have to say what they do.

- As with most of these things, write the synopsis in the third person, present tense. It immediately places the reader at the heart of the story, and creates a sense of immediacy.

- The wording has to engage and create the sense of a ticking clock – something is at stake. Think of what words you can use that will make an impact.

- Brevity is key, with a succinctness that is clear and makes sense – imagine how many synopses producers and development executives read every month. Go for clarity, conciseness and a lively delivery.

- This is your voice. Use active verbs to give the synopsis pace, energy and tension. Think about it this way – where your story has tension, so should your synopsis.

- Use your one-line synopsis to set up your world.

- Unlike a treatment, you don't need to reveal the end, just sell it enough to make someone want to read it to find out what does happen. People like surprises.

•••

FINDING A PRODUCER

All talent needs a champion and the lesson I've learned as a producer is that if I'm not absolutely passionate about something and determined to make it happen, I'm wasting both their time and mine. You need to find people who believe in your project because they're the ones who will ultimately have to sell it. No one means to waste your time – it's just that, frequently, they don't know how to say no.

JOSH APPIGNANESI: I was very lucky. Gayle Griffiths, the first person I really approached for advice, ended up producing my film and she was amazing. The more closely the vision is shared, the more likely the film is to get made and get made well. Everyone needs to feel engaged with it and your job is partly to create that sense of engagement and involvement. The rookie problem is often defensiveness.

SUSAN JACOBSON: I am incredibly blessed to have a fantastic producer, Alex Boden. We have a company that we started together 15 years ago. Having someone who isn't only a work colleague but a true friend is a gift. We understand each other and are totally on the same page with regards to our visions and goals.

MICHAEL KUHN: The most important quality to look for in a producer is good taste in the area that interests you. It doesn't mean you have to do tasteful films but you need someone who has got taste in the same particular area of filmmaking you are interested in. The rest of it you will learn – i.e. whether they are good at something or better or worse at it. That is the defining thing to look for in someone.

REBECCA DALY: We spoke to a few, sent them the script. We met with them, talked about the film and where we all thought it was going, how it might develop. It was also about seeing if we got on with them, their personality – you have to see if you click. Make sure you have a good feeling about the person. Don't feel like they're necessarily doing you a favour; it's a collaboration and you're working together and both bringing something. Don't feel you have to take the first offer you get. You need to have a good connection as you're going to have to spend a lot of time together (especially if you're a director as well as a writer), and you need to trust each other and have a good working relationship. Be careful and be choosy if you can.

JAMES DORMER: In the early days, I remember walking one script to the postbox with my wife and asking her to kiss it before we sent it off. Funnily enough, it didn't work. Though it did almost get me an LA agent. Through Shooting People I made contact with producers and first started to get work. I know everyone says not to work for free, but I worked for free on quite a lot of things until I got going. I worked with quite a big producer recently and even now he's trying to get stuff for free, it never changes. Now I don't have time to work for free, but who knows?

SALLY EL HOSAINI: Getting into the Sundance Labs didn't help me raise money or get a producer on board in the UK. We were rejected and turned down by all the main funding bodies and I couldn't find a producer for a very long time. I pretty much produced myself for many years. I managed to raise some finance, get an MG from a sales agent and then found my producers, who pulled the last pieces of the puzzle together. But you do have that reality check when you think, 'Hey, I've spent nearly five years of my life trying

168

to make this film and I'm still not getting there.' It was when I gave myself that deadline of 'this summer' and decided not to play by the rules. I went against everything people told me (only contacting one producer at a time) and bombarded every producer whose email I could get hold of simultaneously.

MUSTAPHA KSEIBATI: Be clear in who you are and what you want to do. Strong fresh voices are what public funding bodies and others are looking for. May the Force be with you.

PERFECT PITCHING

We've all been there when someone tries to tell us a great idea or story for a film or show. I encourage people, even friends, to send me a one-page synopsis of the story outlining the beginning, middle and end. That way I know exactly what the idea is and it's on paper, protecting them and me. Pitching is a skill and can be uncomfortable. Brevity works – the listener will know in minutes, perhaps even seconds, if they are interested.

MICHAEL KUHN: With *Being John Malkovich*, the main thing I learned was that when someone comes to you with a completely mad idea you should never say 'maybe'. Say 'no' right away, otherwise it might happen. Certainly when that was pitched to me, I thought it was some kind of leg-pull.

ANDREA CORNWELL: There's very much a wrong way to approach a producer: it's not about bombarding someone with information, but trying to make them want to know more. You need a very, very good short synopsis. Something where you can see the potential for casting or a clear audience appeal. Also something about you that is exciting; if you've just won a prize at a festival or come off the back of some accolade (no matter how small), be aware of your own currency and get a bit of buzz going about yourself.

LEE ARONSOHN: Less is more. Tell them just enough to pique their interest – let them ask for details.

CAT VILLIERS: I don't think there's a right or wrong way to do anything. For me, pitching should be to the point and short. The idea isn't to tell the whole story of a film, but to inspire. You mostly pitch to financiers/funders and the aim is to inspire them to want to read it, to make them want to have a conversation with you about it, to get that film made. A good pitch is a seduction. A good pitch should fire intrigue, enthusiasm and interest.

DAVID FLYNN: The biggest mistake when pitching or presenting a project is not knowing the industry you are going into or what is out there already. We get quite a few unsolicited pitches from people who might be new to the industry. A basic mistake is not researching the industry enough. Often things will be pitched that have already been on, or even made by us. What that says to me is that you are not necessarily interested in finding out those things. Therefore, there's no reason I should pay attention to your idea because it's likely to be something derivative. Sometimes people come in and pitch five or six ideas; if somebody doesn't like their first idea they move on to the next and the next. It's really important to be passionate about your ideas and believe they should be made. If you don't have passion then why should anyone else be passionate about it?

KERRY APPLEYARD: Be concise and rehearse. Stick to the relevant points so you don't start reciting the story in minute detail, which can make the whole thing unravel. Better to be brief and answer questions than ramble on for an hour and lose focus. I tend to find I'm more engaged when the writer begins by explaining where the idea came from, why it's personal to them – you know they have something meaningful to say that comes from a genuine and real place. Communicate the premise and episodic form/structure, key characters and spine of their journeys, attitudes and relationships, and be ready to give an example of an episodic story. Know the project inside and out so you can answer any questions on it. I would prefer a writer to refer to notes than get completely lost without them, but don't read a pitch.

REBECCA DALY: I would have thought a lot about the pitch but I wouldn't learn it off by heart as that can be a bit strange. I think about what would interest the person I'm talking to about the project and bring that into it. Usually I would pitch in a fairly informal setting and try to keep it conversational, so I wouldn't stand up and give a two-minute spiel as such.

RICHARD COOKSON: In general (and practical) terms new ideas tend to start as verbal or written pitches that summarise the lead characters, setting, the main thrust of the plot or set-up and an indication of the tone. A sense of audience and broadcaster is useful but not essential.

JOHN YORKE: Pitch with enthusiasm and love.

MUSTAPHA KSEIBATI: When it comes to my stories I just go in and be myself. Reading off a piece of paper never works for me. The projects come from a truthful place that I know inside out, so I feel that I can have those discussions in a 'pitch' scenario. When it comes to pitching on other projects, knowing the source material is key. Prepare! Knowing what to say is as important as knowing what not to say.

ALEXANDRA ARLANGO: Keep your pitch short and punchy. Leave them wanting more and they can always ask you questions about it.

PAULA MILNE: I did some work in Hollywood and I realised I could really pitch the hell out of stuff. So I thought, great, I'm never going to write another treatment, I'm just going to pitch, because a treatment turns into homework and becomes boring. They give lots of material for others to pick holes in before you've even started the bloody thing. Create the best arena for your talent to shine; learn how to work the industry to the best advantage for your work.

KATE OGBORN: Do your homework. Know who you're pitching to and what their taste is. Talk about your ideas, reference ideas and ways of expanding beyond the page so people can begin to see what you're describing. Also, we want to see that people are enthusiastic about what they're doing and clear as well, not coming with a sales pitch. Talk as one human being to another, so we know where the connecting points are and what the potential idea is.

BERTRAND FAIVRE: I'm a terrible pitcher. I don't know how to pitch. I sell projects through a mixture of elements, which involve script, director, cast, budget – never one thing. I am not script-driven, I don't develop concepts. My problem isn't to find which film to make, but how to make this film. This is derivative of being director-led. I have to find the right thing to do and how to do it best.

CAMILLE GATIN: I find passion is always the best pitch strategy. If you sound like you're pitching a movie that you'd love to watch, I'll listen more. If you've done your homework and know other films that are similar in tone or in scope that have done well, either commercially or critically, I'm listening. I love to come out of a pitch thinking, 'What a simple, obvious idea. I can't believe I never heard it before.'

DAVID PARFITT: I'm not sure I know how to do it. If you had asked me whether I pitch, I would say probably not. We often have conversations but it doesn't feel like pitching – it's just about getting someone to read the script.

GARETH EDWARDS: If the pitch isn't funny then why would I be interested? I like laughing! Just be funny and be nice. No one will want to work with you if you are a wanker. It's important not to be. Being arrogant or difficult might be all right for a while, but sooner or later they will choose someone nice over you. Everyone wants a nice day at the office. If you're not going to do that, you better be 10,000 per cent better than the person who is nice to be around.

IVANA MACKINNON: The best way is to imagine you're telling a story to someone in a bar – make it intimate, engaging and make the listener feel they are listening to a story. I don't like the hard pitch; it makes me feel nervous and unnatural. I want to feel I am in the hands of someone who understands their story and can tell it naturally. Be flexible enough to listen to feedback and take it on board rather than being defensive. That's sometimes more important than the pitch itself.

SIMON HEATH: We tend to favour a two or three page pitch backed up with a writing sample. A meeting may follow when we discuss the idea in more detail, so it's important to have fully thought through the idea. Too many one-pagers fall apart under interrogation.

MIA BAYS: Belief, motivation, good social skills, and a healthy ego are all essential to develop and nurture as you go. The top tip would be that you have to develop a good filter, to siphon good advice and feedback from bad. And you also need to learn how to listen and not take comments personally, or at least pretend not to – rant once you've left.

EXECUTIVES ON PREPARING FOR A MEETING WITH THEM

Prepare! It's a meeting, an interview – make sure you give yourself the best chance of success. One of the best lessons I ever had was when I was living in Paris and went for an interview for an administrative job. I had put in my application that I liked theatre. However, when I was asked what play I had seen recently, I didn't have an answer. In truth, I hadn't been to the theatre in six months – hardly the mark of an interested person. I looked foolish and never let it happen again.

RICHARD COOKSON: Come in with passion and enthusiasm. We work in this industry because we love TV, so demonstrate your own feelings. Which shows excite you? Which are comfort viewing? What show would you most have liked to have worked on? What recent shows haven't worked for you, and why not? As mentioned above, be aware of current TV and trends. Devour everything! It's fine not to like British TV – presumably that makes it the writer's ambition to improve upon it – but you should be aware of the British TV landscape. Watch at least one episode of every new series. Have favourite shows from the last three years. Know what's popular and why it's popular, even if you're not a fan of it yourself. Know the competition! What are the new trends in TV? It can also be useful to learn a little bit about us before coming in. What shows have we made? Have you seen them – if so, what did you think? You don't have to like them – but be clear what worked or didn't for you. A meeting might have been arranged about a specific idea, or it might be a general catch up, but in either case it's useful to have more ideas that you want to talk about. They might be worked-out scripts or pitches you're trying to sell, or they might be formative notions: just an arena or interesting anecdote that made you wonder if there was a TV idea to be had. We want to hear it – because it helps us get to know how your mind works and what interests you, and we might also want to buy it! Some people are great at spit-balling in the room, while others need to be prepared, so wherever you fall on that spectrum, know that you can bring more ideas to the table.

DAVID FLYNN: The most important thing with any meeting, whatever level you're at, is to know about the company, the shows they've done and have an opinion of them. Make sure you are well versed in the company and the wider industry before you go in. If you think something's bad, you need to qualify it in a good way. We want to have an intelligent dialogue, for example, 'I really like this because of X.' As soon as you hear someone engaging in your material in that kind of way, it makes you understand the way their brain works, etc. You also need to know what's going on in the industry. If I were having a meeting with someone, I would expect them to have an opinion on the latest entertainment shows.

SASKIA SCHUSTER: Watch the shows that the production company has made. Watch the channels, and read any interviews with channel controllers and heads of genre. Do your homework on who you are meeting. We'll have done our homework on you.

SHANE ALLEN: At commissioning level, you would already want to know what the idea is, what their voice is, what the project is about. Hopefully you would have read something in advance; there would be at least a treatment or a sample of their writing so that you know what their voice or style of humour is. In terms of preparing, it's about being articulate about the project, about the characters, about the story, about the world; if you're a bit sort of half-hearted about it and you haven't quite worked it out, people don't have the confidence in you or your project. Discuss it with loads of people before the meeting and get their input to better address any criticisms as early as you can. This applies to scripts too. Because if you're in front of a commissioner or a broadcaster, that's your one golden shot and you don't want to be half-arsed about it; you want to make sure it's sharp and that you're as prepared as you can be.

KERRY APPLEYARD: Do your research. I would never go to a company without having watched and read up on their productions. If it's for a job on a certain show, read the script and have an opinion. Be able to converse intelligently about what you enjoy watching and what type of drama or comedy you aspire to. I can't tell you how many times I meet aspiring TV writers who claim they are too busy to watch TV. It drives me nuts. If you love it, you consume it and can talk for hours about it!! And what better way to bond with a potential employer?

ANDREA CORNWELL: There's absolutely nothing worse than taking a meeting with somebody who is courting you (rather than the other way around) and having to explain who you are. They need to know why they are trying to meet you, why they think their work might appeal to you – perhaps something in your previous filmography or something which means that there's a connection to the project you are pitching. These days you can find an awful lot of information on the internet. Go in with a lot of self-awareness about your pitch. You can gauge in the room when people's eyes are lighting up and at what points they look interested. Be prepared to be flexible; don't rehearse a script and trot it out to everybody you meet. Watch how they react to you; listen to what areas they ask questions about. If they want to see your film in a certain way, listen and, if that works for you, go with it.

SIMON HEATH: Try to be familiar with the company's output (current and past) and have a knowledge of new TV dramas. Have one or two ideas to pitch – but no more. There's nothing worse than listening to a shopping list of ideas.

ALEXANDRA ARLANGO: There's no excuse for not knowing the people you're about to meet! On the other hand don't go in with any preconceived ideas. Be open-minded and relaxed.

BERTRAND FAIVRE: Make a list of the people to go to, based on how accessible they are and how similar their work is to yours. Your job isn't to be a postman. Don't send your script to 25 people, as it could end up in the wrong hands. I'd rather go to the people who are most likely to go for it, rather than facing endless rejection before I find the right person.

CAMILLE GATIN: If you have project ideas, have a snoop around to check whether there haven't been similar projects in the past; I always feel bad when a writer is very excited about one of their ideas and an almost identical film was made three years ago, which tanked.

DAVID PARFITT: Our meetings are very relaxed. I wouldn't expect people to be terribly prepared. With writers, we are often talking about projects in general. It's rare we will have an early meeting with a writer about very specific projects. It's often more general stuff. The next jump is straight to notes. However, it would be dumb for a writer to go to a meeting without knowing something about who it is they're seeing and what they've done.

GARETH EDWARDS: It helps if you know and ideally like the producer's work. But, more importantly, consider what you think characterises funny for you. What's your comedy writing about?

IVANA MACKINNON: Research the company so that you're not going in blind, both on a business level and also a personal level (if you can). Know what you want to talk about, but then be flexible.

JOHN YORKE: Make sure you know everything about who you are meeting, and what they want. Make sure you know what you're selling and who it's for.

CREATIVES ON PREPARING FOR A MEETING

One lesson I've learned is that you need to make sure you're in the right meeting. In 2011, I was invited to brief a section of the UN on Libya. Led to a meeting room containing 20 strangers, I was asked to introduce myself. I gave my 120-second speech about the Libyan revolution, only to be met with silence until I heard, 'Ma'am, I'm sorry but I think you're in the wrong meeting.' That was when I saw a sign saying 'Kenya'. So I thanked them for their time and made a hasty but composed retreat. When I was younger I hadn't a clue what was expected of me. I just rocked up and spoke. This led to a succession of bad meetings where I was too talky, over-explanatory, generally ill-prepared and lacking focus. I asked for feedback, it was tough to hear and I learned as I went along.

KEVIN CECIL: You don't prepare for a meet and greet, but do research who they are beforehand. If they are a producer who has made a couple of shows, you ought to see those shows. There are other meetings where I have prepared massively. You can't rehearse what you say in a meeting; it's different from pitching.

DESTINY EKARAGHA: Before every meeting I attend, I prepare. If the meeting is about a comedy drama, I'll watch a hundred comedy dramas that week. Or at least I'll try to! My motto is, always be prepared, always know what you're talking about, and if you don't, pretend!

LEE ARONSOHN: To prepare for meetings, I look in the mirror, say an affirmation, then throw up.

LUCY CLARKE: Have a bunch of ideas ready and be aware of what is and isn't working across all the TV channels in the genre you're working in. Then you can say, 'I'm so excited about "my idea" because X is doing so well and I think "my idea" speaks to the same audience, while obviously being completely unique.' Make sure you have something written up – even if it's just a paragraph – so you can leave the producer/commissioner with something physical to take away from the meeting. Then email it to them as well!

BOB BALABAN: Leave your defences at the door and LISTEN to what is being said to you. Take it in. Think before you speak. Also... it wouldn't hurt to know something about the person you're meeting. Look at their CV. Read an article or a book they wrote. Or someone wrote about them. Google them. Don't try to impress them. Be yourself. Try to relax. Breathe. It's really hard to believe this, but I have sat on both sides of the fence and it's true – the person you are meeting with is desperately hoping you are going to be exactly who they want so that they can stop the tedious audition process immediately. You wouldn't believe how much they want this to happen. They NEED your intelligence and talent and creativity. You hold the keys. They don't. Never forget it. And if you don't get the job after you did your absolute non-self-destructive best – you weren't meant to get it. You weren't edgy enough. Or tall enough.

Or old enough. Or blonde enough. You cannot be all things to all people. Stop beating yourself up. It's hard to do but it can be done and it will help you get your next job.

GUY HIBBERT: You have to give the producer or executive producer a sense that you are extremely competent, like you're somebody they will want to work with. You've got to make them feel confident that you're going to deliver the script they are wanting. There's nothing worse for a producer than commissioning a writer who does a duff script, because then the whole project goes AWOL and it takes a lot of time for them to correct that. Collaboration is so important. If you go into a meeting with a sense of entitlement or pride – or anything that makes them think you won't take notes very well – then… well, as a producer I wouldn't employ you.

JAMES DORMER: There are so many meetings where I'm presenting a script and the first question the producer will ask is, 'What do you think about it? What do you think the weaknesses are?' I've learned from experience to throw the question back at them and say, 'I've just delivered this draft; I'd really like to hear what you think first.'

STEPHEN FINGLETON: Before I meet someone, I work out ways in which we might collaborate, and try to imagine what the other person wants from the meeting.

MIRANDA BOWEN: I read the script and anything (if I have time) that might help to broaden my understanding of the script. If it's based on a book I will read the book beforehand too. Likewise I do an image trawl and try to get a sense of an image language that might work for the project.

MALCOLM CAMPBELL: You should treat meetings like an actor treats an audition. Be prepared and absolutely clear why you want to do that particular job, and why only you can do it.

ROCLIFFE NOTES on...

OVERCOMING NERVES FOR A MEETING, PITCH OR PRESENTATION

At drama school, I suffered from nerves before performing on stage that manifested itself as a tremor in my hair. I do a lot of public speaking nowadays and, no matter how confident I may seem, if you look closely you can still see the quiver. As soon as I realised this, I started to style my hair in a different way. That is my coping mechanism. Similarly, if you're a big personality, ensure when engaging in certain professional situations that you don't appear overly confident, monopolise or overwhelm. Many people I've met rely on strategies they know will work, i.e. familiar, 'crowd-pleasing' stories, a way of sitting and a certain on-stage persona. Here are a few specific tips:

- Don't take liquid courage! That can be a very slippery slope, especially if someone were to get a whiff of it and think you might have a problem. Alcohol and nerves don't mix.

- Thirty minutes beforehand, check through your questions. If using a tablet or computer check the battery while you still have enough time to recharge.

- Twenty minutes beforehand, run through the four main points you want to make. Have two prepared questions. Don't over-rehearse the points, but know them thoroughly.

- Ten minutes beforehand, use the facilities – the 'need to go' sensation before or during a meeting is often the body's way of dealing with nerves. It's fear trying to get rid of the anxiety by creating a physical need to flee – flight or fight syndrome!

- Have a fall-back response for any unpredictable questions. I tend to use 'I hadn't actually considered that...' followed by repeating the question in my answer. It allows time to formulate a relevant response. If thrown a left-field question in a meeting, people want to see how you respond: whether you are measured, defensive or flappy, and how well you know your subject or story.

- Try this wonderful centring exercise from my drama school days to slow your breathing down: put your hand on your tummy and breathe in through your mouth for as long as you can before breathing out through your nose for ten seconds. Repeat ten times. I use this for flying in turbulence too.

- Smile – this instantly puts everyone, including you, at ease. Smiling is medically proven to slow down the heart and relax the body as well as releasing endorphins. Even if it isn't at first genuine, it will be, and encourages those around you to trust you. It's contagious too – people smile back and it's free!

- Visualise your introduction – say your full name, repeating the names of people as you shake hands; smile and try to look directly into the eyes of everyone you meet, but don't squeeze the life out of their hands with too firm a handshake. That just seems weird.

••

ROCLIFFE NOTES on...
MEETINGS

I am frequently asked by writers and producers to make introductions. With all meetings it isn't just about you – it's about the part you might be able to play in the lives of the other parties. When I introduce people, I do so thinking it is in both their interests. It's tricky and you hope to God it works out. The worst thing is when people come back to me saying one or other hasn't been in touch, hasn't read their work, or said something they didn't like. You need to look at every meeting as a prospect and opportunity. Don't be disheartened if nothing comes from that meeting – it's a chance to gather information for some future date. You may well have something to offer them, although possibly not today, so see how it plays out. Look at every encounter as another opportunity.

Here are some pointers to help you get the most out of meetings:

- Be engaged and interested.

- Do your research in advance; watch shows they have made or read their work.

- Arrive on time, but not too early – ten minutes is sufficient; put your phone on silent.

- Decide what it is you want from the meeting.

- Don't be afraid to ask about the purpose of the meeting in advance, saying it's because you want to prepare.

- Make sure your mind is focused on the meeting – take the time to pause if asked a question you don't know the answer to, even if it's a few seconds. Use the trusty fall-back – 'I hadn't thought about that, but now you say it...'

- Don't just address the oldest or most senior producer or development executive in the room. Junior members of the team bring fresh ideas and a new perspective to a project. They are hungry too, so may see potential in you that a more experienced person wouldn't. Also, we women notice when the conversation is directed only at the men in the room!

- Come with ideas you think fit the company's brief and some that don't, but prefix an intro with that. Show your versatility – don't arrive with just one idea or script.

- Try to relax, shake hands and smile – there's nothing worse than someone who is stiff.

- Say what you need to say and don't be afraid to ask at the end whether they have any other questions or would like to see more of your work.

FINDING THE RIGHT COLLABORATOR

Finding the right person to work with is essential. Someone who is passionate, who will get behind you and what it is that YOU want to do with this film. Develop relationships with people – connections are not about making something today but planting seeds that may develop into something more in the future.

LIAM FOLEY: The hopeful, natural conclusion, if you want to be a writer, is that you want to be a successful writer. To be a successful writer in film or TV means working in an industry and that means working in a collaborative way within that industry.

SERENA BOWMAN: When we give feedback we try to be very constructive but give a definite 'yes' or 'no' answer so we don't waste people's time. If we think a project has potential and it's something the broadcasters might be interested in, then we can work with the writers on developing the characters and the plot. We'll always explain why we didn't go forward with a script, so hopefully that will help them go away and rethink the writing or come up with something entirely new. If I think someone's writing is really exciting, I will tell them to keep in touch with new ideas and I'll keep track of their progress as well. Someone might not be right when they initially approach me but, if there's some sort of spark or initial promise, in a couple of years they might be the perfect person to develop something with.

KATE OGBORN: It's fundamentally about trust. Trust can be built from respect, shared tastes, finding common ground. With Carine Adler and I, and a lot of people I've worked with, it's a shared sense of humour, knowing that you trust each other enough to take the piss out of each other. You can then lighten situations. Directors want to know that you care, and care enough for the project to fight for it and fight for them. They also want to know that you're going to be the buffer between them and someone else.

183

LUCY CLARKE: I'm a believer in trusting your instincts. Anyone can say they like your idea, but are they excited about what could happen next for your characters? Do they share your vision of where your script fits into the TV world? Do you like the same shows? Do you get the same references? You're going to be working closely with this person so you need to have the same sense of humour!

KAHLEEN CRAWFORD: Find the right producer, someone you can truly collaborate with. Many producers are incredibly creative people and have brilliant ideas. They can help you see the wood from the trees. You can also trust them to represent your project in a professional manner. They will do a lot of knocking down doors for you. Andrew Haigh does an awful lot himself and he's fantastic, but generally I would advise a writer-director not to do everything themselves. Instead, find an amazing team. Use people's time wisely. Your heads of department, if you get the right people, could be the same ones you take with you throughout your career. They will take pressure off you as well as bringing exciting ideas to the table that you wouldn't have had time to come up with yourself.

GLENN MONTGOMERY: Find out who they are and what they've made before you approach them, and from that you'll be able to see if that person might be interested in what you've written. A lot of producers have a creative interest in certain things. Figure out who you're going to talk to. Go in with an open mind because although they might be the right producer for you, you might not be the right writer for them. Be prepared for the fact that they're going to want to have a say in your script if they take it on. You need to be open to that because, even if you've started on your own, at some point it does become a collaborative process; that is the reality of it. You should go with it rather than fight it. At the end of the day everybody, in my experience, just wants to make a great film. Producers want the right one.

NIK POWELL: People do need luck in life – don't let anyone tell you differently. Sometimes you just don't realise the luck you have around you. One of my pieces of luck was that in the village I grew up in there was a guy, Richard Branson, who became my best friend. Most people get into groups because they like each other, but at film school you meet people who have something to offer you that's different from what you're offering. They bring something else to the table and that's what can give you the advantage.

IVANA MACKINNON: Finding collaborators is essential – by whatever means. Finding a network of people to understand you, share information with and support you is invaluable. The most important thing is to keep producing work while getting out there and making connections with other people.

MALCOLM CAMPBELL: I've been lucky because most of the work I've done has come through three or four individuals or production companies. People will stay loyal to you if you stay loyal to them (and keep producing the goods!). Don't spread yourself too thin. Don't feel compelled to say yes to everything. Saying no is better for your mental health down the line. If you write too much it means you are someone who is constantly working and not thinking or living. I'm not precious about my work and I am a pretty good collaborator. I do take notes and I am not confrontational. But then I'm lucky, as I've worked with great people. On *What Richard Did* I was working with one of the best directors around at the moment and that's a huge privilege. You also need a lovely producer who gives you space to do what you want to do. I've been fortunate in that respect.

MIRANDA BOWEN: You have different chemistry with different people. Sometimes a script will come to you that is so beautifully written and chimes so perfectly with your own interests that you end up shooting pretty much what was on the page in the first draft you read. That is rare, however – scripts are not complete documents but blueprints for a story in a world. Mostly I find that scripts are too literary for my tastes – that is, they subscribe to dialogue-led scenarios that eschew the dynamism of the 'cinematic moment' –

and so I try to work out how to make the script sing cinematically. This means trying to engage the viewer viscerally rather than simply intellectually – through the senses rather than just the trajectory of the narrative. To feel rather than to watch.

ROCLIFFE NOTES on...

FINDING COLLABORATORS

- Working on actual productions – for example, jobs on short or low-budget films advertised online – can help you get access to a producer and crew. When I lacked experience, I attended courses and Q&As and approached people afterwards.

- Go to festivals to meet other filmmakers – writers, directors, producers. You get a sense of what producers are trying to do. Watch films you wouldn't otherwise necessarily see. Apply for the talent campuses, i.e. training schemes. You cannot but be inspired and energised.

- Certain initiatives introduce you to people within the industry: BAFTA Rocliffe, Breakthrough Brits, the MEDIA Programme, iFeatures, Creative Skillset, all the regional bodies – ScreenSouth, Film London, Northern Ireland Screen, Irish Film Board, BAFTA and IFTA – have educational events you can meet people on. Sign up to their mailing lists.

- Employ the services of a freelance story editor, who will work with you on a draft-by-draft basis. I suggest you do this when you feel the project needs new eyes and you can't take it any further on your own.

- Funding initiatives like Microwave, iFeatures and the Irish Film Board's Catalyst scheme are great for finding collaborators and meeting lots of industry execs who are more than happy to talk with you.

- Research your local cinema, which may run Q&As. BAFTA and IFTA host a wide selection of events, many of which are filmed and put online. Ask a question, get tips on breaking in from industry practitioners. If someone in the audience says something you liked, introduce yourself afterwards.

- While many companies don't accept unsolicited material, write a personal letter to a junior development executive asking for advice on what they are looking for.

- Courses or writing groups are a fantastic way to meet people.

- Contact film schools, attend their short courses and go to their showcases, or reach out to their producers and director alumni.

- Use social media. Facebook has a group for everything – it's worth joining up. Get onto mailing lists like Mandy, Shooting People, IFTN, etc.

- Guilds have associate memberships for newer talent – Production Guild, Writers' Guild of Great Britain, Women in Film & TV, Directors Guild, and many others. There is a variety of ways to connect and no excuse not to reach out.

- Try agents, diary services and production agencies as they may have production department crew who are looking for the right project to work on. Gems Agency have a Facebook page for jobs on low-budget films and shorts.

••

ROCLIFFE NOTES on...

WHAT TO LOOK FOR IN A DEVELOPER OR COLLABORATOR

Yes, you write alone, but you can also have very supportive people around you. Don't be flattered because someone wants to work with you. Interrogate them as you will be working with them intimately. Be

187

they a producer, development executive or script/story editor, their role is to keep the end in sight and not lose focus, to recognise any problems and help you see where the weaknesses and strengths lie, and to possibly get the film financed and made. And so you should:

- Seek out someone who responds to your material, who has an analytical approach to wanting to help you to recognise and realise the potential of the script, not someone who wants to rewrite it for you.

- Be prepared for a potential collaborator to ask to see samples of your work, a treatment, your CV and biography, and other examples like links to online material you've worked on.

- Ask for examples of *their* work if you haven't managed to find any online. How do they like to work? What are their turnaround times?

- Ask them how they felt about the work and what they like about it. Ask them to define their role and what they see themselves bringing to the table.

- Understand that developing a script is far, far away from actual production and that there are many other steps in-between.

It's not unusual for someone to have read your script at least twice, researched the background to the project, watched your online material and to arrive bearing notes and questions. I've seen industry guests who have prepared lengthy notes, reeled off effortlessly and showing great insight into the writer's story. It's very impressive to see, but that's preparation!

....

APPROACHING A PRODUCTION COMPANY

Most production companies have their own remit and brief, but when it comes to that rare and unquantifiable thing – THE GREAT

SCRIPT – they will generally be more than happy to shift position! If truth be told, there are very, very few brilliant scripts out there. It's a myth that producers and broadcasters are turning down loads of brilliant scripts every day. When a company receives a script and gives it to a reader, it will usually ask for recommendations to fall into one of four categories – Pass, Second Read, Develop and Option/Fund.

EMMA NORTON: If you are keen to approach a production company with a 'no unsolicited scripts' policy, don't try to persuade them to make an exception for you. Think laterally instead. They're big, they're busy – they don't want to tell you 'no' when it already says that on their website. So why not ask them for something that they don't have a policy about? Ask them about their slate; ask them what sort of new writers they work with; what sort of films they are developing. Questions that will give you a better sense of them and how their company works. Play the long game, be informed and make a connection with people by being polite rather than unduly pushy. You still might not get a reply, but if you do it might be more useful than 'we do not accept unsolicited scripts'.

••

ROCLIFFE NOTES on...
WHO TO SEND YOUR SCRIPT TO

- Look at what a company has done – check out IMDb, look at their website.

- Does the production company have a slate of films in development that may be similar to what you are writing? If they do, this may be a good or a bad thing. Sometimes companies post what's in development online, but you can also check out *Variety* and *Screen* for projects in development, or simply ask at a Q&A.

- At what stage does a production company take on projects? Do they want projects they can develop, or ones that are ready to go into production?

- Do companies favour writers or writer-directors? How are they led?

- Do they have a preference for particular types of movies – arthouse, auteur or mainstream?

- So you know you're aiming at the right company, what is the budget range of the films they make?

- Do they develop both film and TV projects?

- How big is the company? Smaller companies can be more approachable than bigger ones but may take longer to read your script.

The companies which, at the time of writing, accept unsolicited material are Red Planet, Red Productions, Palace Pictures, Picture Palace and Baby Jane Productions, but check their guidelines before submitting work. And don't forget the BFI and IFB for development funding.

••

WHAT IS THE BBC WRITERSROOM?

I asked Kate Rowland, Creative Director for New Writing at the BBC, to put together an overview.

KATE ROWLAND: It's a virtual writers' room, and it's a resource and place of inspiration and ideas for writers. I would say we're an internal agent. Our aim is to find talent and to then champion and promote that talent. We're only as good as the amount of people who get commissioned. I remember someone coming in once from an auditing company, as an external consultant, and he was trying to quantify the Writersroom in terms of cost per writer. I said, 'It's a long process, the writer's journey doesn't happen overnight, it might take years.' That's so important to understand. That's our job: we've got to believe in people and try to support them across the industry. I don't think it's just about the BBC, the Writersroom is also very much part of the creative industries and is a partnership organisation.

It works on many fronts. We have the Scriptroom, which is a completely open pathway for any writer who wants to send a script in for any medium. That can be drama, radio, film, children's. You get noticed that way. Secondly, it's our job to talent spot by seeing new plays, readings and short films. Thirdly, we do outreach programmes. Fourthly, we design and create innovative, targeted schemes, which will find and nurture talent in a different way.

Years ago we did a Muslim writers' scheme, with mosques and community centres across the North West, as those writers weren't coming forward. One writer got a TV commission. That's taken a long time, but he's really talented and it's finding the right place for his voice.

We work with all the heads of department and development, telling them to 'read this script, this person's amazing'. We have 'talent meetings' where we will just share names. We do professional training. Sometimes people have the instinct, the voice, but are unsure about moving between one medium and another, e.g. from theatre to TV. There's a different set of rules. Sometimes good writers fail because they don't know enough, they don't always understand that it's a business, an industry, and you've got to work bloody hard. Writers have to have the right work ethic.

DEVELOPMENT

This industry requires patience and commitment. Development is a long slow process of writing, feedback, rewriting, more feedback and writing again. Scripts evolve through a process of investment and development by all parties through to the edit and post-production. When someone is looking at your work, they are assessing if they can live with it, develop it, make it into something workable over time and invest money in it.

ALEXANDRA ARLANGO: It's often a case of finding the best way to work in a collaborative and supportive way. Development will often take the form of the writer doing a treatment or beat sheet for the project. This is a blueprint of what the story is and where it's heading. The writer will then work on a first draft, then revisions follow. The process continues in this way. At some point a director will be attached, and eventually potential financiers will be approached with a solid, great script that excites them as well. If all the planets align, the film will be green-lit and head into production.

MIA BAYS: The development process really depends on the team and project, and if it's documentary or fiction as they have different processes. Experience has taught me to be sensitive and to establish the 'rules of engagement' with the writer and team first. Trust is important to establish, as is your credibility – you can't just breeze in and throw opinions at everyone as that can be overwhelming and also destructive. Bottom line – it's the writer's job to fix the issues. I prefer to be a strident guide. I'm passionate about what I feel is and isn't working but I also create space for the writer to find their own solutions, while offering ideas.

LUCY CLARKE: Development is like trying to put together a jigsaw without being 100 per cent sure what the picture is. Actually writing the script is like finally being let off the leash.

KERRY APPLEYARD: Once we option a property we work with the writer to get it ready to pitch. That involves ensuring we know what the show or the franchise is, what the episodic format is, what the key character relationships and attitudes are, etc. Before taking on a project we always make sure we are on the same page as the creator as it's our job to support and enable their vision. It involves a lot of heartfelt and in-depth discussion. Once we have a project set up with a broadcaster, we work on the deliverables, often creating a bible and pilot script, getting the package ready for consideration for production. We give notes on drafts and work on the deliverables extensively to make sure it's as good as it can be before a broadcaster sees it. Sometimes this will be in the form of written notes, followed up by a call, and sometimes day-long meetings. We'll then revise each draft or deliverable according to the notes. It's all about developing it to a shootable script. Sometimes that is three drafts, sometimes 30!

BERTRAND FAIVRE: I try to work alone with the writers until we feel we are happy with it and then open it up to other people. It's not to reach a consensus early on, but to ensure the distinctive result we are after is possible and shared.

GARETH EDWARDS: You will read the script. If it's something that you like, you might give strategic notes on the overall things you like or dislike about it. You might then follow it up with more detailed notes from a second draft on a line-by-line basis. To begin with, you are trying to ask big questions about what is at the heart of it, what is funny about this, or even how you were bored at a certain point. It's usually the third quarter where I get bored.

IVANA MACKINNON: It's a people business and you have to be flexible with regard to how that writer works best and hears notes/collaborates best. You need to get to know them. Some writers respond very well to written notes, some to questions, others to long dialogues that are more thematic than specific. You need to build a relationship with the writer to know what works best.

JOHN YORKE: Depends who they are and how experienced. There's no substitute for just giving an honest emotional response to what you've read, and then seeing if that squares with the writer's intention. If it doesn't then that's the note.

SARAH GAVRON: I collaborate with writers over cake in coffee shops for months – years, sometimes – reading drafts and giving feedback. I so admire writers and I love working with them. Scripts are incredibly difficult to get right.

REBECCA O'BRIEN: With Paul Laverty and Ken Loach, they tend to come up with the idea between them and then we meet and discuss the way forward. At that point, we'd have been discussing which project we're going to do next and then we alight on the favoured subject. Then Paul goes and spends perhaps four to six months researching, travelling and meeting people and reading. He'll work up some character ideas and share them, at that stage, mainly just with Ken. Then he'll settle down and write the script, once we've all agreed on it. He does that very quickly; it's very straightforward and organic.

WHAT ARE NOTES?

Break down feedback into three types of notes – good notes, useful notes and mad notes. Good notes resonate, flagging things that you hadn't thought of, and make sense. Useful notes are ones that won't impact the narrative but open the script up with suggestions. Mad notes take you off on a tangent that you weren't expecting and need careful consideration. These are the ones to which you should respond along the lines of, 'Let me go away and think about that.' These are the notes to be careful with as they have the potential to damage your script or film. Start a discussion with 'If we do that, then my concern is we lose this' or 'If we make that change then the impact is...' Discuss it as, half the time, when people proffer 'mad' notes, they are identifying a problem they don't know how to address. Listen and explore the feasibility of the note through intelligent discussion. Question, challenge and contribute to a discussion without defensiveness, enjoying the journey

KATE LEYS: What writers and filmmakers need to know is how the story is working and where it isn't, and why; what actually needs changing (as opposed to what looks wonky) and how they can approach making changes. All projects are different and all filmmakers and screenwriters are different. In itself, feedback is based in knowing the work inside out, really thinking about it up close, and having clear, simple notes that are of practical use to a writer. No writer needs to know what I like, or what my opinion is; there are thousands of opinions around every film script. It also depends on when I come into a project: all stages are different from the very start.

CHRIS SUSSMAN: It's always advice, it's never 'You have to change this'. If people don't understand notes, they should ask for clarity; there's no shame in asking. Someone coming into it with a fresh pair of eyes might have some really good points. This is a collaborative business. It's not just producers who will be giving notes; there are going to be actors, directors, etc.

KATE OGBORN: It's a mixture of conversations and written notes, where that's helpful to follow up. Most people find it helpful as it's something to refer back to.

GARETH EDWARDS: There are two rules to getting notes. The first rule is to listen to and carefully consider the notes you get, no matter where they come from. The second rule is you must only ever act on the ones that feel true to you. I think about this a lot as a writer and producer. If you try to write something that you don't believe in in your gut, where will that end up? You'll end up with a project you don't like or even understand. And if *you* don't like or understand it, why should anyone else?

KATE ROWLAND: A lot of writers challenge us by saying 'Why don't you give us all feedback on our scripts?' We get up to 10,000 scripts per year; we could waste so much time and money looking for euphemisms to say something's rubbish or not good enough. A lot of people don't understand feedback. They can't separate their personal feelings from being able to stand back from a script and look at where the strengths and challenges are, and where it's just not working. The thing that frustrates me about some writers is that they don't read other work, they don't read scripts, they don't see enough, or only watch American TV when they want to work in British TV. So you think: watch British shows, listen to the radio, go to the theatre. You don't have to like it, but you have to watch and understand why that works, why that doesn't work. It's very competitive and you've got to look at things and think, 'Actually, will this stand up?'

THE PURPOSE OF FEEDBACK AND NOTES

Feedback and notes are like the best and worst friend – best for the work and worst for the ego. Many newer writers are terrified by notes. At drama school I dreaded end of term 'crits', sitting in a circle listening as each tutor gave their professional opinion of our performances in front of everyone. Sometimes it felt like a blood bath and deeply personal. I wanted the floor to swallow me up but it was essential if I was to get any better. I adapted and developed thick skin.

OL PARKER: I hate it, obviously. Unless it's pure sycophancy. But even then it's never enough. Garrison Keillor said that the only review that will truly satisfy an artist is the line 'Arise, O Sun God, and greet thy people'. Any less than that... still, you get better at it. You learn not to panic. Never take the solution. Almost without exception, when the studio or somebody gives you a suggestion of what could happen in a scene, etc., it's catastrophic and makes you want to have a prolapse when they suggest it. You learn to swerve past that feeling, and think about what their crappy version is giving them that you haven't. Then you can work on your own ways to give them that. They'll forget what they said anyway. They're not wedded to their own solution; they're wedded to change for the better.

LUCY CLARKE: I like collaboration and I'm not precious; if someone suggests something that really does make my idea/script/gag better, I will happily accept it.

DAVID PARFITT: Feedback is vital. For example, if we've been round to multiple sources of finance or out to multiple cast, and they've all pretty much said the same thing, we take that very seriously and adjust accordingly.

RICHARD COOKSON: The best advice I got was to always point out the positives in any feedback. Even the most eloquently worded critical feedback should find space to say which bits you liked. A great script-editing tip is to let writers know your headlines up front – even before a meeting. Nobody likes an ambush.

KATIE GOODSON-THOMAS: I'd like to think I handle feedback with sensitivity and honesty. If it's a pass I like to give a little bit of constructive criticism, pointing them in the right direction. Having been on the other end of it, there's nothing worse than getting material back and them just saying 'No, thank you', as you have no idea why. How can it improve? From one job to the next, I have always asked my employers for constructive criticism. What could

I have done better? What are my strengths and weaknesses? You constantly want to improve. Feedback should be the same.

BERTRAND FAIVRE: I would say don't answer my notes, kill them. If I have a point or question at any moment in the development process, it's your role to suppress it, kill it.

DAVID SIMPATICO: It's important to know when the script is ready to receive feedback. In my first screenwriting job, the producers were not confident in me, as it was my first screenplay. They wanted to read a rough draft so they could 'help' me. They sent a messenger to my house to wait while the last page of the ROUGH draft printed out, and then scooped it away; not even a *first* draft – a *rough* draft, a draft I had not yet had the chance to peruse. I was fired a few days later. As my agent said, 'Welcome to show biz.'

JON CROKER: Even the most auteur-y of auteurs has to collaborate to achieve their vision. Embrace feedback and use it to make the film better. A badly phrased observation might have some truth behind it. And even if you profoundly disagree with a suggestion, make sure you can prove to yourself why it's wrong. Otherwise they might have a point. There's no such thing as 'development' notes. The stages of filmmaking (development, pre-pre production, pre-production, production, post-production) are artificial constructions for legal and practical purposes. Creatively, they are all the same thing. From the blank page to the final sound mix, you are making the film and you should always, constantly, night and day, be listening to feedback and trying to make your film better.

POLLY STOKES: When I read something I don't always know straight away what I think about it. I try to read something twice before I give any serious feedback. I make sure that I've had a night's sleep between having read something and meeting to talk about it, so there's time for the work to settle. I would want to know why *that* producer, writer and director wanted to make *that* film. What is it that they are personally connecting with? If your feedback comes out of that place, you will always be able to give more helpful guidance.

MALCOLM CAMPBELL: I really welcome feedback. I don't know if I'm in the minority there but you have to understand it's a collaborative process. Script editors and development people do incredible work. Pretty much everyone I've worked with has made me think differently and made the work better.

JIM UHLS: The only thing that the top people on the project want to see, when you turn in a rewrite, is a good script that will make a good film – not a motley patchwork that slavishly followed every single note.

LEVI DAVID ADDAI: Feedback is brilliant as you can get tunnel vision. You need to finesse it and make it clearer.

JOSH APPIGNANESI: Encourage feedback and try to realise all of it comes from a valid place. Everyone's encounter with the text is, subjectively speaking, true – although often people's specific suggestions have to be approached with caution because they can be seductive but ultimately misleading. Work backwards and decode them to see what it is that's not quite moving them or grabbing them. Oh, and nod and smile. A lot. Everyone likes a smile.

WHO TO GET FEEDBACK FROM

I once worked with someone who gave me notes and I just didn't get them. They just didn't resonate with me. In recent years, I have worked with people like Ellis Freeman, Kate Leys and my agent, and they have helped me to progress my work, particularly what wasn't working. When we are judged as writers or filmmakers, it's hard not to construe feedback as criticism, and to not feel slighted. It's ultimately down to what you do with the feedback and how you react to it. Comedy writers the Dawson Brothers have said that, in the early days, they did whatever they were told and interpreted the notes they were given. They trusted that the people they were working with knew what needed to be done to get it commissioned, which was their ultimate aim. It helped them cultivate the right attitude to working and they learned that, early on in your career, you don't want to burn any bridges.

TINA GHARAVI: Firstly, it's important to listen (of course!), but decide WHO that person or team of people are. The notes you get aren't always coming from a place that will be helpful. So keep that in mind. People say a host of things for a variety of reasons. They aren't the writer, you are. So choose your 'experts' carefully, but listen. Engage and then decide what you do with this information.

IVANA MACKINNON: Find truth tellers who can let you know when you are barking up the wrong tree, and follow what's happening in the industry. But most of all find collaborators you trust and make things happen with them. Don't take rejection to heart – you have to be thick-skinned – but listen to what people are saying to you and what they aren't.

DESTINY EKARAGHA: When it comes to my work, there are only a few people that I trust for feedback. The person that usually sees my work first is my agent, Fay Davies. She's not just an agent; she has creative insight and I trust and respect her opinions. She knows those out there who are going to like my work and those who will think I'm bonkers. For that I am grateful. I also send my work to writers I often work with, as they never sugar-coat things. They're critical – not in a nasty way but in a way that forces me to do better. I also go to a script group that consists of other writers. We share our scripts and then critique them. It can be hard sometimes when it isn't what you want to hear, but if you trust their opinions it can be really helpful. Don't be too precious with your work; be prepared to change things if, in the long run, it will make your film better. Kill your darlings, as they say!

201

MUSTAPHA KSEIBATI: Don't show everyone your work for feedback. Only a select few. You should never share your work with negative people. Embrace feedback from the right people. It's there to support you. Filmmaking is collaborative and this forms an important piece of that process. Of course, some things will come down to taste so it's up to you to identify that.

CONFLICTING FEEDBACK

One area of concern I hear raised over and over again is that of conflicting notes. Many of our contributors made similar points so I have included a cross-section of their comments here – as a reassurance for the reader as much as anything else!

RICHARD COOKSON: Ideally writers should be presented with a unified voice. When the process is working, all notes (be they from a small development group or an entire production team) should be filtered through one point of contact (often a script editor in the latter case), who has collated and distilled a coherent response. If that process doesn't come about and you're faced with conflicting notes – or if the notes come from unrelated parties offering their own feedback – then you should analyse each note for its insight and value, and make a call based on what chimes most with your own opinion of the project.

DANNY BROCKLEHURST: Working with people you trust and respect is great because you talk the feedback through. Then I go away and write them. I had one occasion where I worked on something and there were just too many people giving me notes. I had to say, 'If you take these notes to their logical conclusion, then I will have to start again.' You have to front people out on conflicting notes. As this is where things go wrong and you can't satisfy every note or it will be a mess and your vision will be lost. So don't try to address too many notes. It's difficult, as you and others want to make it better, but in the end it's your name on it. You have to stand by the work so take the notes you think make it better or make sense and work with those. Ditch the ones that don't make sense, or you'll find you don't know how to implement them.

LEE ARONSOHN: If you don't go in with a shared vision, the producer's vision will always win, so you either accept that or move on to something else. A single vision – even if it's flawed – will almost always result in a better script than something which is the product of trying to satisfy multiple points of view.

LUCY CLARKE: Try not to lose your temper! It largely depends on who is giving the notes. If it's someone you trust then give their ideas a go – even if they don't work it might nudge you towards something else that does. If the person giving you notes clearly doesn't like or get your idea, just nod politely and say you'll try. And then don't.

KERRY APPLEYARD: My experience of this is from two sets of broadcasters, and one of my jobs is to reconcile conflicting notes. Be honest and talk the conflicting viewpoints through. A writer can't service differing visions. I've seen too many scripts suffer as a result of the writer trying to meet notes they don't understand or believe in and completely losing their way. You have to stick to the spirit of what you believe in and fight a note if you believe it's wrong, but you have to pick the hills to die on too. A good writer will have always thought of the many different ways a scene or story can go, and have chosen the route they did for a valid reason. But a good writer will also try a better idea or another route if something's not working, and let go when they know they are wrong. Contesting the note, explaining what you are aiming for and why, often negates it; a small change in perspective can work wonders. Also, a writer and producer's job sometimes means digging a bit deeper to get to the nub of what the note really is. Often notes from execs can point out an issue or a problem, and actually they've pinpointed a consequence of something else. Interpreting notes correctly and thoroughly is a skill that you learn from experience.

BERTRAND FAIVRE: You take many opinions and you just pursue yours. Yours are made of who you are and your opinion. I would say that conflicting notes are not about who has the power. It's more what bounces back positively in your mind.

DESTINY EKARAGHA: Conflicting notes can be the worst things about the development process. There are just so many. My producer, Christopher Granier–Deferre, was really good at preparing Bola and myself for them. We were able to weed out the ones that were useful from the ones that would take us in a direction in which we didn't want to go. Early on in my career I realised that if I only listened to everyone else's voice and went against my own, in the end it would harm me. If the film were to crash, everyone else would walk away uninjured; however, I would be left mangled in the driver's seat. Listen to your instincts – that way, if the film doesn't do as well as you hoped, you'll know that you did what you thought was right at the time, and that's a lot easier to live with. If it does well, great! Pop the champagne!

OL PARKER: Sometimes, some notes you learn to just reject in the room. It's just better categorically to tell people there and then, politely, and with good reasons, why you won't make certain changes. Because, in the end, you learn that it's important to listen to them, but it's more important to listen to yourself. Once you start believing in what you're doing, then you learn that the only notes that really, really matter, are the ones you've already thought about but haven't admitted to yourself. When those notes come in, you're passionately grateful and you'll take them from anywhere. What a note is, is somebody exposing the gap between what you thought you'd achieved and what they've understood from what they've read. So what you have to determine is how big the gap is, whether it's their fault they're missing something and whether you're entirely comfortable with what you've done. Which I would suggest you should never be. Because everything can be made better.

IVANA MACKINNON: The role of the producer is to translate notes from others for the writer and filter them so that the writer isn't overwhelmed or confused. Everyone will always have a different opinion. For a writer, part of the development process is discovering what their line in the sand is, where they can't change things and where the DNA of the film needs to be better explained, so that people understand why a certain note won't work. The writer has to know their work better than anyone and sometimes needs to fight their own corner. Sometimes that is hard to do, and sometimes it only comes through going down a dogleg, but that's why no time in development, even if it feels like you're going in the wrong direction, is really wasted.

ALEXANDRA ARLANGO: If we're working with other development partners on a project we usually discuss and compile notes so that the writer will only get one set of notes. If there are notes that the writer feels are conflicting, then they should absolutely pick up the phone and talk them over. Everybody wants to get a good script in at the end of the day, and unexpected solutions often come from working through issues.

MIA BAYS: So often notes are dangerous – especially bad ones. They might be well meaning but bad notes can be really destructive and throw a project off. It's vital to separate opinions from real technical or structural issues. The solution is to get everyone together if possible, all the key people who need to take on the notes or who have given them, talk them through, come up with feedback, then leave the writer to go away and do their job. It's the producer's job to protect the writer and director when necessary. Just as sometimes it's important to protect the film from the writer and director and financiers sometimes! I see that as my job – working FOR THE FILM, not for anyone or anything else.

ROWAN ATHALE: Don't be afraid to fight your corner – if you feel a note is wrong, articulate your reasons. Conflicting opinions are fine as long as everyone debates their side while being consciously willing to change their mind should the other person make a good case. And that isn't about your prowess in a debate; it's just about finding a way to articulate yourself.

JULIETTE TOWHIDI: I have learned to be honest if I think a note is crap – in a diplomatic way, of course – but that is harder when you're newer to the business. Having worked in development before becoming a writer helps, because you know what it's like to sit on the other side of that desk, with a writer's stony, blank face staring back at you. Your job is to pinpoint the underlying weakness in your own work that triggered their poor solution. Then go home and fix it.

JOHN YORKE: It can be a minefield, but the best answer is don't be defensive; listen to the notes that make sense to you and discuss the ones that don't.

SASKIA SCHUSTER: The reason I give feedback to the producer rather than the writer is to try to avoid this problem. Ideally the producer and I will have good communication and can discuss any potentially problematic notes so these can be sorted, or contextualised, before being fed back to the writer. A good producer will be in constant contact and communicating about all aspects of the production, so note giving will be part of an ongoing conversation, which in theory should prevent conflicting notes between broadcaster and production. That said, when the process doesn't happen in such a collaborative way the note giving process won't be so joined up, and this is where difficulties can arise.

ANDREA CORNWELL: Accept that it will happen, even in an edit: you will get conflicting notes, and if it's a project with multiple partners you have to navigate those and work out what are the common problems. People may sometimes make a suggestion that you don't necessarily agree with, but there's a problem with that area or character. You have to try and unpick that. Often people are right about something not quite making sense. The important thing is to not dismiss it but to try to fathom out why they're saying what they're saying.

MALCOLM CAMPBELL: I know people who have had battles with their script editors and sometimes they just don't get it (to which I'd say, maybe that means there's a problem worth addressing). It takes a hell of an ego to think that what you are writing is definitive. I really enjoy getting feedback. It's difficult when you have seven or eight different voices and you have to understand the hierarchy of who is giving the notes. That can cloud things. But it's about having a sense of the work, what you want to say and translating those notes. You just have to find the way through the conflicts.

CAMILLE GATIN: It's absolutely legitimate for a writer, if faced with conflicting feedback, to flag it up immediately. There's usually a single point person and it's their responsibility to consolidate feedback. Conflicting feedback will be a stumbling block. So the first course of action is to tell the point person clearly to check whether, in the first instance, they can clarify or come back with helpful, constructive feedback that is consistent. Otherwise it may create new, big problems and slow everything down. This usually works.

SIMON HEATH: Address the good notes. Ignore the crap ones.

CLAIRE WILSON: The only notes I have trouble with are vague ones. They cause much more trouble than a note you disagree with. I learned early on to grill the person who is giving the notes so that I walk away with a clear understanding of what they want. 'Slow this down' or 'Speed this up' aren't notes. 'Ending doesn't work' isn't a note. Why doesn't it work? Why is it too slow?

CONSIDER REJECTION A RITE OF PASSAGE

Everyone has faced rejection at some point in his or her career. It's part and parcel of every profession. As creative creatures, console yourself in the knowledge that you are not the only one, and that this is yours... so own it! When someone else talks to you about their worst rejection story, low and behold you have one of your own.

Often, just when you want to give up, along comes a sight of land and you feel on top again. Your deepest lows will be reversed by your greatest highs. You've no idea what's around the corner – that's what keeps you going, so don't give up with the knock-backs. Accept them as a rite of passage. Embrace the lows and the highs – know that, with euphoria, come really hard times. But that you only need one person to say 'yes'.

PETER HARNESS: It's never nice but it's a part of it. What I wish I'd known as a writer starting off is how much it does persist and how much it's part of the course. I also wish I'd known that most writers get sacked several times throughout their careers. It's hard to deal with but it's usually not personal. To be able to succeed as a writer, you end up having to build a fairly tough edge in terms of dealing with rejection. I also think that I'm a bit more careful about presenting stuff to people. If I had an idea that was desperately close to me, I'd rather not sell it so that, if rejection happened somewhere along the line, there'd still be the chance of it living again. I had lots of rejections and knock-backs early on, and that's just made me quite cautious and aware of keeping things where I have some vague level of control over where they're going. It's part of the job.

OL PARKER: You try not to see it as constant. You try to see each rejection as a separate thing and not part of a pattern, and so be surprised and disappointed anew each time. Wilfully blind optimism is the key. Occasionally anger and disappointment can help you write something else, but I don't really function on those kinds of motives. I believe that ferocity works for some people; they put it into their next script and write with an increased passion. Also, I don't really have a choice; I can't really do anything else; I have no other discernible skills. You've just got to throw it over your shoulder and carry on really.

JAMES DORMER: On a feature of mine – which took 12 years to get made – I got fired and brought back about three or four times. Being a writer for TV and film is really all about being in a series of abusive relationships. It has something to do with the fact that everyone else's job depends on the writer putting something down on paper. Some people are comfortable with that – but others find it a bit scary/frightening and perhaps find it empowering to know they can put down the writer or fire them and find another. Look, there's a lot of pressure on them and the show always has to come first. But ultimately I'm not sure that's always the way to get the best end product.

MIA BAYS: Failure is essential. Trying out ideas and having space and time to find your style, your themes, your voice is vital.

PAULA MILNE: What happens more now with me is stuff not getting made, and that's very disappointing because you may spend six to eight months writing something and you have nothing to show for it. It can do the rounds but chances are it's tainted. However, I'm a great one for plagiarising myself. I will take an element out of one script and transplant it into something else, either a character or a scenario, so nothing is ever truly lost. The kind of rejection when you go in as a younger writer or newer writer, and you pitch an idea that gets rejected before you even get to write it, that's really hard. But you have to roll with the punches; it's an industry, you have to learn to take the knock-backs. I remember back in the day I had a file with a big label on it saying 'Rejection', and I made myself look at it so it became part of everyday life like doing your VAT!

HOPE DICKSON LEACH: There's a lot of rationalising that goes into processing rejection, but ultimately it's a blow that takes a while to recover from. My work is always personal and rejection feels personal, even though I know it isn't. Ultimately it makes the work, and my relationship with it, clearer as it makes me decide if I want to fight for a project, or if I agree with the rejection. It's a gut thing, and I've learned that the sooner you listen to your gut, the better. I often get excited about new ideas, but as you develop an idea it can become clear that it isn't going to be a film, or that you aren't the right person to make this into a film. It's hard letting things go, especially if you've worked on them for a while, but it's the only way to free yourself up to make the work you HAVE to make.

BERTRAND FAIVRE: Don't send it out to as many people as possible as a beauty quest to see how many likes you get. They might have a different vision or just reject you. If you send it to 20 people and you are rejected 20 times, it can deter you and be demoralising.

ROBIN GUTCH: No one minds a 'no'. It's upsetting and disappointing, of course, but in the end, actually being told it's not going to work, preferably with the reason given, is better than silence. That helps you in the sense of where to put your energy and time.

REJECTION ISN'T JUST FOR NEWBIES

Rejection isn't a privilege accorded solely to new writers and filmmakers trying to break in; it applies to us all and is a way of life, alas. When I came out of drama school I was fortunate to be signed by an agent. I thought that was it – I was made. However, the process was only just beginning. I found the casting process gruelling. I had to sit in a line of actresses and in my head they were better looking, more talented, more of everything than me. I was a good actress but I didn't have the staying power or the determination and passion to perform. This is why I have such respect for actors and admire their tenacity. What I've learned is that, when things don't work out, it's not always in your worst interests.

JAMES DORMER: Rejection is always difficult. It's easier when you're just working on one project with a company and it doesn't work out and they fire you. What's harder is when you are working on maybe a couple of things with them and you get fired off one, but you have to go in the next day and talk to the people who fired you. That's quite tricky. That's something everyone should be aware of. A lot of writers get fired a lot. I have a friend who didn't know that – he took it personally when he was fired the first time. Got really angry and hasn't really worked in TV since.

TINA GHARAVI: Rejection is painful for anyone. What counts is what you do with that rejection and how you come back.

CHRIS SPARLING: I started as an actor in this business, so rejection was part and parcel of that entire experience. As a result, I developed a bit of a thick skin. Nevertheless, it still sort of frustrates me when I don't land a particular writing assignment or if a spec I write doesn't get the traction I hoped it might. But you take the hits and you just keep coming out for the next round. You'll win one eventually.

DANNY BROCKLEHURST: I deal with rejection badly – usually very badly. I get cross, pissed off at all the work put in. There are different types of rejection. If we have been working on it for a long time it feels like a waste of energy and thought, especially if the reason seems stupid. It's exactly like being dumped. You put your heart out there and you know the chances of selling it elsewhere are slim. It also depends on where you are in life. At the moment I have a show filming and another green-lit so I would be fine with it. That said, I spent two and a half years being rejected and each time it felt like another kick in the teeth and worse than the last. I felt like I was physically moving further and further away from the screen. A writer's life is spent avoiding those periods and, of course, you then

211

become resentful of other people's success during those times, which isn't a nice emotion.

BERTRAND FAIVRE: Rejection can be dangerous. If I am trying to make a film and I send it to the wrong people, they can question you to the point where they take your confidence and make you weaker.

DAVID SIMPATICO: I bitch and moan for a bit; then I go to a movie. As my grandmother used to say,'Wadda ya gonna do?'

DICTYNNA HOOD: Hard! I know the reality is that most of us have to deal with it in the film industry. Sometimes rejection can also help crystallise the project and bring it forward in a positive way by making you think about what could be improved and what you want to retain. Also, 'no' never means 'no'; it just means 'come back later'.

LIAM FOLEY: A good project is a good project and it's painful to close the door on it, but sometimes a competitive project can put the kibosh on it. There's always a passion and excitement for an idea at its inception – that's why it gets on the development slate. We don't want to say goodbye to them and generally we don't. They're always there, ready to be resurrected, even if they're not in active development. It might just mean waiting for the right talent to come along, whether that's a director or cast. We move sideways onto other projects, but we never entirely move off a project. We are very reluctant to say goodbye and put a full stop on anything. It's worth being dogged and determined – if there's a passion for something here, it tends to be seen through to the very end.

GUY HIBBERT: I've got one film at the moment, which I started writing in 2002, so I'm now in my twelfth year of trying to get it made. At the moment, we have a new director attached to it. I have also added a new producer to it to give it new blood. The director and a casting director are now going out to Africa, to look at the casting of the African boys in it. That's 12 years on. If the script's good enough and other people think so too, I will keep going with it until I fall out of the tree. Some of my scripts are just not good enough so I quickly abandon them. I can think of a few scripts that I have written where I have started off on the wrong foot; they just don't work and it's best to bin them immediately and forget you ever wrote them.

JACK THORNE: It gets slightly easier. It never stops. It's always quite bizarre. No one ever tells you that you've been sacked – they just stop talking to you. And then you find out someone new is going on the project.

JIM UHLS: It's important to believe that there are people out there who will connect with your script, although it might take a while to find them.

JON CROKER: Very, very, very hard. Very (very). But always remember it's because you weren't good enough. That it was personal and your fault. So next time, you can do better.

JOSH APPIGNANESI: It's really easy to deal with rejection. I just open my veins in a hot bath, and along with the vodka and Prozac you feel practically nothing. Just a sense of release.

JUSTIN TREFGARNE: Easy! No, it's of course one of the toughest things to deal with. But I once heard Stephen Frears say something like, 'All you need is one person to agree with you and you can make the film.' What he meant was, however many people say no, only one needs to say yes in the end. It's a lot worse for actors. I'm married to one and they get rejected two or three times a week sometimes – that's a pretty crazy way to live. It's a bit like a policeman complaining they have to arrest people. If you don't want the rejection, do something else. So basically, when someone says no, you just have to regroup and come back stronger and better every single time. No isn't an answer in the end; it's just another obstacle en route to the eventual yes.

KEVIN CECIL: It's never easy. It's terrible and horrible. It's very disappointing when a project gets turned down. If you are lucky enough to be working on other things then at least you can get on with them. There's a point perhaps when you realise that you haven't heard anything for a while, and then it's less of a shock. You have to take heart from the fact you got as far as you did. You pick yourself up and get on. Sometimes you just have to go and do something as different to writing as possible for a few hours. Then you can come back the next day to push the next rock up the hill.

KIRSTEN SHERIDAN: I consider changing industries often. Rejection isn't too bad – it's silence that's hard. Rejection is fine. They say 'This isn't for us' or 'This isn't our audience', and you go 'Okay'. Actors say 'I didn't feel this part', and I always think this means they just weren't the right choice in the first place, that I got it wrong. Whichever actor does feel the part must be the right one. It's when you send out a script to 20 people and there's six weeks, or six months, of pure silence. That's the hard thing for new writers. Writing can be an incredibly solitary task.

LEVI DAVID ADDAI: I look for a positive. I believe cream rises to the top, so if it's a good idea it will find a home. It doesn't end with one person saying no. One person isn't the voice of the industry or your only destiny. There are some people out there who will love it, like it, hate it, or be indifferent… we're all human beings. As a young writer you meet producers who seem to be rooting for you, and you think you are on this incredible path to success and production. But then you get to the nitty-gritty and all of a sudden it falls apart. It's a learning process. Not every project is going to be right for the person you are pitching it to. It doesn't mean they are stupid or can't see the merit in your work; it just isn't for them. You have to remain optimistic because this industry can be soul-destroying.

MALCOLM CAMPBELL: I've been sacked many times. I didn't realise you could get sacked from writing! Nobody ever says 'You're fired'. You suddenly find no one has come back to you with notes for weeks or months. It goes dead. It's hard initially and you have to develop a thick skin. The first paid job I had, I was commissioned and I thought that was it, you can give up the day job at last. It didn't work out because I didn't know how to craft stories and I got found out. It made me determined that was never going to happen again. Of course, it has, but I'm more resilient now. Talk to other writers as everyone has gone through it.

RICHARD EYRE: It's extremely painful.

MARC EVANS: I'd rather have a swift 'no' than a protracted 'maybe'. Uncertainty drives me crazy. I've developed a fairly good instinct for gauging in meetings how much of a chance I've got. I'm rarely wrong these days, actually; I often come out of meetings thinking 'I didn't get that', so the actual rejection, when it comes, is slightly mitigated by that. Occasionally I get miffed when I really genuinely think that I would've been the better person for a job. But equally I can often see why another director might be the right person, and I can often see there's a reason why they might get it over me. I don't carry grudges. I just don't want to waste too much time.

MARNIE DICKENS: I'd be lying if I said it was easy.

PETER KOSMINSKY: If it's kindly meant, then I try to take it in the spirit it's given. But for any kind of creative person, rejection is hard. And because these matters are often a matter of opinion – personal taste – it's sometimes difficult to accept a 'no' when it's given. We all struggle with this. If you don't care enough for it to hurt, then it probably wasn't worth doing anyway.

RON SCALPELLO: It's like bumps on the road. If you want to be involved in this industry, you're going to go over those bumps constantly. And every now and again, you're going to hit a big one. When *Here Comes the Summer* failed after two years, it was kind of depressing for a week or two. That's quite a long time for me, but I was in a flat phase. Appreciate the process. Rejection does happen, your script might not be made, your film might not go through. There'll be a day or two days of being a bit sulky, but don't allow that to dominate your approach. Don't let rejection be the default position that you carry over onto the next project. You know – feeling that it will never happen. Rejection can turn to hopelessness, and before you know it you've given up.

ROWAN ATHALE: It's not easy; it's fucking awful. Getting a film made, particularly your first, is a process where you pitch your heart out to 50 financiers/producers/production entities over a long period of time, hoping that eventually four will say yes. That's 46 people saying 'NO'. No one likes rejection. If the fear of rejection is something that weighs heavily on your mind, do something else for a living. Everyone, no matter where they are in their career, gets rejected. I dealt with those situations in the age-old manner: I was working with producers who felt just as disappointed, so we went out, drank a few pints and said, 'Fuck it, it's just a bump in the road, we'll start again Monday.' A thick skin is essential in making your first film.

SAM WASHINGTON: It's never fun. It's all part of the deal, though, so you just have to suck it up and move on. It does get easier over time, as your skin thickens, but I don't think it'll ever stop stinging entirely. I hope I get to be a wrinkly old director, and I'm sure, even then, that being told I haven't won the pitch or that my idea sucks will be a kick to the balls.

TONY JORDAN: It's tough. Anyone who says they take it in their stride is lying.

TONY GRISONI: I got knocked back only the beginning of this week. You offer up, you try to get the gig, give it your best shot and then someone decides whether they want it or not. It's as simple as that. How do I react? Usually my immediate reaction is a kind of fury, but I'm very good at channelling that and saying. 'OK, fuck them. We're going to make this work some other way.' You go back to the drawing board. Usually I'm with a producer, but I've sometimes been in a situation where it's me, a producer and a director, and

216

we're going in to pitch to someone – convince them that this film has to be made. If you get knocked back, you've got to get on and figure out your next step. Sometimes it just doesn't happen. But the projects are never dead. A friend of mine talks about this dark warm shelf, meaning they are still alive, a sort of body in the swamp. At some point, they will be pulled out and it'll be, 'Yay, you're alive!' You'll maybe dress them up differently so they have another chance. The trick is to be working on about five things at any given point. If you've just got one treasured, beautiful child and somebody rejects that, you're really stuck.

••

ROCLIFFE NOTES on...
WHY YOUR SCRIPT MIGHT BE TURNED DOWN

- It isn't in the right medium. The script is a feature film when a TV mini-series or movie is what's required.

- It doesn't have a strong, rounded protagonist with complexities that engage, and who is right for the genre.

- The protagonist doesn't have clear goals and a clear character arc, or the stakes aren't high enough.

- It's not clear what the premise and theme are.

- The script is a dull read – it doesn't have pace and it drags. To repeat the commonly used refrain: come in to scenes late and leave early.

- The structure of your film script, although written in script format, feels more like a novel with things going on inside the characters' heads that can't be portrayed on screen. Films and TV shows are about what happens *between* characters. Things need to be filmic.

- There's too much telling and not enough showing; the script tells us what we need to see in the action. This is particularly so with the dialogue. There may be long monologues.

- It doesn't fit into a clear genre, starting off as one thing and then turning into something else. This is as much to do with expectation as anything. If the script doesn't deliver what we expect, then it has to deliver something much better.

- Don't second guess what a producer or commissioner wants or send them a script that is too similar to something they've already made. Allow whatever you write to be your take on something. Nobody knows what they want, so it's best just to write what you want to write and what you believe in. What will shine on the page is that it's coming from a truthful place, and no one else can tell that truth except you.

••

PROCRASTINATION

My form of procrastination involves cleaning, going for walks, buying whiteboards and making 'to do' lists. When I start writing, however – or editing or filming – I don't want to stop. Like my father I'll just keep writing until I fall asleep. And now I've adopted my mother's way of working too – rising early to work on things. When she was writing her dissertation (she was a mature student who took up education to escape her teenage children) she would start writing in the early hours of the morning.

JAMES DORMER: I procrastinate a little bit but not much. I tend to work best with deadlines and under pressure. I've been lucky enough to be busy over the last few years so there's no time for putting things off. Actually, I tend to put off everything else – paying bills, etc. Everyday life stuff.

JULIETTE TOWHIDI: How do you deal with procrastination? I have learned to trust it as the unconscious needing time and space, and so I take myself off for a guilt-free shopping trip. Usually I'm right, sometimes I'm wrong.

LUCY CLARKE: It's not really a problem with gag writing because of the fixed deadlines and the fact that you're usually working in the programme's offices. But with sitcom writing it's easy to do. As I only work two days a week I often find it hard to get myself into 'the zone'. I now accept that it's unlikely I'm going to start doing any actual writing until 11 am as I will be finally getting round to answering emails, hanging up the washing, nipping to the post office, etc. Basically I have built 'faffing' time into my work day. I did try turning off my phone and email once, and it happened to be the one day the school was trying to get hold of me because my daughter was throwing up everywhere... GUILT!

PETER HARNESS: It can be worrying if you're a new writer and you hear about other people's level of commitment, as I think every writer falls prey to procrastination and finds it painful. I know how difficult it is for it to be something that completely consumes you and utterly exhausts you. I do the best I can to put off getting into that inevitable state; it's kind of like mania. I think everybody writes in a different way. I'm always a bit afraid of writers who get up really early and do it in an orderly way and I think, 'I don't do that; am I not a real writer?'

MOIRA BUFFINI: It's the difficulty of beginning. I force myself not to leave the page until there's something on it. Quell the voice that tells you whatever you put on that page will be crap. Try to put something on the page and say yes to it. You'll come back the next day and there will be a couple of lines that work and might be good. Those lines may spark something else worthwhile. You have to force yourself not to leave the desk until you have something. Say to yourself, I need to have a scene, or a character. Listen to them speak. It's so important to listen.

SUSIE CONKLIN: Procrastinating? Let me just say that my house is never cleaner than when I've just been given difficult notes.

MALCOLM CAMPBELL: I do procrastinate a lot. Who doesn't? But since having children (I have two under three), you know that your working day is limited to crèche hours! There are certain windows when I can work and I am pretty good at sticking to them. And I try not to work evenings, unless I am on a deadline for an episodic TV show, in which case you know you will have to work around the clock. And I rarely work into the night, just because I don't get much sleep anyway with small children. I am quite disciplined in terms of my working days. However, sometimes I find myself looking at articles online and then go, 'Oh God, I've spent 15 minutes reading about a football match I've already watched!'

OL PARKER: I try to see it as part of the process, if only to forgive myself, and not finish every day with self-loathing. In the end, the thing that gets me writing is actually self-disgust. You go through all your bookmarked pages several times, you respond to a couple of emails, you talk to a few people, you play games, and then finally you think, 'For fuck's sake, just write something.' But I do view all of that faffing as part of it. If you're really late and you have a deadline, then obviously you have to crack on a bit more, but I don't really beat myself up. I'm not sure that getting angry at myself has ever worked as a spur to anything good in my life. Would I have written more without the internet or procrastination? Without question. On the other hand, I don't know how much better it would have been. I find that when I actually start writing, it turns out that something has been going on in my subconscious, and I sort of know where to go next, even though when I first sat down at my desk I didn't have a clue.

GUY HIBBERT: If I write 12 hours a day, I'm probably actually writing about five of those hours. The other seven hours, I'm wasting time, dithering about, looking at the *Guardian* website, looking at emails and seeing what the cricket scores are, not just in England but some game in Bangladesh too. And I'm being distracted by a neighbour or looking to be distracted by a neighbour. I know some people can write in a very concentrated period of time but, unfortunately, I can't do that.

DESTINY EKARAGHA: My writing process frustrates me sometimes because I'm still so rubbish at it! I'm most inspired at night as that's when all the ideas come to my head, so I always thought that would

221

be the ideal time to write. I gear up, I open the laptop, I'm all good to go and then BAM! Five minutes later I'm asleep. Useless. I would try Redbull to try to keep me awake. It worked for a little while but it wasn't healthy; I'm sure that all that caffeine was making me twitch. Now what I try to do is write first thing in the morning and when that doesn't work I leave the house. I actually get more done when I'm out of the house as the opportunity to procrastinate isn't as great. When I'm at home, I'll wash my clothes, wash the windows, hoover the floor. I'll do everything but write! I perhaps don't write as much as other writers I know but once I have an idea I have to write it down because, if I don't, the voices of the characters whirl around in my head. I feel almost schizophrenic until it's on the page. Only then am I free. It's a form of madness, writing – perhaps that's why some writers are considered a little crazy.

CLAIRE WILSON: I find it easy to knuckle down for long periods of time but when I switch between projects there's usually a day of procrastination. The internet is the bane of a writer's life. If I start the day online I will lose a day. I have Mac Freedom so I block it out for hours at a time to avoid distraction.

RESEARCH

On every project I do there's some level of research that's part of the preparation. I spent six months researching this book. With the films I work on, I explore the topic with such intensity that I often feel I've become a minor authority on that subject, albeit for a short period. On *Pressure*, I read up and watched everything on deep sea diving, from pressurisation to the bends. With *No Deposit, No Return* I explored the process of sperm donation and fertility to such an extent that people even started asking me for advice! If you reach out to people in a field you are looking into, many are more than happy to share with you what they know and it enriches the project.

PAULA MILNE: Researching *Endgame* was extremely challenging and fantastically rewarding. It was amazing to talk to people – white and black – whose country had gone through a seismic change almost overnight. I'm currently writing about the Berlin Wall dividing families in the 70s; again it's the same sense of the weight of history and how it has affected people's lives. That's incredibly exciting. There are a few places you can talk to people about that, where you can talk about individual shame. But to have this collective, national sense of something is really a huge canvas to focus on, and that's really exhilarating.

MALCOLM CAMPBELL: You have to research to get into a new story world. That usually entails going out and meeting people, understanding what they do. For example, I did a short film with young girls on the Falls Road, which is the nationalist side of Belfast. I'd no experience of what their lives were like. I needed to meet them and understand what they were into, what they did and how they felt in relation to issues regarding the Conflict. I needed to understand their accents and know how to write for them. I spent two weeks getting to know them and learned about them inside out. I didn't want to be a guy just observing and thinking I knew what was going on in their heads. This way I had a better understanding of them.

GUY HIBBERT: There are two projects I'm doing at the moment, which I haven't started writing. One is about the UN in New York, and the other one is set in India. A producer asked me if I would be interested in doing something about the United Nations, I said yes, we took it to the BBC and they commissioned it. We then had a lot of discussions about what it should be and I did a lot of research, read a lot of books and we both went to New York to spend some time at the United Nations, talking to people working there. I went out there with a story and then realised that it wasn't working and changed it on the research. Reality is always different from what you imagine it to be, which is why research is so important. When I feel ready to write the script, I will just get up one morning and start writing. It's not necessarily a planned time; I just think, 'I'm fed up with researching this and I know what my opening scene is so let's go.' I usually need to know what my opening ten minutes are and what my end is.

SIMON CHINN: It depends what kind of docs you're talking about. A lot of the docs that I've done are retrospective in that we are creating a film from a pre-existing story. These kinds of films comprise the retrospective testimony of all the key witnesses to, and participants in, the story, and are then crafted out of that testimony with archive and other visual elements such as re-enactments. In terms of the research, it's about: getting access to those characters; getting them to feel utterly comfortable with you; building trust in such a way that they're prepared to tell you their story in a way they never have before. It's about getting brilliant archivists to scour all the available sources, and winkle never-before-seen material out of the unlikeliest places, finding people and material that has never been seen before. The research process is quite specific in documentaries. You can't compare it to academic research in any way. Although, clearly, journalism and getting your facts right is important. But in the feature docs I've done, it's not about dry reportage. They are often in some ways about people's different versions of truth.

KEVIN CECIL: A lack of research is something that I've noticed in the work of newer writers. People writing about subjects they don't know, so nothing seems real or believable. Don't get me wrong; write about whatever you like, but find out about your subject matter. Even if you want to do something weird and veer off of that, it's still good to know what you are writing about.

ROB BROWN: It took four years to write and direct *Sixteen*, a film about a troubled former African child soldier, so it was important that I had a story whose potential was rich enough to hold my attention for those years. Initially, with every film, I do secondary research from books to understand the characters and the world they live in. Then, when I feel confident enough, I speak to experts in the field. Then, if I can, I speak to people whose lives are as close to the lives of the characters as possible. I was lucky enough to speak to two former child soldiers when developing *Sixteen* and that helped give me the confidence to write an authentic script.

DAVID FLYNN: It's really important with factual and documentary – the research is the most critical part of the project. We often see ideas come through which are responses to something from a newspaper, though sometimes they haven't necessarily taken that extra stage to dig down and find the reality or the truth behind the story. It's when you dig down to that deeper research that you find the really interesting things that might surprise people.

FINISHING WHAT YOU START

Nothing you write is ever a waste of time. Even if you don't finish what you start, it may be of use to you later on. I started this book about four years ago but put it aside. Then someone suggested I create a blog, so I used it as the content. The book was then mooted and, bar interviews, it was already half written. So nothing is ever wasted – only abandoned until you need it.

ALAN MCKENNA: I used to bowl straight in and fire up Final Draft with only a rough hint of a story, character or scene, foolishly believing that the rest would somehow magically come together once I started typing. Needless to say, it didn't. Some great scenes, sure, but no real story. I have a bunch of scripts that never got beyond page 30 and those are the longer ones. More than anything, this 'fools rush in' process leads to half-finished scripts or scripts that remain destined never to leave the privacy and comfort of your hard drive. Luckily, my writing process has evolved somewhat and I'm a firm believer in the 'treatment first' method. Get it down, see if it works, know your beginning, middle and end. It's my way to ensure the story is worth telling and, if you have that, nothing will stop you finishing that draft.

REBECCA DALY: You always feel like you're getting to the end before you get there, both in the writing and the editing process. You're winding down and you're checking along the way, 'Am I really at the end?' You just know. It just feels right.

PETER HARNESS: I always advise finishing things. Keep doing it and get it finished, even if it's the most painful thing in the world. Drink a bottle of wine, sit and crack something out until it's finished. Once you've finished, you can do something with it, edit it – you've got something there, rather than a trail of half-finished things. Writers finish things. People who aren't writers don't finish things. That's the difference.

TINA GHARAVI: I finish all the scripts I start. I am lucky or unlucky in that I don't know how to give up.

JAMES DORMER: I got a piece of advice from some crappy astrological book my mum gave to me to not give up – finish things. Actually it landed so hard I went and got a tattoo of my Chinese sign. A goat. Which is still with me – for better or worse.

GARETH EDWARDS: The phrase I come back to a lot about writing is 'A thing is finished, not when there's nothing left to add, but when there's nothing left to take away'.

CLAIRE WILSON: I finish every script but not every idea. I have a folder of sparkling gems that never see the light of day. When I go back over them for inspiration I often understand why.

ALISON MILLAR: I'm never completely happy with the films I make. There are always bits that just needed a wee bit more work. You stop because you collapse, run out of money and time, or hit the transmission date. Afterwards, no matter how many awards they win, and even if critics write positive things, I often think to myself,

'Oh, I feel that could have been a bit better.' Having someone supportive and strong working with you, such as a great exec, will help encourage you to stop and may even utter the words, 'Leave it now, Alison, it's grand... it's done... leave it... no more...'.

SIMON CHINN: The thing with filmmaking generally, and documentary-making specifically, is that you always feel, at the end of a project, that you are just walking away or being dragged away from it. A film is never quite finished. I've just been to Sundance with a film of ours. I sat through the screening wishing we could get back into the cutting room and change this and fiddle with that. I always feel like that. As it happens, Malik claims he spent 1,000 days cutting and editing *Searching for Sugar Man*. He literally had to be dragged away from the edit suite; we were screaming at him to stop. We felt there was a point where the film started to get worse, not better. That's often the case. That process for him had become something other than making the film; it was like falling in love. Malik had fallen in love with the story and had spent four years of his life with it, suffering for it, loving it. The end of that process was painful for him and still is in a way. He gained so much from making that film (he won an Oscar, for Christ's sake!) but he also lost something when it ended. I sometimes wonder whether he feels he may never find it again – which is really how I felt after *Man on Wire*.

REWRITING AND SELF-EDITING

Rewriting is my favourite part of the process. It's where the real ideas come together.

DAVID FREEDMAN: All writers know, or find out eventually, that writing is the art of rewriting. The odd genius can barf out a perfect first draft first time, but there isn't an executive brave enough to green-light it. They need to tinker so, genius or not, you will rewrite, and the delete key is as important as the full stop. As a writer, I build into my schedules time to sleep on my own work and look at it with fresh eyes a day or two later. The more sleep the better. Most important, I always re-read my own material as if I'm a complete moron, which I find very easy to do! If I'm confused at any point, or bored (reading my own stuff!), I scribble all over it with a red pen. Time to rewrite.

JAMES DORMER: Whenever I'm writing a first draft I take it for granted that it's going to be shit; the fun for me is rewriting it and making it better. The worst experience is working on a show where for one reason or another they don't have a script; they're going to shoot and you have to write it that minute. Then your first shit draft goes out to all the heads of department and everyone that works for them. Frankly you wouldn't even want a producer to see that kind of raw stuff. But there it is – out there for a crew of 200 to read. Naturally they think it's shit (which is true) and they think the writer is shit (which is debatable). Avoid this if at all possible.

JOSH APPIGNANESI: You go back and forth between big ideas – big visual ideas, tonal ideas, all that sort of thing – and story or script. Put your script editor head on and be tough with yourself. The two have to suit each other, one emerging from the other, with an aesthetic coherence that's related to story. The problem with most writer-directors is they're directors first and their scripts are weak. Fellini wrote 20 screenplays before he ever directed a film and even his most visual films are informed by that.

SHANE ALLEN: Some people write a first draft and think, 'That's it, that's a masterpiece'. They're not open to input or collaboration, to taking other people's notes on board. But you need to be open to good advice. Sometimes people's notes are there to prod you or to ask you a question. The way Chris Morris and Damon Beasley and the *Peep Show* guys work is that they'll write a draft, then do two or three read-throughs with the cast. Then they'll rewrite and rewrite, they'll take on board notes, they'll get three or four different people

– Iain Morris, Robert Popper, the people from the channel – to give notes. They'll cherry-pick the best of the notes so it becomes more of a collaborative process. Nobody is necessarily right on the whole process, but you can inspire people and push people to do better work, write a better joke, make the storyline make a bit more sense, make that character more consistent, and all this is really about opening yourself up to feedback.

SALLY EL HOSAINI: In terms of self-editing, you do have to share what you do. This is something that the Sundance Labs really helped me with. Going through the Sundance Labs process, where you get a lot of feedback on your script, made me realise that everybody has an opinion. And it doesn't mean that just because somebody has won an Oscar their opinion is more valid than yours. Your opinion is what matters most. If something doesn't click or work for you, ignore it, stick to your guns. I had potential producers and investors say that they'd come on board or invest in *My Brother The Devil* if I changed the ending, or made it about one brother and not the other. I refused and was faithful to my initial vision, which is hard when you are desperate to get it made and people offer you money. But in the end I was so glad I did and so proud that I was able to make the film I most wanted to make.

KIRSTEN SHERIDAN: There's different types of self-editing. There's the self-editing you do when you're writing ten pages and the next day you're reading those ten pages and cutting them to eight, or cutting out lines here and there – that's easy. Then there's the career editing, which is totally different. It's when you look over the last ten years of your career, and you spend a day watching three of the movies or something, and you start to see a pattern of some sort. I do think you keep telling the same story to some extent. When you realise what that is, you can start to maybe change that or open it up so it's more accessible to other people. In my case, the stories that I've done up to this point have been very personal. In a weird way, *Disco Pigs* was personal, *August Rush* had a personal quality to it, and *In*

America was obviously very personal, but *Dollhouse* was the most personal thing I've ever done, so I've kind of gone backwards. Now, for the first time, I'm wanting to make a movie that's both social and personal, whereas they've always existed before in a kind of personal sphere. Now I'm more ready to do something which says more about the world. What the hell that is or whether I'll ever get that financed or not is a whole other story.

SUSIE CONKLIN: One thing that script editing taught me before I became a writer is that rewriting is absolutely essential. It's in that process that you figure out what you've actually got and refine it. The first draft can often be this very fun exploration – although some writers hate the first draft and love the second, so it really depends on the writer. I find second drafts are where you start to discover what the heart of the story is; where you begin to consciously develop some of the more interesting ideas that sprang out of the first draft and, just as importantly, abandon the ones that aren't serving the story (even if you're rather taken with them, which you often are!). It's rarely a smooth process – sometimes there's so much you're trying to do in the second draft it gets baggy and loses its focus, but then the third draft can feel like a huge leap forward. Yes, it's true that you can get too many notes or do too many drafts – development hell is a destination most writers have been to at some point. But hard notes aren't necessarily bad notes – rewriting is a difficult thing. What's vital is to understand them; why it's going to make something better, clearer, richer, deeper. If you understand then you can gird your loins and get engrossed again. If the notes don't make sense it's easier to get lost and lose the will to live. But rewriting is part of the process, it really is.

MAKING A LIVING OUT OF THIS

Being a freelancer, on the lookout for your next job, is hard. It can be feast or famine. I worked in the City as a personal assistant to bankers. During that time I invested in myself, making three short films and building up a CV by doing additional photography reshoots on feature films. I travelled to film festivals and attended training courses. In 2008, an opportunity arose to take voluntary redundancy. I took it and committed to a full-time career in film. With that step, I told myself that if it didn't work out I could always go back to temping. That threat keeps me going!

MUSTAPHA KSEIBATI: If you're a filmmaker, it's in your blood. TV and commercial gigs and paid development on projects have kept me afloat. As well as Kinder Eggs. I love Kinder Eggs. But there's no shame in having a day job.

MIRANDA BOWEN: I have been very lucky to have found a parallel career in commercials which sustains me very well. It puts me in the fortunate position of being able to pick and choose more as I am not reliant on a living wage from film and TV. That has freed me up to only embark on the projects I feel most passionately about.

JOSH APPIGNANESI: A living is when people get paid regularly, no? You have to call filmmaking a vocation rather than a living. It's clearly not a rational choice to have made, so I don't see how the way I think about it can be taken at face value. Don't underestimate how impossible it is to make any real income doing this.

GLENN MONTGOMERY: It took six years to get to the point where I thought, 'Okay, I can try to do this full-time.' Being in Ireland I've been quite lucky with development funding. The film development programmes have always been good here; they always help people get started. I've had one feature made and I have three in development at the moment.

SARAH GAVRON: I have a partner who works in film and we have kids – we take turns with childcare and work. It's a juggling act.

REBECCA DALY: Another director told me when I was starting out, that 'life is too short to do a project you don't love'. I don't mean to sound flippant in saying this – I know we all have to earn money and sustain ourselves financially – but I've been surprised how sticking with what really interests me has led to different opportunities and kept me working. Usually, between writing and directing, from project to project, I do OK. I also do some workshops with actors in acting programmes. But generally the work of writing and directing keeps me going, so I'm lucky.

JAMES DORMER: I worked as a civil servant for 15 years and then made a bit of money on film work, and thought that would be plenty while I got my career going. Then I ran out of money and was unemployed for about three or four years; my wife supported me. I've written scripts for ministers and such, and recently had to write a speech for the ambassador in a TV show, which was kind of weird. I thought: I've gone from writing for a real ambassador to a pretend one – is that really a progression?

ROB BROWN: In terms of what I do for a living, I lecture part-time for Bath Spa University on the MA in Feature Filmmaking two days a week. I mentor students, using skills and experience from my own filmmaking. The university funded my debut feature film so they are very supportive of my professional development as a writer/director. The rest of the week I develop new feature scripts and go to any meetings with film and TV execs whom my agent wants me to see. My producers and I have a production company, Seize Films.

ALAN MCKENNA: There's no infrequency as far as I'm concerned. There's always something waiting to be written; having the time is the bigger problem. Making a living and keeping the wolf from the door is a much trickier prospect. The more you write, the more you've got to sell. Like most creative industries, only the select few screenwriters earn the big, big bucks. Coming from an acting background, however, I love that, as a writer, you're not waiting on someone to 'allow' you to work. You can start something without needing anyone's permission. You can knock out a spec, option a book, craft a treatment, all off your own bat. You don't have to wait diligently by the phone, hope that it rings, hope the work you've done in the past leads to more work, hope someone you've worked with before wants to do that dance again, hope that the casting breakdowns and director's vision align and land for you. Get out there and make a short film, put on a play or, better still, write one. You have to be proactive. The work won't find you – you have to find it.

STEPHEN FINGLETON: I worked in an office for many years while writing spec scripts and making short films with my earnings. I made the decision early on that I wouldn't work in a junior position in the creative industries as I didn't feel I would work well lower in the chain of command, and the hours and intellectual resources you need to put in would be a drain from what I really wanted to do. I've been a professional for several years now – mainly writing for income.

TENACITY

The vast majority of the people I went to drama school with have long since left the industry and I don't blame them, but I held fast to my belief that this was where I wanted to be. I've never lost sight of that although there are times when I think I'll retrain in another field. I suggested once to an SFX supervisor that I could be a nurse, and he laughed and said my bedside manner would do no end of good for the NHS as it would drive people back to health! These moments of doubt come with the territory. That said, I love what I do and will stick with it as long as it sticks with me.

SARAH GAVRON: It's a rocky road. It requires lots of luck and masses of effort and persistence... I have learned that some ideas won't happen even after years of work, but others will if you believe in them enough – keep pushing, keep refining.

MUSTAPHA KSEIBATI: 'Never give up and good luck will find you.' This comes from a character named Falcor in *The NeverEnding Story*. What he's saying is that we have to remain steadfast in the pursuit of ambition and, by doing so, opportunity will present itself to us. Filmmaking is a constant battle.

CHRISTOPHER GRANIER-DEFERRE: It's not a sprint. It takes a lot of time, effort and energy to stay in the race. If you think you're running the 100 metres, you're going to get worn out pretty quickly. You need to pace yourself and find a rhythm to what you do. Understand the rhythm of the industry, which is dictated by festivals and other business-led calendar points that dictate how and when people are interested in seeing scripts and films.

SUSAN JACOBSON: Other than obviously having talent, learning from everything you do, and respecting the industry, you need TENACITY! Tenacity is what keeps you in the film industry. There are so many of my peers who are now in their 40s who have stuck with it and are finally getting the success they have strived for. It's the 20 years' hard work that they have put in that is paying off for them now. This is ALL about the journey. If you can hang in there and stick it out, it will pay off.

BERTRAND FAIVRE: Hold tight. It's not about how successful you are at a specific moment, but about how you endure over the long term. The point is how to last.

KATE OGBORN: There can be that paranoia about being exploited. Generally the newer writers and directors that I've worked with have embraced the process, and have worked incredibly hard to do that. One of the truths about the industry is that it can take a really long time, you have to be in it for the long haul. This can be really hard at the beginning, but it's about knowing when to stop with something and accept that it's not working and that you need a new idea. That can be really difficult when you feel like you're solely responsible for carrying the idea around and trying to make it work.

DESTINY EKARAGHA: The film industry can be a very hard one to function in. Sometimes it's feast, sometimes it's famine. Sometimes you're working, sometimes you're not. Sometimes it feels like the end of the world, sometimes it feels like you're on top of the world. It can be a real rollercoaster ride. Savour every moment of it because, however we measure success, my hope is, when we get there, we'll look back on it all and laugh.

ANDREA CORNWELL: People will tell you about their journey, but you have to adapt these things to your own skillset, and look to people you admire and try to follow in their footsteps. Certainly a number of people talk of the value of resilience and sticking to it. That's the number one thing in the film industry: it's very tough and you're not going to build a career as quickly as you initially think you will. But the ones who stick at it are the ones you see around five/ten years later. It's keeping going and not letting go of what you want to do that is the most important thing.

RICHARD COOKSON: Persevere: sometimes a TV idea just needs to wait for the industry environment or zeitgeist to be right. *Spooks* and *Life on Mars* spent many years in development. Writing is a sport, a discipline. Practice will make you better. Experience will make you better.

CONFIDENCE AND SELF-DOUBT

There's not a single person I have met, in any industry, who doesn't experience self-doubt. There are times when it's so tough you wonder whether it's worth it or not. Before, during and after each film I do, I question why I'm putting myself through it. Especially when I feel so exhausted. This industry is daunting. There are so many hoops to jump through – fighting against low budgets, lack of opportunities, different personalities, and trying to stay afloat and be recognised for the job you do. It can be hard to stay on top and be the best you can be, and there are no guarantees that the fruit of your labours, i.e. the film, will be any good. I'm passionate about what I do and I'd like to think I'm a hard worker with a good work ethic, but that's for other people to decide – I can only do the best I can. God knows, I've made sacrifices, missed weddings and birthday parties, although never funerals!

JOHN MADDEN: It's part of the creative process and, with experience, you learn that it doesn't help to banish it. You have to embrace it and question what it is that you doubt. I've often said that the most enviable position to find myself in would be that of a Dardenne brother or a Coen brother, so that you actually have someone standing beside you who has exactly the same interests as you. It's a dialogue, whereas, of course, if you're a single director, as most of us are, then you need to have that dialogue with yourself. I think that process needs to go on all the way through the making of a film. The amount of confidence and experience you can build up is a key part of that, as you're no use to anybody if you're dithering and haven't really decided what you're going to do when you step onto the floor to direct a scene. The point is that you need to lead at that point and say, 'This is what I want to do,' and be able to validate that case to whoever might challenge it for whatever reason, whether that be a cinematographer or an actor or a studio. Confidence is your fuel and the fuel that you offer to others. It's about belief and accepting your belief in what you're doing. You can't be afraid of doubt or pretend it doesn't exist. It will be there, you just have to be able to ride it.

CHRISTINE LANGAN: When you are on a creative journey, there are times when you need to hold your courage and move forward very determinedly. You have to grit your teeth and you can't let self-doubt eat away at you. I think that you need to stick to your guns for a stage of the process, and once you are creating you need to step away and look at it analytically to see if it has some sort of shape. Then you can be questioning of the work itself, which is incredibly healthy, rather than self-questioning. There's a big difference between creative sensitivity and self-doubt, and somewhere along that scale you need to find your anchor. You need stability from which to operate. Strong collaborators and a team can help each other with this. Sometimes you don't have this luxury and you are on your own. It's very easy to sabotage all the good work you've done by allowing too much self-doubt into the process, but you can't be complacent either. Perhaps look at each stage as a draft: go through each phase and let it gestate, then see how it feels, what its strengths and weaknesses are, and have another go – right through the production process.

DAVID FLYNN: Getting into the media generally as a new talent is one of the most daunting things. It brings out all of the fears in you. It's an industry that doesn't require firm qualifications or hard skills. It will take you three or four years, even of solid working in a place, before you stop thinking someone is going to tap you on the shoulder and ask you to leave. You always think you shouldn't be there. One of the things that I would say to any new talent is you genuinely are good enough if you put the effort in and you work hard. It may seem tough at first, but it absolutely is an industry where people can make good careers and have good continuity of work. If it's your passion I'd really urge you to follow that passion and really give it a go.

SAUL DIBB: I would be amazed to hear anyone say that they don't have moments of self-doubt. If you don't have that you are not on your toes. You must question yourself, try and do something you haven't done before, and that can be hard. Any human being has those experiences, whatever they do, and if they say they don't, I don't believe them.

ALAN MCKENNA: The first draft is when I'm at my most self-assured. It's a masterpiece waiting to be read, isn't it? Well, more often than not it's gonna need a lot more blood, sweat and tears for that to even be a remote possibility. But I remain undaunted, brimming with confidence – that is until I finally read it, and then the 'self-doubt' kicks in. 'It's bad, isn't it? It's shocking. What was I thinking? I'm terrible at this, who am I kidding?' But at first-draft stage, the truth probably lies somewhere in the middle. You need the confidence to write in the first place, but the self-doubt makes you a better writer, because it forces you to question your choices and hopefully improve on them. Embrace both and work with them, but just make sure confidence wins out in the end.

RON SCALPELLO: What you've got to realise is that you've come into a kind of conveyer belt of anxiety. First anxiety: are you good enough? You have to say to yourself constantly that you are. Second anxiety: which project are you going to get and who's going to endorse you? Third anxiety: somebody does endorse you and says, 'Right, deliver me your script, deliver me your film.' Then you actually have to make the thing. Fourth anxiety: you get to the set, it's all there and you've got 30 days to film. You shoot the thing and then you go into the edit space to see what you've actually got. By the time you finish the film, at the end of the day you might have made a film you're really proud of, but as soon as it's finished you're back to anxiety once again. Where's the next project going to come from? Am I going to be good enough?

TINA GHARAVI: The biggest obstacle has always been my own confidence in myself to do it. Once I resolved that, the film happened. The next challenge was dealing with difficult people on set... but that merits a much longer answer.

MICHAEL KUHN: It's very important to have in mind a map of the landscape you are operating in. You should develop it with input from those in the know in finance, marketing, development, production, post-production and networking. Once you have this in mind, if you decide to deviate from the beaten track, you will at least know you are doing so and (hopefully) why. If you just set off without developing this mental landscape, you fully deserve the stress, pressure and probable disaster you will encounter!

PETER HARNESS: Everybody goes through the self-doubt and criticism; everybody finds it hard. Don't worry if you do.

PAUL ANDREW WILLIAMS: I don't get moments – I get one long moment. It never goes. All the time, I find myself questioning why I am doing this. There are so many people taking the decisions out of your hands, where creativity means nothing. The creatives have very little say. It's so hard but that is part of the whole deal. There are some great things about this industry too and I've met some wonderful people, made great friends and had amazing experiences. There's always the part of you that will say, 'I can't be arsed doing this any more.'

ASIF KAPADIA: Every time, with every film, I have moments of self-doubt and insecurity, generally just before I am about to shoot, before an important meeting or a screening. It's scary; you think you are useless, that you don't know what you are doing. The challenge is to learn to trust your instincts. You may end up disagreeing with people, people may not like your films; we have all made films that haven't worked. The main thing to say is that that's not going to stop me doing it again. I am just going to try again. It's perfectly natural and I don't know any filmmaker who doesn't feel that way. Anyone who doesn't get moments like that probably doesn't care enough. I only make films that I really care about that feel personal and say something about the world we live in. You must choose projects you care about because it can take three to four years out of your life to get a film off the ground. With every film you are putting yourself on the line, you are risking your reputation (if you have one) and your talent – do you have anything to say? There's a hell of a lot of self-doubt in every film you make, but for me that's an exciting thing. That's the thing that makes me want to come to work every day and say, 'We're going to make this better.' Hopefully at the end you have something you are proud of, but in-between there's a lot of doubt, drama, your hair turning grey, arguments. That's the nature of creating something. Particularly if you want to challenge yourself with your work, you are going to put yourself in a danger zone, an unknown place which I think is what you should always do. I interviewed Ken Loach in 1997 before I did my short film *The Sheep Thief*. I asked him about this. He told me he was thinking about retiring, that he didn't know how many more films he had in him, and so he'd made the decision that he would only make films without a safety net. Walk the tightrope without a safety net so you put everything into it, because it may be your last film. It was the same with Scorsese. In an interview he said that, when he was making *Raging Bull*, he was sick and thought it was going to be his last film, so he put everything into it. He thought no one would ever let him make a film again. Whenever you read interviews with these great filmmakers, or if you are lucky enough to meet them, they all have this self-doubt. So just imagine this is your last movie and make it the best you ever do.

KNOW YOUR AUDIENCE AND STAY PLUGGED IN

When people say they have a great idea for a screenplay or a book and are desperate to tell me all about it, I ask them to write a one-page overview and send it to me as I relate better to things in print. And then I ask myself whether the story is one that people would be prepared to tune into or pay to see because, first and foremost, this is an industry, with a marketplace. So look at the film listings or TV guide – stay attuned to what's going on. You need to decide who you are making the film for – yourself or a viewing public.

PAULA MILNE: Never write anything you don't want to see. The main opportunities reside in popular and continuing drama on TV. That, pragmatically, is where I'd say the audience appetite is. If you never watch them and don't think they have a place in British TV, then you can't write them. Sometimes I feel like watching an episode of *The Street* or *Shetland* because I'm in a certain mood. Then I might want to watch something more challenging the next night. Audiences aren't compacted in a departmental way, and writers have to be the same.

LIAM FOLEY: A script is a template for a film and a film should be made for an audience. Not every film has to be so broadly commercial that it has a life outside the UK. However, a story that is going to grab a reader and then, by extension, an audience has to deal with universal themes, conflicts, and dilemmas. It's tough; it's very hard to get the balance right. It's increasingly important for new writers to be tuned in and aware of the marketplace that they hope to enter. By following the Twitter feed of deadline.com or *Hollywood Reporter* or *Variety*, new writers can keep up to date with what sorts of films are getting made, what TV is being commissioned. Market forces shouldn't necessarily dictate what a writer is writing, but it's crucial to be aware of what's going on out there. Knowledge is power. That doesn't mean you have to be inside the industry; you can do it easily with the click of a button. New writers need to remind themselves they are not alone. You don't have to look very far on Twitter to find people who will give 140-character, bite-size pieces of insight and advice that can help you through a dark time or a blank computer screen. Look to places like Twitter to follow writers, producers and directors whom you admire. Writing can feel quite isolating, but one doesn't have to exist in a bubble.

SASKIA SCHUSTER: It's impossible to create content in a vacuum; we are all influenced by what we watch, see, read, etc. However, with newer writers it's not uncommon to be able to read their script and then be able to list that writer's favourite comedies. What I mean by that is that newer writers can be too influenced by their viewing tastes and habits – possibly through lack of confidence – to allow their own voice to really inform the script. It's their individual voice that is going to sell the script. Newer writers can also find it harder to take notes than experienced writers, and I have known great projects not progress for this reason.

ANDREA CORNWELL: I have worked with a number of first-time feature directors. Certainly a huge problem is making films for yourself rather than with an audience in mind. Often the subject matter is simply not one where you can understand how it might engage or excite an audience. It doesn't matter if you are intending to work in a very art-house world (which will have a small audience) or whether you are looking to do a commercial genre project – they both have audiences and you have to know who they are. There are films that fall between the gaps and feel too small or too like TV when you're trying to make film, or vice-versa. People absolutely need to have an awareness of others working in similar territory to themselves, how they put their projects together and what the likely audience and budget for those films are.

KERRY APPLEYARD: The old script guru adage is true – what is it about? Know that and keep coming back to it to give your work focus. Some writers don't have any appreciation or understanding of how their writing might impact an audience. Over complication and lack of clarity lead to confusion for a viewer or reader. Often new writers are not clear what the story is about and consequently bring in too many elements, which can make the storytelling unwieldy and unfocused. You are aiming to make the audience feel with the drama, so each choice and dramatic turn should be written with an intention. If the end result is evocative and powerful, the audience will take away so much more.

GO DO IT

Whatever you choose to do – a play, a radio show, a sketch show, a short, a low-budget feature – the important thing to remember is that you *can* do it and you don't need permission. There are various routes – through shorts, working on other people's films, writing a script. Everything is at your fingertips. It really is about having the confidence to do it. For many years, my mantra – and don't ask me where I found it – has been 'To do is to be said Aristotle, to be is to do said J-P Sartre, do be do be do said Frank Sinatra'. The main thing is to try!

SARAH GAVRON: As a director, you learn by doing. However basic, however small, it's worth making stuff, and lots of it, before you are exposed to the real world and the pressure to get it right. I believe the most important thing is to work out what kind of filmmaker you are, and you only discover that through making stuff.

DANNY HUSTON: Bernard Rose and I were sitting around moaning and groaning. His girlfriend said, 'Why don't you do something? Go out and make something?' We responded by saying it was too complicated. She completely dismissed this and told us to just go do it. So we did with *Ivansxtc*. We felt like an early punk band, doing it on our own without permission, with only a digital camera. It felt revolutionary. We didn't expect it to get the reception it did and it was a surprise when it got so much attention. As an actor, that was my beginning.

DAVID SIMPATICO: Don't wait around for someone to say 'yes'. Either go out and make it happen, or do it yourself. Learn skills, try new things. Shoot some short films and then learn how to edit them. It will make you a better writer if, at the very least, it teaches you what you don't need. It will also teach you about the three versions of any script: the script that is written; the script that is shot; the script that is edited.

CONOR BARRY: Get out there. Don't be shy. Work on other people's films. If you're trying to make a short film, you should be working on other people's short films. If you're trying to be a producer, you should be working in production offices. Whatever it is that you're trying to do, you should be willing to work on other people's stuff to learn. You basically work your ass off and, as a result, you can't help but grow. You naturally move up.

THE VALUE OF SHORTS

Short films were my way into the industry. I helped my friend Antonio Mendez make short films with a Super 16 camera and fell in love. It paved the way for my career, especially working on other people's shorts, which led to my own. The process of making a film – short or feature – is the same, but the money and time factor is different. You have more creative control on shorts. They are a solid starting ground to build a showreel, ultimately saying, 'This is what I can do.'

SAUL DIBB: Shorts did play a role for me, but less so for most directors I know. I found them quite frustrating in a way because they work best as the distillation of an idea or mood and I wanted to work on something that was longer. Mostly the films I made before moving into features were documentaries.

PAUL ANDREW WILLIAMS: They were useful to learn how to direct, manage a crew. They got me meetings, an agent and opened doors that led to my first film.

SARAH GAVRON: Shorts are vital. Unlike the other jobs in film, as a director you can't really work your way up. You can learn and benefit from working on films, but that won't get you a job as a director. You have to show you can direct in order to get a directing job. Short films are a great way, or commercials or theatre – whatever it is that shows your work as a director. I made nine short films and it was with the ninth short that I had my break – it won some awards, got me an agent and meetings with film companies and broadcasters. I made that short while at the National Film and TV school – having fellow students, equipment and expert guidance on hand helped enormously.

JOSH APPIGNANESI: A good short can get you noticed, but also it's a nice way to make mistakes in relative privacy at a low cost. But I'd say to people, don't spend too much time or money on your first few shorts. Do them fast and cheap and you'll learn more with less disappointment. Don't sit around waiting.

KERRY APPLEYARD: Producing a short-film version or trailer of the longer form demonstrates the story and your directing talents. There's nothing better than having proof in the pudding, to stand out from the crowd.

CONOR BARRY: It may be old-fashioned, but if you're a writer/director or producer, you should make a short film using your natural network and then use it to make a better one, which will hopefully get into a film festival or generate funding for another short film or development. Shorts are a proof of your ability to hold responsibility and a remit. As a writer/director or producer, you're involved with a particular style of filmmaking, not a copy of other things. You should be able to go, 'That's what I'm about.' It's a calling card in terms of the tone or style.

ARAB NASSER & TARZAN NASSER: In every director's life, creating a short film is the first important step at the beginning because the short film is made with the simplest tools. These are the first baby steps of going forward with a career in the world of cinematic direction. There's also the trust you create through the film with the audience and producers who you hope will continue to support and finance your next film. The most difficult thing is presenting the story because, unlike feature films, time is limited and the director has to squeeze everything into this short, whereas with feature films you have more time to expand the story. Ultimately, though, it comes down to storytelling and both types of films need to be convincing for the audience.

MIA BAYS: I love short films. Having an Oscar-winning one as the first film I produced (*Six Shooter* by Martin McDonagh, 2005) really helped establish a new career path (from distribution to producing). I have a lot of affection for short-form work. I made another two recently after only doing features for the last few years and it was a breath of fresh air.

TINA GHARAVI: Shorts are great – they are such an important part of building your storytelling confidence and testing yourself.

BERTRAND FAIVRE: They cost very little money and the risk is limited. This means you are much freer as a director. You can try out, be bolder, and experience filmmaking. You need to use this calling card as a way to find your voice and distinctiveness.

REBECCA DALY: I can't imagine doing a feature without ever having made a short. I cut my teeth making shorts and learned so much about the whole process. It really is like a micro-version of a feature.

PHIL ILSON: Short films have existed since the dawn of cinema (the first films were shorts), and every single filmmaker in the history of film will have made a short in some capacity, whether it's playing around as a kid or coming from an ad or promo background. The role of short film is to develop the filmmaker's talent. Many decide to stay with shorts or go back to shorts, particularly in the world of experimental and artists' cinema. There's no doubting the importance of short film in the creative industries.

ROB BROWN: I made six short films before making a feature and I don't think *Sixteen* would be as strong a feature-film debut if I hadn't made all six. You learn your craft, but you also learn about festivals, distribution and the industry as a whole. It's very important to have this grounding before making a feature if you haven't at least directed TV before.

KIRSTEN SHERIDAN: It gives you a concept of how hard it is to sustain an interesting story arc over an hour and a half. When you realise it's quite hard to do it over ten minutes, you see what you're up against in terms of a feature. In saying that, I've seen people go almost straight to features and I've seen it work for them. It's up to each individual. If people continue to be better at shorts than they are at features, you can build a career out of that and not consider it a bad thing. Now, with distribution changing to such an extent, you could probably build an incredible online following from good shorts.

DESTINY EKARAGHA: Short-film funding schemes helped to jump-start my career. Southern Exposure, a borough fund, funded *Tight Jeans*. *The Park* was funded by Film London. The funding and support that I got from each of them enabled me to make the films exactly as I intended and for that I will always be grateful.

MIRANDA BOWEN: People do things in different ways. Depends what you ideally want to write and direct. If you want to be directing returning series you are probably better off directing a soap, but even then you probably won't get the gig unless you have a competently made short film under your belt. I suppose it's important to be able to demonstrate your grasp of narrative, film language and working with actors. And there's no other way of learning your craft! Some directors come up through ads and music videos, and that is another valid path, but it doesn't quite prepare you for working with actors in the same way.

STEPHEN FINGLETON: If you're a director and you're not making work, you're not a director. If you're a screenwriter and your material isn't finding its way on screen, you're not a screenwriter. Short films are both practice and art, both of which are things you should be aspiring to do throughout your career.

MUSTAPHA KSEIBATI: Understanding story and structure is something you learn on a small scale on shorts when writing/developing. When it comes to directing, it's an important place to build your craft. We are not all geniuses off the bat. Directing is a craft and skill developed and strengthened over time.

HOPE DICKSON LEACH: I can't imagine trying to write a feature without writing short films first. And if you're not a director and you're not shooting your films yourself, then having your short scripts MADE is invaluable to you as a writer. A screenplay isn't created to exist on the page, so unless you can see how it plays out in time, large and human and colourful, then you don't really know what you've got in you.

SALLY EL HOSAINI: After university I made a lot of shorts with friends on zero budgets and they were a great way to learn. I would never show these shorts to anybody and we never pushed them into festivals or anything. They were made for fun. We did all the different roles ourselves – acting, lighting, costumes, props, and then edited them ourselves too. Later, after over ten years of working various jobs, and when I quit working for other people, I thought I'd do that classic thing of starting over with shorts. So I made a 60-second short, then made another longer short film. I then tried to make some much more ambitious short films but never got the funding together. I then realised that I was putting so much into trying to make these ambitious shorts that I may as well have been trying to make a feature. I stopped and put everything into *My Brother The Devil*. The only reason I made shorts later in my career was because I kept getting told that you have to make shorts in order to show what you can do in order to make a feature. So, for me, short films were always a means to an end.

SUSAN JACOBSON: For a director, a short is PARAMOUNT! Writing perhaps not as much as you can showcase your work on the page.

But for a director, you need to demonstrate your storytelling skills, how you get a performance from an actor, your vision. There's no way to do this other than visually, and that is through a short.

MALCOLM CAMPBELL: The first two things I had broadcast were part of a series of 10 x 10-minute films on BBC2. *Black Cab* was short stories set in the back of a taxi and *Table 12* was ten films taking place at the same table in the same restaurant. I learned how to write economically and got an awful lot of story and character development into those ten minutes. I can tell when reading a short script where the fat and the unnecessary stuff is. Though I favour looser, fluid storytelling in features, the better short films are concise and precise. Those shows really helped me with TV screenwriting; how to get a point across and move a story on quickly.

ANDREA CORNWELL: Short films are essential for writer-directors. Better a fabulous short film that starts winning prizes than a feature film that is neither commercially nor critically successful. There's a current move into doing low-budget features: other people will have different opinions on this but I personally don't like them. Very rarely do you have enough budget and resources to sustain production values that you would want to have as your calling card. It's very difficult to engage cast and crew for enough time to make 90 minutes of material, as opposed to begging favours to try and get a really polished ten minutes. Anybody who is going to be looking for a feature film writer will want to see how you handle story over a length of time. For that, people are much keener to look at radio or theatre work or spec scripts. That really is the only way you're going to break through. However, for pure writers short films are not particularly helpful.

JON CROKER: As a writer, I'm not sure if short films are that important as the director gets all the credit. Why not take the time to write a feature-length script instead? It costs nothing but hard work and time. And it gets you a lot more attention.

ASIF KAPADIA: I wouldn't have a career without shorts. I got interested in making films by working on short films as a runner for other people. Before that I had no interest in either watching movies or making films. My passion and interest started with shorts. I learned by being part of a crew and realised that I wanted to make films. I started to make films with my friends. We didn't know what we were doing so we made it up as we went along.

CHALLENGES OF MAKING A FIRST FEATURE FILM

Getting to the first day on set is a road paved with hard work but it's magical. Look around you because this is where it all begins. The easiest part is behind you. Now you have to really prove what you're made of.

CHRISTINE LANGAN: Making your first film can be many different things depending on how you go about it, how much support you have and who you are working with. You need to have fire in your belly and be really determined to get the film made, otherwise you will run out of the energy you need to take you through this demanding, tiring and frustrating process. Keeping your excitement and joy in the story alive, in any way you can, is important. It's all about bringing a story to life, and you have to understand that it's a layered experience and you will go through different phases to get to the end. You get interesting phases, tough phases and ground you have to break through. It's about stamina, It's not a sprint.

SAUL DIBB: There were many and various challenges to making *Bullet Boy*, my first feature. The biggest was that I couldn't make it the way I did documentaries – capturing moments. It was having to bring these moments, from a scene that existed theoretically on the page, to life, with actors, and to make it feel like it had the same veracity and truthfulness as the documentary stuff I had been making before. We also set ourselves a hard task with that film because the script was only 40 pages as I felt it was best to capture the dialogue and turn of phrase of these young kids living in London through improvisation – and about half the cast were non-actors. That was very challenging and difficult, turning up every day not knowing what I was going to get and how I was going to create the moments.

MIA BAYS: I've worked on a ton of debuts and always enjoy helping to find and expose new talent but my frustration lies in the perception of what 'new talent' means. You're not suddenly a veteran once you've made one feature – the definition should be more 'stretchy' than that. What often happens is we focus too much on debuts and then much of that talent struggles to get further support. That's a hard space to be in – when you've done a good film but it's not won big prizes or got the commercial or public sector buzzing around you for your next one. I find that very difficult and a real waste of talent and funding – you can't drop talent because their first film didn't hit. If it's good then they deserve more support. If it's bad, then that's hard to justify. But plenty of filmmakers considered geniuses now didn't find their voice and their feet until several films in.

SARAH GAVRON: I hadn't done it before. I hadn't even been on a real film set. I wish I had shadowed someone or been an assistant. I knew about directing to some degree from shorts, but I didn't know much about the process of making a feature: casting professional actors, schedules, pitching, the list goes on... Making short films can get you a job, but it doesn't prepare you for many aspects of long-form filmmaking.

STEPHEN FINGLETON: Nobody gives a damn about you until the following happens: you have made a feature film that someone else has told them about.

JOSH APPIGNANESI: My youthful naivety really helped. Wish I could have some of that back again. Don't imagine there's a Big Daddy out there who's going to come along and see your great big masterpiece and say, 'You've arrived! Well done – you're such a genius, I love you, and now please let me help you do anything you want at all.' That person doesn't exist. Not for anyone, not even for people way more talented than you. Try not to go mad waiting for that person as you'll only do yourself an injury.

DESTINY EKARAGHA: Making my first feature *Gone Too Far!* was one of the proudest moments of my life. There were so many obstacles in the development process that Bola Agbaje (the writer) and I were beginning to think that it would never happen. I still can't believe it sometimes. It was a dream come true. The first thing to know is that, in this industry, rejection is a part of the job. Once I got my head around that, rejection became a lot easier to deal with. However, it was still difficult at times, especially when trying to get *Gone Too Far!* made. When it came to funding my shorts, the process was pretty straightforward. We got rejected by some but accepted by others; you win some, you lose some. However, with *Gone Too Far!* it was just constant rejection for two and a half years. It was the most difficult time of my career. It wasn't long before Bola, Christopher and I clocked that our film was seen as risky because it had black characters who didn't go down the usual route of anti-social or criminal behaviour. It felt to me like some people just couldn't get past the concept of a film being based on black youths going about their day-to-day lives. This was not a narrative that most people were familiar with, so it was seen as risky. Thankfully the BFI stepped in. I couldn't believe that they had read the script, got the humour and backed the project. That was amazing to me. It still is.

TINA GHARAVI: What is clear is that you need to 'cast' your crew as much as you do your actors. Your collaborators are key. But as Persians sometimes say about a marriage: they are like a watermelon… you don't know what you get until you cut into one.

ROB BROWN: The difficult part is making the transition from writing to directing your film. Especially as you may need to rewrite the script during pre-production or even, as I did with *Sixteen*, on set when you're about to shoot the scene! The biggest challenge was getting the money to make the film and casting the film well on a micro budget. Be creative in how you fund your film (I got my employer to pay for it) if the usual industry funding channels are exhausted. If you believe fully in your project then you will get it made no matter what.

MIRANDA BOWEN: Lack of time is a problem. On *Gozo* we wrote and shot the script in under three months. Then it took two years to edit because the script hadn't worked as well as we had imagined. With hindsight, it's clear we were so keen to galvanise the enthusiasm to produce the film on no budget that we didn't allow ourselves enough time to develop the script properly. Then lack of time on the shoot meant that some scenes felt compromised and we were all run ragged by trying to accomplish anything upwards of ten pages a day in order to complete the schedule. And fatigue is your worst enemy on anything where your time is limited. Although, having said all that, I'm sure that some of the energy of the film comes from a 'gung-ho', unprecious shooting approach. There was very little waiting around ruminating over dialogue while lights were set up. It was more a question of making sure the camera was in focus then shooting whatever was in front of it. (I exaggerate, of course, but it felt like that at times and those confines bring a great energy to the process while also, inevitably, being disabling too.) However, we chose this route as it afforded us more creative control and freedom. The obstacles are the same as something that has been conventionally funded but you just don't have anyone to disappoint but yourselves should it all go wrong.

KATE OGBORN: Making your first film is exhilarating and terrifying. It's good that you don't know what you don't know, as you can jump off the deep end and you don't know just how far you could fall. *Under the Skin* was Carine Adler's first film as a director and writer, and mine as a producer. We made a conscious decision that we would stand shoulder to shoulder, and we wouldn't let people drive a wedge between us, whether that was financiers, crew or anything. We stayed united and that was a really important decision. We backed each other and we kept to that. It meant we really trusted each other, and we worked really hard not to let each other down and not to let any situation get divisive. The other crucial fact was that I worked with a brilliant production manager, who was very skilled and never undermined me and taught me a lot. I couldn't have done it without her. The decision Carine and I made to stick together and be rock solid was absolutely vital. On that film, one real bonus was that I'd previously commissioned a short film with Carine called *Fever*, and she'd started developing the feature film on the back of that. I'd begun the development with her, when it was just an idea, and went all the way through the development process with her right through production. It was a very easy decision to make, to say we needed to stand by each other on it, as I really felt like I could speak for her absolutely confidently. I knew it from the inside out and that was crucial. It would be much harder to come onto a film as a first-time feature producer when you're not as intimately connected with the film and what's going on in the director's head.

SALLY EL HOSAINI: Like many first-time writer-directors making their first film, I kept hearing that it was a great idea, but execution-dependent. Of course it's going to be execution-dependent when it's your first feature! It's hard to get people to take a risk and believe in you. *My Brother The Devil* took five years up to the point when we started filming, six to when the film was finished. It wasn't an overnight process. Before I found my producers, I had told myself that 'If I don't shoot by next summer, then I'll stop'. It had been four and a half years of trying to get the film made. When do you stop? I'd nearly spent half a decade pushing it. I had this sense of defiance that I was going to show everybody that hadn't believed in it, so that spurred me on. My big message for writer-directors who have a script and are trying to get their films made is that you have to get out of your comfort zone. Put yourself out there and don't give up, don't depend on public money. If you get rejected by those sources of public funding, there are films made every day with private investment. It's a business. It doesn't mean that your idea isn't good or your script isn't good or your film isn't good. In America they don't have public money so it's a completely different attitude. British filmmakers could benefit from having more of that attitude. For me, the most amazing thing was when it was so well received, critically and by audiences. That felt really good. I felt that I'd believed in it for all these years and that that belief had been justified.

THE PROCESS OF MAKING SOMETHING

Communication is key. My advice is prep the hell out of it. Meet with your heads of department, talk to them, get their input, talk to your actors. Do as much as you can to give yourself the best advantage. Producers, make sure your paperwork is in order because it's hard to get that sorted after the production ends. Then begins the edit, trying to piece it all together, followed by post-production and sign off. Then comes the film festival premiere – sales, distribution, reviews, commercial success and hopefully an award or two.

ROB BROWN: There are three things to concentrate on when you're on set: What do I tell the actors? Where do I put the camera? How will it come together in the edit? It's a real struggle to concentrate on these things when there are so many things happening around you, but if you've got a good first assistant director you're shielded from a lot of these so you can focus on your job. I only shot for 18 days on *Sixteen* over three weeks, but even that felt like a marathon in terms of exhaustion. So persistence is just as important as creativity. When I hear about people shooting for three months or more it sounds like an insane amount of time to be in such a pressured role.

But equally I wouldn't want to be doing any other job, no matter how much I moan about it. Seeing my debut feature have a Leicester Square premiere at the BFI London Film Festival and compete for two awards more than made up for the struggle of making the film!

KATE OGBORN: Getting the green light is always good. I love the first day of shooting. I love the edit. As terrifying and exhilarating as producing your debut film is always the moment when you first put it in front of an audience.

SALLY EL HOSAINI: What I love about filmmaking is that each stage of the process requires you to use a different part of your brain. That makes it a really exciting journey because it's constantly changing and evolving. I do love writing too, but it's a love/hate relationship. Much of the time when I'm rewriting, I'm problem-solving and it's hard work that makes your brain hurt. But actually my very favourite part of the filmmaking process is the first day of the edit. That's the day when you have to forget everything that you've previously invested in the script and the shoot. You have to lose all of your preconceived ideas of what you wanted to achieve. You have to draw a line in the sand and face reality and say, 'Right, this is what I've got. It can only get better than this.' It's like being reborn and looking at your film with new eyes. These are the raw building blocks and you have to remake the film again with what you've got. That's really exciting.

JOSH APPIGNANESI: My favourite part is the excitement around the initial idea. I also love looking at the rushes: however painful they are, something finally exists.

REBECCA DALY: *The Other Side of Sleep* didn't have a particularly low budget for a first feature, so we weren't as squeezed as other productions might have been. You have to make sure that the momentum and the enthusiasm for the project is sustained throughout and that everybody is brought on that journey. That's part of your job as a director on a film, regardless of the budget. You have to keep that momentum going.

MIRANDA BOWEN: I love the edit. The edit is where the film is shaped and reshaped, rewritten and given inflection, nuance and finesse. I have an editor I am good friends with and have worked with for years and that helps a lot. It's where you finally see the audio and image coalesce to hopefully create something distinct and engaging. It's like doing a jigsaw puzzle, but with multiple ways of arriving at the end result, and you somehow have to weave a path through the footage, through trial and error, to find the most powerful synergy of elements. The shoot is probably my least favourite part as inevitably things are compromised and you have to continually struggle to preserve integrity in the face of limited shooting time, compromised funds and a huge lumbering machine that is necessary to the shooting process, and idiosyncratic characters and egos. It's probably the most alchemic part of the process, however, and it's wonderful when the 'magic' happens – moments when it feels there's some sort of mercurial serendipity at play. Sublime moments that really bring a scene or a moment to life: an actor's performance, the light hitting a building in a certain way or an unexpected weather condition that contributes perfectly to the scene.

OL PARKER: You've got to let it go. You have to recognise that it's a different discipline, and that by definition there will be frustrations, of course there will. You've shot the film in your head already, in a very weird platonic way. The faces of the actors are not quite clear to you, the settings aren't quite clear, you know there'll be beautiful music but you're not sure of the tune. The process of the film being made is the process of all of those things becoming real. And in that reality inevitably comes mundanity. On the other hand, what you also gain, if you're as lucky as I've almost exclusively been, is the fantastic amount of things which have been improved and helped, of which you could never have conceived. There's an enormous amount of smooth to go with your rough.

HAVING THE WRITER PLAY A ROLE ON SET

Many people exclude the writer from the set but, in my own experience, having them around has helped the project rather than hindered it. Many directors don't feel comfortable having the writer present but, in my opinion, once the boundaries are set I can only see the advantages – but it depends on the individuals involved.

OL PARKER: I'm incredibly involved in the filmmaking. Or as much as I'm allowed to be, which to my enormous good fortune has worked out fine so far. I was in India for two months on *The Best Exotic Marigold Hotel 2*, for the entire shoot, except when my baby was being born, but that was the first time I've ever missed a shoot day of anything of mine. John Hodge said that the writer on set is like an English monarch, consulted on everything on the understanding that your answer will be yes. And he's not wrong, although the degree to which you're listened to will vary, and depends on the director, and to a degree the producer too. There's a chain of authority, and you have to respect that. If an actor came to me and said, 'This line should be said sadly, but the director wants it angry. What do you think?', even if I thought that yes, it should be sad, I would never say that, not to the actor. Even if I went to the director and had a quiet word, and the director then said let's try it both ways, if the actor then thanked me, I would never admit to having done it. Which is tactical to a degree; you'll get a lot more accomplished if you know your place. But hopefully those kinds of games aren't necessary anyway. In the case of the *Marigold* movies, the director, John Madden, is a lovely, utterly secure guy, who had no worries that I would ever betray him or sell him out.

LEVI DAVID ADDAI: You can't do everything. I've seen it where the producer and director go off in production; they don't ask or involve the writer and inevitably wrong decisions get made. You have to respect that it's a special triangle. It needs to be right. If one person is going off and doing his own thing, then it's not going to work. I am very involved; from casting to post-production I'm there, even with costume and locations. With my show *Youngers* I have to respect the privileged position I've been given by Big Talk. They know how unique the world I've created is and, to get it right, they listen to the creator. People know they can ask me the smallest of questions, to the biggest of things. I'm very appreciative of that with them. They recognise that it's important to keep the writer engaged and they want to get it right, so they involve me. That is the best way to work. We all want the same end goal – a great show. My advice to producers and directors would be to involve the writer; as the creator of the world they are an asset, and their input should not end until the finished product gets on screen.

JAMES DORMER: Seeing a script as a finished film is exciting and horrifying. Nine times out of ten, whatever you've written is going to be changed a lot. Sometimes that can be really thrilling, as it makes it better, and sometimes it's absolutely horrifying, as it makes it worse.

GUY HIBBERT: As a writer, I am constantly frustrated by not having a larger role once the script is completed. I'm quite fortunate in that I do often have an executive producer role, so I do get a look-in at the edit. In TV you can have that role, but rarely in film. I'm not interested in directing, I have no skills as a director, but I just think that, as so much of writing a script is editing a script, for a writer not to be involved in the editing process once the film's been shot makes no sense to me. I actually enjoy the editing process the most, when the story is being put back together again.

SO YOU WANT TO MAKE AN INDEPENDENT TV PILOT...

Every year the New York TV Festival (NYTVF) accepts pilots from around the world. This isn't something I see a lot of in the UK or Ireland but it has huge potential for launching you. The craft talks alone at this festival are worth making a pilot for. I asked Terence Gray, the festival's founder and executive director, to offer some tips for creators looking to take the plunge.

1. ***Don't just look at what's on TV now.*** When writing or developing a TV show, it's important to research what networks are looking for. Look at what's on TV now, but also look at what networks are developing and acquiring – both domestically and internationally. If you have a clear sense of where you want your show to eventually air (even if that is as vague as 'broadcast' or 'basic cable'), it will be easier to funnel your creativity into something productive.

2. ***Do create a show you would watch.*** It's important to see where TV is headed, and I encourage creators to think outside of their comfort zones in terms of subject matter and even genre. Some of the greatest successes I've seen have been from scripted and comedy creators who moved into the unscripted/ doc/factual/entertainment space. However, if your show idea is successful, you will be required to sell that idea in meetings and amongst your friends and peers. Make a show that you would watch or enjoy, even while being conscious of the marketplace.

3. ***Do watch TV.*** This may seem extremely simple, but you wouldn't believe how many scripts and pilots I see where the writers don't seem to have an idea of what a TV show looks like. So, watch TV, and watch it critically. Think about act breaks and scene lengths,

see how much story is unravelled in the half-hour or hour, and look at the way characters deliver exposition and interact with one another. Also, look at shows that have great pilots to see how they establish relationships, tone and story.

4. ***Don't rush development and pre-production.*** Production is expensive, and often those costs are unexpected. The best way to minimise costs in production is to spend time before, making sure that everything is as ready as possible. Look at your locations to see how and when scenes will be shot, think about possible delays (actor commitments, weather, union rules), and look at your script to see what ideas might not be feasible. A huge snowstorm raging while your characters ride in a perilously small aircraft might read well on paper, but it may be too expensive or complicated to shoot.

5. ***Do be quick and simple.*** If you're creating an independent pilot, think about what you're going to shoot to get your main idea across and highlight your voice and the tone of the show. Don't be afraid to edit your ideas or shoot a shorter tape – no development executive has complained that the tape she's watching is too short.

6. ***Don't forget to keep your crew happy.*** Many independent creators are working on a shoestring budget, which means that often the crew and actors are being paid less than they should be or nothing at all (calling in favours is often a necessity). So, when you're on set, make sure that everyone is happy – this can be as simple as making sure everyone is fed. And don't discount the importance of a wrap party – people may be more willing to work with you in the future if they had a good time.

7. ***Do make your show seem real.*** You're making an independent pilot, with a much smaller budget and fewer resources. It's not expected that the final product will look completely polished.

However, when you're looking in the camera or walking on set, think about how what you're making will look in post-production. If something seems odd or out of place, remove or modify it. A show doesn't have to exist in the real world, but it should feel real... lived-in. Creating a cohesive vision in production will cut your time and stress levels immeasurably.

8. ***Don't be too tied to your idea.*** Inflexibility can be the death knell for any creative endeavour. While you are the voice of the pilot, there are other voices as well. TV is a collaborative medium, and other people's opinions should carry weight. Listen to your actors and your crew, even if you don't always take their advice.

9. ***Do hire an editor.*** You are closer to your pilot than anyone else, and that's a good thing. This is your baby. However, because of all that love and closeness, it can often be difficult to look at your tape objectively. Hiring someone to work with you on the editing process is a useful step in creative distance, in looking at your project from an outside angle.

10. ***Do think about digital.*** Making a YouTube video that becomes a TV show seems like an unattainable dream. With more and more content on the web, it can feel like there are fewer opportunities to make an impact. However, even if your video doesn't become an overnight smash, online distribution can be a great way to test the waters, to see how the show hits with audiences. Make sure that you're emotionally ready to see how people react, though. Even *Citizen Kane: The Web Series* would have got its fair share of negative comments.

UNDERSTANDING CASTING

Actors and casting directors are great supporters of writers and writer-directors, and their opinions matter. I've included a section on casting as I've known newer writers and producers who have tried to attach or approach actors before a director is on board. Casting directors often talk of this and it's an essential element to understand. Casting directors open the door to talent and ideas you might never have imagined – their role is invaluable when the time is right and Rocliffe's resident casting director, Laura Dickens, has changed the perception of the event by both industry and actors.

KAHLEEN CRAWFORD: We get a few scripts every year by new writers saying they don't know what to do next with their project. The thing is, I'm a casting director, not a producer, so, before you do anything, find someone who will work with you to get this made and then I'll be more than happy to read your script and cast it. A casting director adds legitimacy, there's a trust built up and we are a familiar name. It gives a project access to talent so much more quickly, but for a new writer-director it just expedites things.

DAN HUBBARD: Each project, you go on a journey with people, and sometimes they're learning as they go along. Everybody needs to be given an opportunity; we need to support our young first-timers and not just the same old list of names. I like to see people listen, take advice and demonstrate a bit of humility. There's a tendency with those fresh from drama or film school to have another idea of the way it should be, that old-school overconfidence. I like people who are humble, and particularly when it comes to casting, not those who say, 'I want Robert De Niro or Tilda Swinton or James McAvoy.' It's very unlikely you can get to those people so you've got to keep an open mind. Listen to the casting director and their suggestions instead of going off on these tangents; they sometimes stop a film being made in the end because you just don't get anywhere.

KAHLEEN CRAWFORD: I would always read the script if it feels like it's actually going to happen. We do get quite a lot of approaches from people who don't have any plan for financing, a director or a producer attached. They don't even have any contacts with financiers. It would just be wasting the actors', the agents' and your own energies. When a producer comes to you and says it's low-budget but that they have 70 per cent of the money in place and mention legitimate sources of finance being attached, I will really consider the project even if they've never done anything before. Casting directors are backing a horse. We're not scared of coming on board but you need to have paved some sort of path ahead.

CATHERINE WILLIS: Writers tend to write with people in their head. They think if they can get X to play that role, their film will get made. That closes everything down too quickly. The issue with inexperience is I have no reference for them. I have to love the script as, without catalogue or showreel, it's going to be a labour of love. When someone says, 'I've written this, I want to make it,' it's quite hard. I don't know them, the agents don't know them, the industry doesn't know them – you're starting at the bottom of a steep hill. So I have to love it and love them to be prepared to embark on that journey.

DAN HUBBARD: There's a project I'm working on where the producers approached me about a year and a half ago and said, 'Let's have Robert Pattinson play the lead.' I explained that we're not filming until next year and we don't have a director so don't know what the budget is, so we don't know what the fee is either. I can't go to his agent without that information. One thing that always makes me scratch my head is approaching me before a director is on board. No actor is going to sign up before they know who is at the helm – it could be an absolute disaster. Agents and actors are reluctant to agree to something so far ahead of time because they need to keep their options open. You don't want to commit and then have Steven Spielberg come along, and you end up missing the opportunity of a lifetime.

CATHERINE WILLIS: There's nothing worse than reading a script and thinking to yourself, 'I know these people – this feels a bit obvious.' Whereas when you read a script that's a bit more believable, perhaps slightly intangible, you ask whether they could be darker, could they be lighter. I'm often presented with scripts written with a certain actor in mind, but when you have something to play with as a casting director it's nice to be able to say, 'Well, how about looking at it in this way?' When something gives you scope to play and use your own imagination creatively, that's what makes me go, 'I want it, can I do it?'

DAN HUBBARD: It always looks good if you've got a good casting director on board. Agents know they're dealing with people who will get the film made at the end of the day. I think the problem with this industry sometimes is that we're too oversaturated with too many people, and some of these people really don't know what they're doing. Along the way it can create nasty experiences and it makes the agents more guarded of their clients. So, once we come on board, the agents know that it's good material and that it will be a good, respected production team who will deliver on their promises.

APPROACHING ACTORS

Casting can make or break a film from financing to final product – you must know how to approach actors.

LEE ARONSOHN: Bad casting can ruin a good script, while great casting can save a mediocre one.

CATHERINE WILLIS: You only offer one person at a time. You can investigate other people's interest, but an offer means just that. It's so important to get it right. Actors are at the mercy of directors and scripts. Respect the fact that they are putting themselves in the hands of someone they don't know. Offer one person at a time, give as much information in terms of the people involved, giving them the opportunity to meet people. If it's a young director or young writer or inexperienced production team it's about meeting those people and going, 'You know what, they've got something exciting going on.' People with a profile are being offered a lot of roles so sometimes they don't have the time to pick up your script the minute it's sent. Have realistic expectations. Yes, your script is fabulous and may win awards, but they probably have 12 more of those that are waiting to be read. That's not to say you shouldn't be passionate and excited, but have a perspective on what else is going on in the industry.

DAN HUBBARD: When people don't play by the rules, they backfire mentally – like sending out three offers at the same time. You just can't do that. For actors at that level, if two say yes to the same project then you have a dilemma and it could be a career-changing thing; an agent could get fired. The thing about casting is that you have to be politically correct in your actions on behalf of the production so the agents take it seriously. I've seen directors offering parts to actors in the room and then completely denying it afterwards. That's something that should never really be done. Even in that magical moment in the room, directors and producers know not to offer the part on the spot. Particularly if there are other actors coming in for the same part that day. It's just disrespectful, really.

JOHN MADDEN: I'm a believer in auditioning, or reading the material if they're very well established. This is simply because it tells the actor whether it's going to feel right for them and whether the process is going to feel right. It may be that the ideas that you've got in your head become revised by hearing an actor with the material. Sometimes you can have an idea of exactly what you're looking for and then a person comes in and makes such an extraordinary connection with the part that you completely throw all your ideas and assumptions about the part out of the window. However, you can't throw your assumptions out of the window unless you have the assumptions in the first place. You have to educate yourself about what you want and what you're looking for.

BOB BALABAN: I don't like taking candy from strangers, so you should try to get someone who knows me to introduce you. Or become my relative. If that doesn't work, seize your opportunities as they arise. They may not come again. If you see me at the gym, politely ask me if I'd like to read your script. Do it quickly, and simply. I might say yes if it sounds interesting. But I'd make you sign a release saying you could never sue me, even if I ripped off the entire idea for your movie and made a trillion dollars from it. But here's the really depressing part. If you happened to be in the next hospital bed, and I was lying three feet away from you about to have my appendix removed, and you had my night nurse deliver me your script with my Percodan, and I read it and LOVED it, I probably couldn't get it made anyway.

PAUL ANDREW WILLIAMS: With well-known or high-profile actors, go through a different route than the agent, especially as a first-timer. You haven't done stuff before and your work might not be known to them. I'd find a way to avoid going via an agent. Agents of successful actors have so much stuff coming to them; they won't take your short film or low-budget feature seriously. However, if the actor isn't so well known, go via the agent.

ANGELINE BALL: Approach each actor as the one for that role. As an actor, the test is to convince myself first, then the director, and then the producer that I can be that part, become someone else, have different reactions, emotions, lead a different life. It can be wonderfully exciting to be presented with this challenge and dive into a character. There's nothing worse for an actor than to see a director become visibly disappointed as you walk into the casting room, because you're not how they imagined the character to be. It's a painful experience on all sides; you both know you're just wasting each other's time with pleasantries. Another thing is, I like to read in the script where the character is emotionally, or know a bit of her past, rather than just her physical looks.

DANNY HUSTON: It's best to approach via an agent but that raises its own difficulties. I started as a director; I had no intention of becoming an actor. Attaching talent is so difficult and there's no science to it. As legitimate a form of approach as possible is recommended, i.e. via an agent or casting director. Alternatively, find someone close to that person, i.e. a producer, who can pass it on. There's a small probability of it being put on the pile, but it's still a possibility. What I look for is a unique vision, originality and something I can connect with emotionally. Sometimes a script will come to you just when you want to do something different, or something classic, or there's something you want to revisit. You hope that the stars align, creating the time and space to do it.

KATE ASHFIELD: Scripts come through my agent, so they tell me if they thought it was good. I often won't know who has written something when I am reading it, but it's always the script – the writing and the story – that grabs me; if the part gives you something to do, even better. Poorly written characters, stereotypes, expositional plot can be off-putting. A character breakdown is great, but only if there's some evidence of it in the writing. An approach through an agent makes the work feel more legitimate. If you approach actors directly then it feels like you are asking for a favour, and they view the script differently. Hopefully the writing will always speak for itself. I have found it harder sometimes to get friends in the business to read my things.

MANJINDER VIRK: What attracts me to a role is the sense that they exist not only in that scene but before and after, a roundedness. It doesn't matter how big or small the part is – it's what is possible with what you have. I'm drawn to strong characters who aren't who you expect them to be. Stereotypes put me off – it's very lazy to create the same person over and over again. It's the people involved and the story that make me want to consider an independent project.

WORKING WITH ACTORS

The way a new or seasoned director works with an actor is incredibly important. You want it to go well, but there are times when it won't.

SAUL DIBB: It's about painstakingly casting the right person in the first place. After that, it's less about rehearsing the lines again and again and making them 'perfect' than it is about looking at the big picture. It's more about trying to understand that person, so that you can access whatever thing you need to get to in order for the actor to be able to inhabit the part in a way that line readings don't deliver.

JOHN MADDEN: Find the language that the actor uses, as it were, and approach each actor differently. My own personal belief (I'm talking about working on film here as opposed to the stage) is that you're unlocking a character. If you cast accurately or sympathetically, meaning you see in the actor's audition something in their make-up or their approach to the part, like they are inhabiting that role, then I would use the role itself as a means of communicating with the actor. In other words, mediate what I have to say through the part as it's written. To me, that's about opening doors for actors. You can't shut actors in. You're wasting your most precious resource if you do that. Avoid telling actors what to do in film, beyond obviously blocking them carefully and telling them what the shot will be. I try to open actors to the material, while at the same time giving them as clear an understanding as I possibly can about what the theme means, what the work in that scene has to do and the deposit that the acting needs to leave. If they have a comprehension about all of that, then they're free to discover within the context what you've set up for them. In film you want to catch the discovery. You don't want to see something executed according to a narrow set of definitions.

KIRSTEN SHERIDAN: I talk to actors about moments and scenes, and get under the skin of that. I am a little bit too nosey when it comes to people. When I see a performance I always want to know how they personally got to that moment. I want to know how they accessed that or how it was for them. There's a degree of psychology in that, but it's a bit of a magic, dark art really. Actors know how much I respect what they do. I know that it's so much harder than what anyone else does and I'll always be honest with them, even if they don't like that. That's how I prepare with actors. I get to know them as people and let them get to know me. When you're directing, almost everything is a let-down from the get-up; you don't have the budget or the schedule. The only thing that's not a let-down is the actors, finding a moment with them that you didn't even know existed, or a look. Usually, for me, it only occurs in small moments, but it's those that keep me going through a gruelling shoot.

ANGELINE BALL: I like to discuss the story, the journey, the pace and pathos of the piece. Inspiring film comparisons, likes, dislikes, etc. It's almost like checking that musicians in the orchestra are all playing the same song, not to mention being on the same page. As an actor you can have the most cerebral, uplifting meeting of minds at an audition, skip out of the meeting planning how you'll juggle childcare, etc., 'when' they call you with an offer. And then you never hear from the filmmaker again! Unfortunately, it's rarely down to the one person, the one you had a wonderful connection with, to have the final say on casting. I've also encountered the mindset where actors are just puppets to help bring a 'masterpiece' to life.

It's collaborative work, a give and take dance between each actor and the director, a process of bringing out the best in each other. Trust has to be there, from the get-go! Indifference is a pet hate.

DANNY HUSTON: Give me as much backstory as possible. If it's a real character I can generate that through research, but if it's original I want to know the genesis. If the characterisation is blank on the page, like a Pinter play, that can be great to create – as you don't know who they are. In some cases the key is the dialogue and you take every clue you can. Were I to ask you a question about the character and you floundered or didn't know the answer, hadn't formed an idea, etc., it would ring alarm bells. It would mean you either weren't connected to the material or couldn't substantiate what you wanted to make. We actors can be cautious. Directors can get too involved with mood drawings or visual ideas. Fascinating that you are going to have a handheld style but that doesn't tell me how I should approach the character. Actors are looking for keys into the characters.

ROB BROWN: You need to almost pretend you didn't write the script and interrogate the script with the actors. Ask them and yourself, is what I've got on the page the best we can do? Do the characters' motivations feel believable? Sometimes I've made changes just before shooting a scene, and I'm glad that I made those changes, even though it was very stressful. It's important to create an atmosphere on set where the actors feel comfortable so they can be creative and do their best work.

PAUL ANDREW WILLIAMS: Get good actors and tell them what to do! If you have a good actor your job is half done. You've got to be as collaborative as possible with everyone on the set, including crew. They want to be okay with failing, with getting it wrong. It shouldn't matter if they make mistakes as long as you are open. I am open to suggestions about how to get to grips with the characters and suggestive comment. I may not always agree but I am approachable in how I work. I don't stand for any diva shit – everyone is on the same level.

271

GETTING AN AGENT

Many of us want an agent because we feel having one will validate us as professionals. Agents are seen as gatekeepers of new talent and taste. Many companies rely on agents to filter the work of lesser-known writers. This is a fact and probably why so many of us see representation as the holy grail of the industry.

No agent is going to turn away great writing – the reality is a great script will always find an agent. However, when you send out your work, be prepared to wait. As a new writer you have to be prepared to accept that your script, compared to those of an agent's fee-earning clients, will not be a priority. They need time to read your script and prepare notes, so expect to wait six to eight weeks.

MATTHEW BATES: There are only so many ways you can find an agent or they can find you, BUT there's also a time not to go looking. A common mistake is approaching agents too early – either without a compelling body of work, or with a script that needs work. Have at least one piece that illustrates a compelling, original voice, and hopefully more than one piece, just to show that the first isn't a one-off and that, in claiming to be a storyteller, you do, in fact, have lots of stories to tell. Take what people say at face value. 'We don't take on many new clients, so there isn't room for you' means they don't take on many new clients, so there isn't room for you. 'Your script isn't strong enough yet' means your script isn't strong enough yet. Some people believe that we can create a brilliant career for writers and directors, but people create their own brilliant careers. Make relationships by yourself. It's hard, but possible. Thousands have managed it. And then talk to the people you've made relationships with about representation – do they think it's time and, if so, would they be able to recommend you to anyone?

....

ROCLIFFE NOTES on...
HOW TO APPROACH AGENTS

- Many agents take on new clients through recommendations or referrals. This is the most likely way of getting an agent. Someone who they trust and respect may recommend you.

- Should you work in some aspect of the industry and regularly deal with agents, ask the agent's assistant you are dealing with to give you advice, look at your work.

- When you have someone interested in optioning your script, approach an agent and ask them will they represent you on the deal. It's unlikely they won't help you when they stand to make money out of it, even if it's only on this one deal. This is a foot in.

- Look for a newer agent who is hungry and building a client list. Call around, find out who is looking for new clients. It may take 50 calls but one may pay off, be it the first or the last.

- Enter competitions or go on a course such as those run by the NFTS, in order to get noticed.

- When looking for an agent be clear what you want. Someone who loves your work, believes in your voice, who wants to go the distance.

- A good covering letter will show your personality and make you seem interesting. With an impersonal, mass, blind mail-out, be prepared to face rejection even when you've contacted 50–100 agents.

- I've known plenty of talented writers who've written strong scripts but wait years to be picked up by an agent. It wasn't until they created opportunities for themselves by winning a competition, making something, or making connections that they got a recommendation or referral.

....

AGENTS ON WHAT AGENTS DO

When people *do* get an agent, sometimes they've waited quite a while, and have managed for so long without one, that they don't use their agent effectively. When a deal comes along that they found themselves, they don't want to share the proceeds and so exclude the agent from negotiations. I've seen writers sign away rights, fair payment and credits. It's perfectly acceptable to say, 'I'll let my agent negotiate the money side of things.' They know the art of the deal, can negotiate, advise and give feedback.

MATTHEW DENCH: To a certain extent, we're one part development exec, one part lawyer, one part therapist, a dash of used car salesman. It's one of the things that makes the job fun. There are such myriad skills involved and an awful lot of things to juggle. It's an interesting choice. It's a tough world, it always has been, and with various changes in the industry it gets tougher, particularly for newer writers. Being an agent isn't just about getting the best deal. One of the main differences between an agent in the UK and an agent in the US is that an agent in the US is going to be very dedicated to the deal and you'll have a separate manager to guide your career. Here, we basically do both. It's about getting you the best deal, but it's also about guiding your career. That's what we're here for. You try to be across as many producers and production companies as possible, finding out who's making what and working out who you've got that can fit those slots.

CHRISTINA PICKWORTH: A literary agent represents writers and their written work, with the aim of selling such works or the rights in those works, for development or production. They then also negotiate these deals and are paid on a fixed percentage commission basis.

JEAN KITSON: An agent's work is fourfold: to nurture and develop your work; to represent your work to the industry in order to sell your original scripts or get you work on an existing commission; to negotiate deal terms and contracts, and to manage those contracts, and invoice for payments due and chase late invoices; and, finally, to be a mediator if and when your relationship with a producer falters. An agent is paid a percentage of your actual income, so they only make money if you make money.

JONATHAN KINNERSLEY: Ideally, you would be tailoring a career to an individual writer. I don't think there's a particular template. It would entirely depend on what genre the writer was writing in, what kind of writer they were and the personal ambitions of the writer themselves. Whether they want to move across from film to TV to theatre or not makes a huge difference in your long-term plan for them. Work comes in to us in a number of ways. Producers do, in meetings, say, 'We're looking for a particular type of writer, or a particular voice.' Mostly, they're not actually expecting us to bombard them with lots of new writers when they say that sort of thing. When we first look at spec scripts, we're looking for a particularly strong voice. The first couple of stages of representation is offering support to those voices. It used to be easier, as the BBC used to offer much more support at an early level.

KATIE WILLIAMS: Beyond the deal, or even the project, it's also a case of protecting a writer's intellectual property and keeping track of the myriad ways in which work is used now. I make sure that is part of it, as well as what you're getting paid or produced today. It's quite a broad range of things, beyond that initial deal that's on the table. It works two ways really. We have lots of meetings with producers, and they'll call us up or email us about their latest projects. They might tell us that they have a new series, or a book that needs adapting, or they might want to do a project about a real-life person or event. When they are offering these jobs, they do tend to be looking for a writer with experience and credits to their name. Alongside that, we have long-running series, which are more open to new writers. We also have projects that are created by our clients, which you then pitch to producers, trying to get them work that way.

TALENT ON AGENTS

I have two agents, one for production work and the other for my writing work. Generally, my literary agent doesn't find me work, but she does negotiate my deals. It's a waiting game. You must believe in yourself and in your ideas.

MOIRA BUFFINI: I have been with my agent since he started at his agency as a college leaver and since my first play, nearly 20 years ago. It was the first thing I'd written and he took me on. He's become a friend and a tremendous support and I don't know what I'd do without him. I have no skill in negotiating deals. I'd be hopeless. I have to say he has been responsible for my earning a living so I am very grateful to him. When you begin your career you need them so much more; they send your work out to everyone and you both hope for the best. Nowadays he is my gatekeeper – I get offered jobs every week that I cannot possibly write. He filters the jobs that he knows will speak to me.

BOB BALABAN: I will read anything recommended to me by an agent. Anything that's financed.

CLAIRE WILSON: I am with my third agent now. My first was excellent but left the business. My second didn't get me any work. My current, and hopefully last, is brilliant. We were introduced by a producer and we get on personally as well as professionally.

JAMES DORMER: I rely a lot on my agent to advise me on what to do and what not to do. I suspect that there's some stuff that comes through that never reaches me, as he doesn't think it would be wise for me to do it. It's difficult for me, as I see things I'd like to do, but then have to step back, calm myself down and question whether I've got too much on.

ROWAN ATHALE: Nowhere does it say you can't start without one, but I wouldn't want to navigate the industry without mine. There's an agent stereotype fuelled by Hollywood movies; a suited, slick, cut-throat bastard who cares for nothing but money... Don't believe what you see in the movies. They are exceptionally creative people. They don't write the scripts, they don't direct the films, nor do they star in them, but they do have a honed creative understanding of these aspects of filmmaking that exceeds that of most others in the industry. The agent's job is to work hard to make their clients successful; to keep their clients protected; to fight your corner, so you don't have to. Of course, the more successful the client, the more successful the agent, the greater their reputation, etc. But that doesn't detract from their passion and hard work any more than being paid as a writer and receiving acclaim detracts from yours.

JOSH APPIGNANESI: It's important and becomes more so with the passing of time, like any other relationship you depend on. The sounding-board aspect is key. The agent helps you get over a lot of delusions and misrecognitions.

KEVIN CECIL: You can definitely write a script without an agent, but sooner or later in your career you will need one. We have been very lucky with our agents. They've done a lot for us. Agents can find you work and some give advice on drafts of scripts. Then they negotiate deals and chase money when media companies have forgotten to pay you six months after you gave in the script. As you get established, some work will come to you directly rather than through your agent. It's important that you still involve your agent in those deals. You have to go all in.

JON CROKER: I am very lucky to have three great agents. They give me practical, creative and tactical advice, and help remind me that, as well as a passion, this is also a job and a business that needs to be done right.

JACK THORNE: My agent is hugely important to my career. But initially too much emphasis is put on finding one. Finding a good reader who'll make you better is as important.

MALCOLM CAMPBELL: When I met Ben at Curtis Brown I felt that my career was lagging. I wasn't getting a great deal of work and it didn't feel like I was progressing. It was time for a change. The first thing Ben said was that I needed to stop doing things I didn't want to do and do something I was passionate about, kind of starting again. I took four or five months off pursuing any paid work and wrote a script that I'd always wanted to write. That was a massive calling card mid career, and that script, although never produced, got me all the work I've done since.

DANNY BROCKLEHURST: When I was trying to break in, I didn't know how to get an agent. A friend who was also a new writer had one and she suggested I write to him and send him a spec script. He must have liked what he read because he took me on. I've been with the same agent the whole way through. I do a lot of moaning to him; he's like a therapist and talks me down as he has a very calm approach. He's not like Ari Gold. We talk things through a lot.

JIM UHLS: It's important for your agent to 'get you' – to understand who you are as a writer.

LEVI DAVID ADDAI: My agent is very important to me; he was one of the first people in the industry to believe in me. We work well together. He listens to my rants, my ambitions, shares my highs and lows, and is there supporting me to be the best at what I do. I came fresh with very little knowledge bar what I knew as a viewer. We're really close; I believe we know how to conduct business together. He knows what I will be into and he's brilliant, and he will always check with me anyway.

CHRIS SPARLING: My relationship with all my reps is very important. My manager and I speak just about every day, at least once. As for my agents, I have two who represent me for feature projects, one of whom I am in touch with more often than the other – which works out fine. I have been with my reps for about five years now, so our relationship is a nice mixture of business and friendship. As for how my agent found me, it came as a direct result of them reading my spec script *Buried*. They really responded to the material and, while they didn't think it would ever actually be made into a movie (surprise!), they felt it would be a great writing sample for me.

ANNE HOGDEN: A good agent will always be sniffing around for the kind of talent that they represent. But you have to remember that it's a two-way street. Your agent will take between 10 per cent and 20 per cent of your income from writing for the rest of your life, and 70 years after your death! Even if you change agents, you will still be obliged for any work that was commissioned while they represented you. A good agent will get you a better rate than you would without them.

AGENTS AND PRODUCERS

Whenever a producer is looking for talent, they usually start with agents, either to find material, directors and crew or to recommend someone they have come across.

KATIE GOODSON-THOMAS: You can't underestimate a good relationship with a good agent. A good agent should be your script editor. That should be part of their job and part of your relationship. They should be helping you get your first draft up to the standard where it would be taken into consideration. One of the things that's very hard is getting people to look at things twice. When you do give it in, it can't just be a pipe dream. It has to feel quite concrete, quite real. You have to have shown it to people that have said it's ready. Once that bad coverage is on file and it says 'Pass – badly written, bad story', it's going to be very hard, no matter how much work you do, to convince people otherwise and to get people to look at it again.

MATTHEW DENCH: We've been here dealing with these producers for a good few years and, generally speaking, they'll respect your opinion. That's what it's about; it's about convincing XYZ producer that what you have is worth them looking at. To a certain extent, any time we're sending out a script, we're putting your reputation on the line. It's got to be something you believe in. If you keep on sending out stuff that isn't good enough, pretty soon people aren't going to be willing to look at your client's work.

LIAM FOLEY: We don't take unsolicited material, so we usually have the benefit of the literary agent being the ideas-filter, so to speak. We rely on introductions from agents, who might have spotted someone before we do and have taken on an interesting new writer or director.

SIMON HEATH: We generally only read scripts submitted through recognised agents. But we're constantly looking at new writing in theatre, cinema, TV and novels, etc.

LAWRENCE COCHRAN: I have a development co-ordinator who had someone call in with their mum pretending to be their agent. That's the saddest example that we've ever had. We asked what other clients she had and she didn't have any. It can be a little bit embarrassing and awkward. If you're genuinely talented then people are willing to read your scripts and submissions. If you genuinely believe talent will out, then there's no conspiracy or need to be tricky to get anywhere, you just have to be good.

DAVID PARFITT: Good agents don't put stuff through that isn't worth a read. For a writer, producing a spec script is absolutely as valid as any other route, and we read spec scripts that come through agents.

KATIE GOODSON-THOMAS: It's about having a good relationship with agents, and knowing that you trust their tastes. When they say 'Please will you look at this short or read this screenplay?' you trust them and know it won't be a waste of your time. I have never in my career to date taken on a project (which I didn't generate) that didn't have either an agent or producer attached to it.

POLLY STOKES: We read work from new writers that their agents send us. We read a lot of books pre-publication, which is a great way to discover both material that we could adapt and new voices writing in prose, people who might just as easily be able to write screenplays. We only accept material sent to us through producers or agents.

JONATHAN KINNERSLEY: To get your untested clients read, producers need to trust you. You can only be so persuasive over an email and fundamentally what it comes down to is you saying 'this person's really good and worth reading'.

CAMILLE GATIN: I would usually meet with a writer I have discovered through an introduction by an agent. We'd discuss their ideas and, if one hits a chord with me, I will find some development finance to enable them to take their idea to the next level.

GETTING NOTICED BY AN AGENT

Agents are looking for talent, professionalism and commitment to the work via their network, at festivals, screenings, theatre, radio and watching showreels.

MATTHEW BATES: The large majority of my new clients come as recommendations to me from other people in the film and TV business – producers, distributors, and existing clients.

JEAN KITSON: I get approached by people, I get recommended to people by producers, and I keep up with new playwriting and short films, as well as trying to attend film school screenings.

ANNE HOGBEN: Often agents will find a writer. Big agencies go to places like the Edinburgh Fringe Festival and have talent scouts. For example, the student writer of the West End play *Chimerica*, Lucy Kirkwood, was discovered early on at Edinburgh. It's rare but it does happen. I'm always trying to steer writers to try out writing radio dramas. New writers could also try to work in theatre, make short films, all kinds of things. There's no set path. Nobody starts from nowhere and gets commissioned to write *Sherlock* or something. You make a path for yourself, explore different genres and find what you can do when you stretch yourself.

NORMAN NORTH: Nowadays, it's a personal reference from producers or other agents. But, when I was younger, I went to a lot of theatre (mainly fringe) and let it be known amongst my peer group of producers and editors that I was on the lookout. It's going to take up a disproportionately large amount of my time, so I need to be sufficiently impressed by their ability and/or potential. I also need to see that their interests and strengths augment rather than clash with those of my existing clients.

CHRISTINA PICKWORTH: I accept submissions from time to time. I am also recommended people by script editors, development execs and producers.

ALEXANDRA ARLANGO: The most important thing for a writer is getting an agent. That way their work will get to more producers and development people. Get noticed – enter competitions, put on plays, find a director to make your short, go to festivals, and have coffees with people. There are quite a number of schemes (e.g. Creative England), competitions (e.g. BAFTA Rocliffe, Wellcome Trust) and courses (e.g. NFTS Screenwriting) that we cover to see who is fresh out there. While you're doing all of these things, keep writing. Practice really does make perfect!

DAVID PARFITT: We don't get a lot of people approaching us but when we do and we like their work we may help recommend an agent or someone to help them.

JEAN KITSON: Recommendations from established writers or producers are an excellent way to get noticed, as are any previous commissions or prizes. Screenwriting isn't being shut away in a room, and anything that you can do to show that you have been engaged in actually making drama – whether a short film, a play in a pub theatre, a published short story – is very helpful.

CHRISTINA PICKWORTH: *Contacts* is a directory updated and released on a yearly basis. Look at the agency websites for the types of clients they represent. Some focus on established or new talent, or theatre, film or TV writers, so approach the right kind of agent for you, your work, and your career stage. Take note of submissions policies and only send what is requested when the agent is accepting submissions. Agents will constantly be reading the work of existing clients so time for anything else is extremely limited. Never email a lot of agents at once with a generic email – target who you are approaching carefully. Do network. If you can meet an agent at an event they may be more likely to read your work, as long as you haven't stalked them! Don't expect them to come back to you quickly, and certainly don't pester them for their thoughts. Be patient and remember that their existing clients are (and should be!) their priority.

IVANA MACKINNON: The industry wants to see people who are active – agents want to take on clients who are already self-generating. So it's not enough to make something and then wait for the world to fall into your lap. Talk to everyone. Share the things that make you specific even if they are tangential to film – we all want to find people with a unique voice.

SIMON HEATH: Getting the right agent is incredibly important. If a new writer has a good idea but no track record, it may be necessary to write the script on spec. It will open more doors.

KATIE WILLIAMS: I've taken on people at the absolute beginning of their career, but generally it's a slower process. There's only so much I can do. You need the material there first and foremost. Sometimes you find that writers really haven't found what they want to focus on, or they haven't quite found their voice. If I have a writer who sends me a range of different scripts from different genres and settings, that either means they're very versatile or they haven't quite found their voice or invested in something they feel passionate about. When you have a specific voice, it's easier to follow it across from a play to a TV show, for example. For me, there isn't one particular way I find new clients. It's a whole combination really. If I enjoy a play and somebody mentions that the writer is unrepresented, I might then contact them. People are recommended, through existing clients or a producer. Obviously, something that comes with a personal recommendation is helpful because it's somebody whose taste you trust. Then you're always going to want to take a look at the writer they're talking about. People write in to us 'cold'. If you've got a great script and it sparks off something in my mind where I think, 'They'd be brilliant, I could do this, this, and this with them,' then I'm going to be interested to read more or meet them, but it doesn't happen very often.

WHAT IS THE WORKING RELATIONSHIP BETWEEN AGENT AND CLIENT?

My relationship with my agent is very important to me. It's a professional relationship. I have absolute faith in her notes and in her ability to do a great deal. When working on my biography about growing up in Libya, I was embarking on something deeply personal that needed an objective ear from someone who understood that, however painful the truth, I needed direct answers. Her feedback was clear and constructive. She also listened when I struggled with the emotional, aching moments of self-exploration. In the end, the timing wasn't right for me, or my family, to explore that story, but the experience taught me that, when baring your creative soul, a good agent is important.

JEAN KITSON: When it works, client and agent are working together towards the same goal. An agent cannot get you a job – your script does that alongside how you pitch yourself and/or your project in meetings. An agent gets you those meetings, and lays the groundwork. Agents often beaver away in the background. It can sometimes feel like they're not doing any work for you, but it isn't helpful to be in constant contact with your agent as that takes them away from doing their job. I probably talk to my clients on average once a month although we communicate by email more often. It's useful to have a mutual understanding of what sort of feedback and reporting you expect.

MATTHEW BATES: Things take time. Writers struggle for money. I won't be able to find them work, just find them people who will find them work. They need to work hard. If things go well then I will be a solid, trustworthy companion on a VERY long journey.

NORMAN NORTH: Relationships differ (slightly) from client to client depending on their character, level of experience, confidence/neediness, etc. But, generally, my view is that the agent, as well as looking after the business aspect, should be the primary but highly partial sounding board for their clients.

JEAN KITSON: You also need to keep your agent in the loop with what you are doing and projects you are talking to people about. When it comes to agreements, it's worth again working out with your agent how involved you want to be – do you want to see every step or just hear the headlines?

CHRISTINA PICKWORTH: Your relationship with your agent will depend on the kind of writer you are, and the agent you've picked. Some agents are heavily involved in the development of your work, and others a lot less. The level of contact varies with the amount of work you generate and the number of projects you have on the go at any one time. Depending on your agent and the size of their agency you may also find that you deal more with their assistant than the agent themselves – never underestimate how much assistants know and can help you. Always be polite and always say thank you. Remember, you need to work hard for your agent so that they can work hard for you. Certainly don't think that, because you have an agent, you can sit back and the work will flood in – if anything, you need to work even harder!

JEAN KITSON: Many agents and clients become very good friends but it's also a professional relationship – you need to be able to disagree and to challenge each other. Some agents like to work very collaboratively with writers, others like them to go and get on with it. That's the sort of thing to work out when you meet a prospective agent. In writing, clients don't tend to chop and change agents often so it's worth taking your time early on to get a good creative fit.

WHAT TO LOOK FOR IN AN AGENT

When you meet with an agent, ask them what are they are going to do for you. Go in with your list of questions. They will sell you, and you are entitled to ask them how are they going to do that, and how the relationship will work from both sides.

JONATHAN KINNERSLEY: You might be flattered to meet an agent and flattered by their interest in you, but if you get a dodgy feeling about them, suspect that they don't know what they're talking about, or you don't feel that their personal taste matches your style, you might do well to keep looking. Fundamentally, an agent's list is going to reflect their personality and, through that list, the producers will get to know their personality and taste. It's a personal relationship. It's not just a personal relationship between, say, me and writer; it's then a personal relationship between the writer and the audience member, or whatever medium the voice is going to go through to entertain. That's where it starts. Everyone gets something different and wants something different from their agent. It's totally fine to ask 'What would you do for me?' 'Why would I need you?' '*Do* I need you?'

JEAN KITSON: Talking to other writers about whom they would recommend is the best bet! Have a look at the *Writers & Artists Yearbook*, Spotlight's *Contacts* or *The Knowledge* for listings of literary and script agencies, and look at their websites. Have an idea of writers whose work you admire and research who their agents are. Make the approach according to their submission guidelines. Look for someone whose opinion you trust and who understands what you would like to achieve with your career in the long term. It's very important to meet agents, as in an ideal world this will be a long relationship. You might not always agree with each other, so it needs to be someone whose taste and experience you can rely on. Someone well connected – your agent is your gateway to the film and TV industry.

CHRISTINA PICKWORTH: All agent-client relationships differ. Do you want someone who is going to be involved in the development of your projects, or just someone to negotiate your contracts? How much contact do you want to have with your agent? If you are generating a lot of scripts and looking for a lot of input from your agent then have a look at the size of an agent's list. If they represent a lot of clients their time is going to be split across more people.

MATTHEW DENCH: I've read scripts which are great, then I've met the writer and there hasn't been that spark there. So much of this business is about personality and relationships. The writer-agent relationship is a very particular one; you're going to be working together for a few years. If you can't stand to be in the same room together, it's probably not going to work. You want to know that people are serious about this. We're not interested in someone who's got one story to tell, we're interested in someone who's got a lot of stories to tell and is passionate about this. Passion is absolutely key.

....

ROCLIFFE NOTES on...

MEETING WITH A PROSPECTIVE AGENT

- Do your homework, look at their client list. Do you know any of their clients?

- What are their industry contacts, i.e. which of their writers have they placed and where? You want to know their success stories.

- How long have they been an agent? Who did they work under?

- What are the three key things they look for in a new client?

- What kind of work are they expecting from you?

- How do they not like to work?

- What will the workflow be like between you and what is their turnaround time, i.e. if you send them your work, when can you expect feedback?

- Do they give notes in written form or meetings?

- Be clear about your time commitments, i.e. do you have a day job/children, etc. What is your output?

- Ask them whether they keep an eye out for competitions, or are you expected to look for opportunities? Which ones do they rate?

- What kind of path or plan of action do they have for you?

••

WHAT IS AN AGENT LOOKING FOR?

Agents are not machines. They are looking for people with potential that they can sell so their investment will pay off.

MATTHEW BATES: I'm looking for something I remember, that surprises me and illustrates a distinctive new voice. 'Compelling' is one of my watchwords. Was that script compelling? Do they have talent? Do they have commitment? Will I enjoy working with them for a long, long time? And, by extension, will people in the industry enjoy working with them?

NORMAN NORTH: Some writers have such a strong affinity with a particular genre that they should probably not be encouraged to stray from it. For others, though, evidence of versatility can be a strong bonus.

JONATHAN KINNERSLEY: Like any job, send your CV around and wonder if anyone reads it. People do get signed from sending 'cold' scripts, just not very often. Debbie Tucker Green was picked from an assistant reading her script and signing her up. It happens. If I'm reading a script that's come 'cold', the first thing I'm looking for is a voice, whether I can hear the characters in my head. You know that within the first two or so pages. If it doesn't do that, there's very little chance that it's going to grab anyone else. That's true across the board, in theatre, film and TV. Also, if someone has something in their history that sets them apart, that's always going to get a tick from me. It can be anything, some weirdness they've picked up to become an interesting person. Being an interesting person is what it's going to be about.

MATTHEW DENCH: I look for a voice. Something about a script which makes it exciting, different. There are lots of people who are perfectly good writers, but I want something special. Once you get beyond the page, if I find I like someone's writing and want to meet with them, then it comes down to personal relationships.

JEAN KITSON: Most importantly, have a killer script to show. Agents get a lot of submissions every week and will not be able to read everything they are asked to, so you need to give a compelling reason in your covering letter about why they should read yours.

WHERE TO GO WHEN YOU HAVEN'T GOT AN AGENT, BUT YOU *DO* HAVE A DEAL

There are several options open to you if you haven't got an agent and it depends on your circumstances. I would always say to writers that, if a deal is on the table, they should seek advice no matter what, and there are various ways to do this.

- Contact an agent, explain you have a deal, and ask if they would represent you on this one (they will take 10–20 per cent of your fee).

- Get a lawyer, which is very effective but costly.

- Sign up for Candidate Membership of the Writers' Guild of Great Britain – about which more below from Deputy General Secretary, Anne Hogben.

Anne Hogben explained more what the Writers' Guild is and the role it plays in the industry:

The Writers' Guild of Great Britain is an association that allows writers to connect with each other or with industry people. The

Guild represents theatre writers as well as film and TV writers. There's some overlap but, generally, most writers tend to specialise in one field. There's a great deal more artistic freedom in writing for theatre and radio, as opposed to film. We also provide legal advice where necessary, so when a member has a problem we assess the situation and then offer guidance.

We have a weekly bulletin, which we started about 14 years ago. I am proud to say that this e-bulletin has gone out almost every single Friday afternoon for all those years. There's a list of opportunities and jobs on there. All of our agreements are available free from the website. Writers can get a lot of information there if they do their homework. New writers need to know about the business side of writing as well as the writing side, and most writers tend to accumulate this business knowledge as they go along. We do prefer people to join; we need the support of writers to keep going.

Newer writers should absolutely join. The Guild has two categories of memberships, Full and Candidate. The Candidate Membership is for those who haven't yet been paid for their work or had it produced or published. Anybody who wants to be a writer can join for £100 a year. They get a good service. As soon as they get their first credit, they can upgrade to a Full Membership. Agents aren't usually interested in taking on writers until they have a track record. New writers often complain about not being able to get an agent, but there are other ways of building a career and the Guild helps with that and gives advice.

We also host events in London and have small, thriving branches in Birmingham, Glasgow, Edinburgh and Cardiff – basically wherever there's a group of writers who want to get together to make something happen.

HOW *NOT* TO APPROACH AN AGENT

Charlotte Knight from Knight Hall Agency has provided these tips on how not to court an agent:

While we're always on the lookout for new talent, please, please remember that Knight Hall Agency isn't a public service. If you really want to put us off the idea of representing you, here are a few tips (some may raise a smile but we've had them all – yes, even the last one – and some are commonplace):

- After checking with the post office that your recorded-delivery package has arrived, phone us to ask if it has arrived. Call again a week later 'not chasing, only wondering' if we've read the script and consider you a genius but have just forgotten to mention it.

- Phone us repeatedly before you've written anything.

- Turn up at our office, barge past the receptionist and inform him/her that you know we say we don't arrange meetings before seeing a prospective client's work, but as you're here… (NB: No one likes anyone who's rude to the receptionist, and anyone who is gets caught out here – we don't have one).

- Phone, cupping the mouthpiece, to say you've got a brilliant idea but for legal reasons can't tell us what it is. Or who you are.

- Send us a wooden guitar-case packed with scripts written in a vast array of exciting fonts and illustrated throughout. And forget to enclose return postage.

- Enclose a bunch of kind rejection letters from producers and/or other agents.

- Write 'Dear Charlotte Night, My name is [insert] and I am a writer', enclosing photos of yourself in fancy dress.

- Having already received two polite letters from us explaining that we don't feel we'd be the right agents for you, submit your third 'spec' adaptation of a copyright novel to which you have not obtained the relevant rights/sequel to someone else's hit movie/ episode of an existing TV series.

- Send a 'zany' letter that runs to several pages, or a one-liner that tells us nothing about the work you'd like us to read.

- Inform us that a spirit guide dictated your masterpiece to you, and you can prove it by your remote-control healing powers.

FUNDING, TALENT PLATFORMS
AND SHOWCASES

Every talent showcase or funding initiative for emerging filmmakers I have been part of has led to great connections and information. A key element in my career still is learning new things. Rocliffe, in partnership with BAFTA, showcases screenwriting talent. To be a part of the early stages of someone's career is fantastic. I went on a Raindance course on low-to-no budget filmmaking that made entering this industry seem possible. The advent of short-film schemes via the BFI (then the UK Film Council) made it possible for me to obtain financial support for two short films that benefited my career hugely. Attending the BFI's 'Think-Shoot-Distribute' gave me great opportunities. These are just a few of the opportunities you can avail yourself of. In the List Section are a few suggestions to get you started. The following pages have a few detailed breakdowns of BAFTA initiatives, the Brit List and *Screen International* Stars of Tomorrow, amongst others. Look up SkillSet's website (www.skillset.co.uk) for more, as well as Screen Training Ireland. Sign up to all mailing lists.

REBECCA DALY: I was lucky, as the film was selected for a residency in association with Cannes, as a development project, at treatment stage. I wrote the first draft in Paris as part of this. It had that stamp, so when I came back to Ireland and we were talking to producers about it, there was already a level of interest in it. We found a producer quite easily and at that stage it was probably easier than it is now to get a relatively small film with no stars in it off the ground. Once it was written, it happened within a year and a half.

SHANE ALLEN: Be realistic: there are specific opportunities and schemes and targets and goals, everything from Rocliffe to Comedy Feeds to other initiatives – and it's your job to seek those out. A lot of the best people who are the superstars of today started out in bite-size shorter-form ways. Most comics began with a 3–5 minute set. Last night I saw Miranda [Hart] in the Brighton Centre and I remember seeing her 15 years ago in a small club in Shepherd's Bush doing a short set in front of 20 people – there's a journey there.

AMANDA BERRY: For an emerging talent to win a BAFTA is beyond doubt a wonderful game-changer in a career, as it's an internationally recognised seal of approval, endorsed by industry professionals. It's the first major milestone, you watch and hope that they build on that success. It's great to see careers grow and develop. The awards are what many young filmmakers aspire to, but BAFTA also offers support in the forming and attaining of goals through masterclasses, scholarships and showcases, both in the UK and overseas. Initiatives help assist and inspire people from all backgrounds to realise their career objectives.

SARAH GAVRON: The NFTS showcased our graduation films and on the back of that screening I got my agent and first job. When making shorts I entered every initiative and scheme out there. Just the process of submitting a project focused my mind. I learned how to deal with rejection and when I did get accepted I always got something out of it.

SERENA BOWMAN: There are not many ways that a very new writer can get their work out there. I recently went to the NFTS showcase and then later met a writer who was showcased at that event and who I thought had a really distinctive voice. Without that, I probably wouldn't have heard of her for another couple of years.

STEPHEN FINGLETON: Channel 4's Coming Up is very significant. Northern Ireland's New Talent Focus scheme is also great for giving new filmmakers from Ulster a chance to make a film. Competitions are useful deadlines for creating work – even if it doesn't make the grade with a particular competition, you've still created something, and in creating something have grown in yourself.

PAUL ANDREW WILLIAMS: I had a kind angel, who helped us fund the shorts, fund London to Brighton and set up our company. He was integral in getting it started. Unfortunately he has passed away now. The only scheme I got on was the Fox Searchlight scheme, which gave me $2,500, and the name got me a couple of phone calls.

GLENN MONTGOMERY: Talent showcases haven't played a role, not directly, but funding has in a big way. It was about establishing relationships with the people on the film boards, and nurturing those. To the point where I would approach them and tell them I had two or three ideas and ask what they thought of them, and they would respond on those. That played a bigger role with me, taking on their advice, etc.

JOSH APPIGNANESI: It's useful, yes, to gain some visibility, no matter how.

TINA GHARAVI: There have been a few programmes that I have been on. Some have been great because of the access they give you to successful people, but the best thing really is the other people you meet on the programme – your peers – and the endorsement you get personally.

SUSAN JACOBSON: I have twice had completion funding for two shorts from the BFI. I am a Guiding Lights alumnus and had the privilege of being mentored by Gillies MacKinnon. I never stop applying for/ attending initiatives and showcases. They are essential.

BERTRAND FAIVRE: It's very hard to convince the first person. The more recognition you get, the easier it is to get someone to embark on a journey with you. The world is full of wannabe filmmakers with white gloves or shirts on them. You need to be shinier than anyone else around. You need to get distinctions and badges at competitions and festival recognition, as they will help you to get more attention. Plenty of people have good ideas that don't necessarily get made, so you must focus on how to get attention.

WENDY MITCHELL: Talent Spotlights are great for helping people cut through the noise and get noticed. The industry is always looking for new talent and new voices. We don't want to watch the same films 20 times; we want to see something different.

CONOR BARRY: The experience of being part of Cannes' Producers on the Move was that I was able to work with people who had a lot more experience than I had. It's a constantly expanding natural network and a constantly expanding knowledge. That's what those things are, basically. Sometimes there are opportunities that you might have experienced previously, but a lot of them are just from encountering like-minded people. You get to know them as a human, rather than a name at some festival. As a result of that, you're able to work on their projects.

MIRANDA BOWEN: Nearly all my shorts were made through initiatives to help new talent. C4's Cinema Extreme was probably the most helpful as it was really high profile. It's a pity it doesn't exist any more.

ROB BROWN: Lab test your script with actors. I have done this through the ICA Lab (which no longer exists, sadly) and was lucky enough to have an extract of my script performed at the BAFTA Rocliffe New Writing Forum 2011 at the Edinburgh Film Festival. This is incredibly valuable as it helps you see where your script works and where it doesn't. You get an audience perspective before the film is made.

SIMON HEATH: The Coming Up strand on C4 is excellent. There's always a buzz around the NFTS graduation films. Most companies now keep an eye out for the winners of the various scriptwriting competitions.

SALLY EL HOSAINI: The Sundance Labs were a nurturing experience for me. They were about learning and gaining confidence in myself as an artist. As you do work in isolation for so long, certainly early on in your career, you feel like what you're doing may not be ready or good enough to unleash on the world. For me, the biggest thing I got from the Sundance Labs was confidence in my script, my ideas and in what I was doing as an artist.

RICHARD COOKSON: We do pay attention to other competitions and spotlights – the Red Planet Prize, Channel 4's Coming Up, the BBC Writers' Academy, BAFTA Rocliffe, etc.

DAVID PARFITT: There are great showcases. A lot of people get to see new people through those routes. Finding the time to attend is often difficult but I do go if pushed. We all try to keep an eye on who is new. We keep a running list going of the new people who are coming through.

ANDREA CORNWELL: Schemes are very important, especially for writers. It goes back to the cover note and the approach: it can single you out from the very many other people who want to do this. You start building a bit of a career for yourself if you've taken part in a competitive workshop or if you've been selected for presentation at a work-in-progress event. No one cares if you've paid to attend things, but if you've been filtered out as a talent to watch then that's really important. Things like the Black List and the Brit List, people pay quite a lot of attention to, even if they are aware that they are not entirely impartially drawn up. There are fewer showcases around now, so it does make you special if you are singled out. If you're BAFTA nominated for a short film or some of these other programmes, then it means a hell of a lot. Generally, if you put on a screening of a short film you will tend to get a good turnout from the industry. Writers shouldn't go into this thinking that nobody wants to hear what they've got to say or that it's no use approaching producers. People are always looking for the next talent but you need to try to get their attention in the right way.

CLAIRE WILSON: Any way is a good way in. But I would always check out schemes that ask for money to be sure. You can usually find out if they're a con with a quick search. I have entered a fair few in my time with varying success. What you do get is a new piece of work to enter each time. And that can never be a bad thing.

WHAT BAFTA OFFERS NEW TALENT

BAFTA offers something for every level of talent; we're all about levelling the playing field and giving people access to networks and knowledge. This means we host masterclasses on specific crafts, run inspiring events featuring screen heroes and heroines, and create new talent platforms to enable people to be discovered. We run over 250 events open to the public each year. My job is all about finding and connecting with the BAFTA winners of tomorrow, giving them chances if they need chances, and connections where they didn't have any previously. It's a hugely inspiring place to work. The awards have the biggest profile but our spotlights and platforms that draw attention to new and emerging talent within every field are growing in size and stature. With Breakthrough Brits, BAFTA Scholarships, BAFTA Rocliffe New Writing Forum and BAFTA Crew, our aim is to support outstanding talent and help them forge professional, sustainable careers. *Alex Cook*, *New Talent*, *BAFTA*

Every year BAFTA recognises major new talent in film, TV and games at its awards ceremonies. Gongs include: British Short Film, British Short Animation, and Outstanding Debut by a British

Writer, Director or Producer at the Film Awards; Breakthrough Talent at the Television Craft Awards; and Debut Game at the Games Awards. That said, it's not just about awards; there are talent showcases and spotlights, and BAFTA runs hundreds of events throughout the country. You can sign up to their newsletter and attend the incredible Q&As and masterclasses – most of which are filmed and streamed online.

Here's a selection of BAFTA events and initiatives:

- *BAFTA Breakthrough Brits in partnership with Burberry:* an initiative that supports and celebrates up-and-coming British talent by entering selected industry newcomers into a year-long mentoring and guidance programme that will shape their future careers.

- *Scholarships:* BAFTA's Scholarships Programme in the UK makes awards to students in need of financial assistance to enable them to take a postgraduate course related to a career in film, TV or games. In addition to funding towards their course fees, each BAFTA Scholar also receives mentoring support from a BAFTA member, and free access to BAFTA events around the UK.

- *BAFTA Crew:* a networking and skills development programme for below-the-line talent based outside of London that places participants at the heart of a professional network, with access to the best industry talent working in film and TV today.

- *BAFTA Rocliffe New Writing Forum:* helps new writers develop their work under the guidance of the very best in the business and introduces them to the industry.

- *BAFTA Creative Skillset Guest Lecture Programme:* sees some of the UK's leading craftspeople in film, TV and games share their knowledge and expertise with students on Creative Skillset accredited courses across the UK.

- *BAFTA Brits to Watch – The Screenings:* aims to support talented individuals, strengthening their already promising careers by building a lasting and durable partnership with the top industry professionals in the US.

- *BAFTA Guru:* online learning resource aimed at career starters in the film, TV and games industries looking for advice, insight and inspiration from the best creative minds working today.

To find out more visit *www.bafta.org*

AN OVERVIEW OF SCREEN INTERNATIONAL'S STARS OF TOMORROW

WENDY MITCHELL: Stars of Tomorrow started in 2004 to spotlight talent in the UK. Everyone knows that the UK is a hotbed of talent and the people we feature are just on the cusp of being known. We have highlighted people like Carey Mulligan, Robert Pattinson, James McAvoy, Andrew Garfield, Benedict Cumberbatch and Andrea Arnold before they were known. We help give them a profile that will propel their careers – writers, directors, producers and actors.

It's a huge process and we have one curator each year. Firstly, we talk to the agents about who they are signing and which of their clients are heating up. We talk to casting directors and companies looking at writers and directors who are making interesting films. We look at which short films are making waves. We ask production companies which scripts people are wanting to sign. We talk to a lot of industry experts. It's very heavily curated. Sometimes we might get 800 names suggested and we narrow it down to 30. It's also down to personal taste – we look at who we want to put *Screen*'s stamp of approval on. We don't get a lot of people directly approaching us but we are open to someone nominating themselves, especially if they have had a short do well in festivals.

Stars of Tomorrow is one of the things we do that I am the most excited about each year. With any new talent you want something singular about them; they have to have a vision to share with the world. It doesn't have to be avant-garde, just a confidence in what they are doing. We are not looking simply for a director for hire. They need to know what their voice and vision is, and be ready to share that. With actors, we're looking for someone who lights up on screen, someone that we can see has longevity and won't fade away.

THE BRIT LIST

ALEXANDRA ARLANGO: The Brit List is a list where the most well-regarded unproduced screenplays written by non-US writers is generated and voted on by the British Film Industry. Nominated scripts are submitted by participating producers, sales agents, financiers and distribution companies. Those scripts with three nominations or more then appear on that year's list. Nominated scripts have all been very varied. If there has been a common denominator, it's that the scripts have been original and aimed at a particular market. There's no specific way to get noticed. Nominations are all anonymous so there isn't any way to petition participants. Its aim is to highlight and help generate interest in projects that have yet to make it to the screen. Some of the previous scripts which have gone on to be made include *The King's Speech* by David Seidler, *We Need To Talk About Kevin* by Lynne Ramsay and Rory Stewart Kinnear, *Salmon Fishing in the Yemen* by Simon Beaufoy, *The Best Exotic Marigold Hotel* by Deborah Moggach and Ol Parker, *Nowhere Boy* by Matt Greenhalgh, *Jane Eyre* by Moira Buffini, *Never Let Me Go* by Alex Garland, *Attack the Block* by Joe Cornish, *My Week with Marilyn* by Adrian Hodges, *The Debt* by Jane Goldman and Matthew Vaughn, *Wuthering Heights* by Olivia Hetreed, *The Scouting Book for Boys* by Jack Thorne and *Men Who Stare at Goats* by Peter Straughan.

WOMEN IN FILM & TV (UK)

WFTV is the leading membership organisation for women working in creative media in the UK, and part of an international network of over 10,000 women worldwide. Members of the organisation come from a broad range of professions spanning the entire creative media industries. WFTV hosts a variety of events throughout the year, presents a glamorous awards ceremony every December, and runs a mentoring programme for women in the industry. Over six months, selected participants receive six hours of mentoring contact with an experienced industry figure, combined with an intensive programme of seminars, training workshops and networking opportunities. They also host networking evenings, collaborate with industry bodies on research projects and lobby for women's interests.

www.wftv.org.uk, *@WFTV_UK*

SKILLSET

Creative Skillset is an industry body which empowers the creative industries to develop skills and talent, helping businesses to grow. They help manage investment from both industry and government to ensure the UK remains a world leader in creative talent. They help train the next generation of creative professionals through mentoring schemes such as Guiding Lights; by offering bursaries to support training through international partners like Rotterdam and the Berlinale; and their Tick accredited courses. They are learning and evolving all the time, undertaking research into the needs of companies and individuals, looking into what's working now while preparing for the future.

www.creativeskillset.org

SCREEN TRAINING IRELAND

Screen Training Ireland, part of Bord Scannán na hÉireann/Irish Film Board, is a unique resource for the Irish screen industry, offering training by professionals for professionals. It is committed to providing customised, state-of-the-art training to support the development of the Irish screen sectors.

The Creativity and Creative Collaboration training strand focuses on providing development opportunities to creatives. It places storytelling and the unique voices of Irish creatives at the heart of the Screen Sectors. Screen Training Ireland provide emerging talent with the opportunity to meet and collaborate with experienced practitioners, creating a cohesive progression process for emerging talent, and new creative approaches for established practitioners.

Screen Training Ireland offer development opportunities for screenwriters, directors, actors, creative producers, programme makers and visual creatives. They aim to provide emerging talent with exposure to key creative trainers on a national and international level. For more established talent, the aim is to provide a less structured approach where new ideas and the collaborative creative process can be explored.

Screen Training Ireland also support international training through the Bursary Award scheme enabling experienced Irish professionals to participate in training opportunities on the international circuit and where necessary design a development opportunity customised to meet their individual needs.

www.screentrainingireland.ie

CATALYST

Launched in 2007 and run by Bord Scannán na hÉireann/Irish Film Board, the Catalyst Project is a low-budget training initiative which offers three teams of emerging filmmakers the chance to produce a feature film. Successful applicants have access to industry experts who will offer mentorship and guidance. In order to be eligible to apply for the awards, applicants must attend a two-day training seminar where forming new partnerships is encouraged. To be eligible, you must have at least one credit on a produced piece. Irish residents take priority.

www.irishfilmboard.ie/funding_programmes/Catalyst_Project/58"

UNDERSTANDING A FESTIVAL

I was really keen to highlight the importance of festivals as this is something writers and writer-directors shouldn't overlook but many newer people do. They're where my education in film began. Watching film nuggets you will never see again, or meeting filmmakers from other places, opens your mind. Sometimes we concentrate so much on the script or the shoot that we miss what happens afterwards, in the marketplace. Most films begin their journey at a festival premiere, and this plays an important role in the life of a film in terms of reviews, buzz, sales and networking.

CHARLES GANT: Film festivals are important depending on the scale of the film, but particularly important in the case of films that might struggle to get a theatrical release. So the only time they will be in a cinema is during a festival. Even if you do get a theatrical release, you may not get enough exposure, as you can be up against other, bigger films, even bigger independent films, which will get the lead reviews. Festivals are where you connect with invested audiences so they can be a much better platform.

WENDY MITCHELL: Festivals are crucial as it's hard to get a theatrical release, especially for a first-time or independent film. It's a way to connect with an audience and answer questions. For a new writer or writer-director, it's the chance to meet industry people at the same level, or you get to meet mentors. Without film festivals, important independent films would not exist. You feel like you have succeeded. You get to have your party for the film in the cinema – you are the hero and champion and are celebrated. As for good festivals for beginners, go to smaller festivals where there's a 'hub'. You will meet lots of people. Maybe it's better to go to something like the Hamptons Film Festival than Sundance (depending on your career, of course). Look for a festival that's not in a major city (so not London or New York, for instance) – you have a better chance of networking with visiting industry if they are in Reykjavik or somewhere, as they aren't so distracted – and then look at those that seem to invite lots of filmmakers to come with their films. You want to meet other people so, if you're going to a local festival where you're just meeting local audiences, that might not be worth the price of a flight. Do some homework about the filmmakers you admire and see which festivals have supported them in recent years.

GRAINNE HUMPHREYS: As a curator, I try to impose a coherent structure on the wide and increasingly diverse art form known as film. As the programmer of a film event with a high level of public attendance I am trying to satisfy multiple audiences, from the dedicated cinephile to the more casual monthly cinemagoer. I attend approximately 15 international film festivals a year and I borrow and steal the best ideas, as well as the best films! Through our international work we aspire to bring some of the JDIFF seasons and programmes, which I have created, to other international festivals. As a programmer I am trying to bring both new names and new films to Irish audiences, to create a relationship between filmmakers and their audiences. The selection of venue, the timing, etc., can be key. As a film matchmaker, it's important to remember the responsibility to the artist whose work you are showing, to always maintain the integrity of the work and to maximise the possibility for profile, platforming the work both locally and internationally. Finally, the director is also the 'face' of the festival, the spokesperson whose ethos defines the event, the single person who is feted for their genius or damned for their incompetence but who must provide vital support for both the emerging talents and the more established filmmakers.

MASOUD AMRALLA AL ALI: It's an interesting, beautiful job. At the same time, it's very hard and tough. For me, it's more than a job to be honest. It's something that I've loved to do for years, watching and analysing different types of films. This job offered me that. The good thing is that you are paid to watch films. The hard thing about it is chasing films and trying to find a strategic look for the entire festival and bearing in mind so many factors which may apply. At the same time, it's all about taste and finding good cinema. It's so hard to describe what good cinema is. You always try to push the boundaries and find new waves, ideas, voices and new approaches to filmmaking. With the recent production situation in the world, and with the digital revolution in film, we receive a lot of submissions. The tough thing comes with trying to identify what suits this festival and not that festival. At the same time, watching films. Sometimes you watch films that you wouldn't watch normally – you are forced to watch them. Making the decision of why you will take one film and reject another is hard. The difficulty is finding your own voice in the festival and giving it the maximum push so that when people attend the festival they see what you have selected and like or dislike it. Finding this voice is sometimes hard. It takes years until you find your path. You have to watch everything and then put aside your taste and look at it as a programmer, as someone who has so many things on their mind. One of them is the audience; another is the filmmaker and their reputation and the direction of the festival. You need to separate yourself at a certain stage.

PHIL ILSON: My semi-official title is 'festival director', but I have 'fallen' into this, as it was me (and a friend, Kate Taylor, who has since left the festival) who set it up in 2004 as more of a hobby. But 11 years on, I don't fill the traditional role of festival director as my main role is festival programmer, a lot of what is traditionally done by the director being handled by the festival producer. I'm looking to change the festival structure this year, to bring in more of a festival director so I can be overall artistic programmer. My personal role on London Short Film Festival (LSFF) is to select from the films that are entered via open submission, and to put these into various ordered programmes; in 2014, we received 1,200 submissions and I selected around 375 (though I also have a separate documentary programmer who works independently). I also decide on retrospectives, special events, partner programmes, and decide what goes in which festival venue. I also oversee the look/design of the festival, as I'm very much about public perception of the festival and its personality. The films are only a percentage of the artistic side of the festival.

GRAINNE HUMPHREYS: I am looking for something I haven't seen before, something which feels new and different – even with genre films an old story can feel fresh when told in a new and innovative way. Integrity, passion, energy, a sense of humour – an interest in challenging audiences and making bold, creative and dynamic artistic choices to provoke emotions and debate.

MASOUD AMRALLA AL ALI: The problem with festivals is that you cannot focus on everyone. The director is at the core of the film but that doesn't mean that the other professions are not important – they are. We hold sessions here where DOPs, editors and scriptwriters come and do workshops with the filmmakers. With the Dubai Film Festival we invite three people from each film. The director comes by default, then we invite actors, writers, producers and so on. It's fair: for a filmmaker to make a film in the healthy, normal way, it takes around one to two years. For the other professions, they might work on five films a year. A filmmaker might take a year to make a film, whereas the editor can do maybe three a year.

309

GRAINNE HUMPHREYS: Directors are most often nominated to accompany films to festivals by distributors, sales agents and production companies – they are also generally more media friendly for press purposes. There are exceptions, but generally writers don't travel and, if this changed, there would be an immediate change in the perception and profile of writers.

PHIL ILSON: Festivals are much more immediate; audiences are significantly smaller, but they're more focused. If a filmmaker is accepted by a reputable film festival, the film industry can take notice; even if the industry person doesn't attend, they will scour the lists of accepted films to pinpoint new talent, so the festival can act as a gatekeeper. Of course, there are also thousands of festivals, and films can be equally lost if they do lots of tiny festivals that may not have an industry connection, and this can cost the filmmaker money entering and attending. Sometimes smaller festivals in more remote places can be equally rewarding for a filmmaker, with the film getting a big local audience who wouldn't normally engage with such work.

MASOUD AMRALLA AL ALI: A festival programmer will travel around the world to different festivals as well as meet with production companies and look at all the films, looking at the new generation of filmmakers. With Dubai, for example, we have 24 programmers and scouts who follow up who is making films and who is shooting what in their region. We are new wave, new ideas, new blood that is coming up. At the forefront is Arab, Asian and African cinema. Then we have sections for international filmmakers. All of our programmers are looking for artistic films and for something different. At the same time, we mix these with some films that are more appealing to the audience.

GRAINNE HUMPHREYS: When a film gets accepted by a festival, ask questions – what can they offer you as a filmmaker and what do you want from the festival in return – and try to get as much information

310

upfront as you can. The festival's screening offer shows that they are interested in your film, but be smart and don't be outrageous in your demands or you will get a reputation which will dog you for years.

MASOUD AMRALLA AL ALI: If you've got into a big festival, it's worth travelling to that festival. Some films get into 50–60 festivals, so pick three or four to go to; it would be mad to travel and honour every film festival. Look for a festival that has a market, good PR and a good audience. A lot of deals get made as a result of contacts filmmakers make networking at festivals. See how people react in different countries. It's an experience for the filmmakers as well as a business opportunity. I often hear writers and directors say how the reaction here is different from the audience reaction in their home countries. It's a new experience.

PHIL ILSON: The explosion in social networking via Facebook and Twitter is fantastic for letting the world know that your film has been accepted by such-and-such festival. And, if it's a reasonable thing to do, the filmmaker should attend.

CREATING A FESTIVAL STRATEGY

The festival circuit is filled with great people. If your film is selected, go to as many as you can afford – they rarely pay for your flight but they may contribute towards your accommodation. When filmmakers realise the importance of getting their films seen, they ask me about creating a festival strategy for shorts. I recommend starting with the BAFTA accredited festival list and the Academy accredited festival list – use Withoutabox (www.withoutabox.com) as it simplifies the application process. I also use the British Council's online festival directory.

PHIL ILSON: Make a good short film. A lot of time the packaging is opened by an intern and everything but the DVD thrown away.

Online submissions help to stop this – there needs to be a short synopsis, clear contact details, and a decent still for the brochure if accepted. LSFF uses Withoutabox, as everything is in one place, but there are other platforms, such as Reelport.

MASOUD AMRALLA AL ALI: Preparing a good package for your film festival submission is a must. Every festival will ask for the same. You need the film, the poster, the trailer and the complete information about the cast, crew, synopsis, plus maybe the tagline and director's statement. Most of the time, our struggle comes with the filmmakers who don't complete the submission form. Then we spend days, weeks, months chasing them for an image in low resolution. We print a catalogue so we need promotional materials for the film. If you have the materials from the beginning, you are relaxed in submitting to universal film festivals as you have everything they need. One of the important things that we struggle with is the dialogue list. If you are screening in this part of the world, for example, we need to translate the film into Arabic for the audience. If we don't have the dialogue list, we screen the film with English subtitles (if it wasn't an English film). If a submission is poor, you think, 'This guy is careless, they will not answer my emails when I write to them, or answer when I call them.' If you have a good submission, the festival will notice that you really want your film out there. I remember once we had a film submitted; the title was *Orange*, and in the synopsis he wrote 'Orange'. How can we sell or promote the film on the website and social media if the synopsis is only one word? We then have to write our own synopsis, which then sometimes the filmmakers don't like.

GRAINNE HUMPHREYS: The advice I give to filmmakers about which festivals to enter is, when looking at a festival, see what they showed the year before – if they showed a film like yours then they may be interested in your film. Be realistic – film festivals need films but they also need professionals. So do your research – don't enter a food documentary into a horror festival unless it's about cannibalism. I once got a film about the history of the pooper-scooper – which was not a joke and was 90 minutes long. Why on earth did they think we would want to show it? In relation to the first festival you play – be very careful, take time with deciding which one.

PHIL ILSON: Encounters Short Film Festival in Bristol has been the UK's premiere international short film festival for 20 years. Even if you don't have a film screening, it's worth attending to see films, network and get the lie of the land. Clermont-Ferrand in France is the world's biggest short film festival and market, attracting international industry and filmmakers, but it can be daunting and I've known filmmakers who felt they were swallowed up. But it's worth coming to see how big a short-film festival can be. BFI London and Edinburgh are the two big international film festivals in the UK and have strong short-film programmes, though they're a small part of a much bigger festival. But, if accepted, it's a high-profile gig, and both festivals offer services for short filmmakers such as networking sessions and talks. In Europe, there's a whole circuit of respected short-film festivals. If you are making documentary, then Sheffield Doc/Fest is essential to visit, even if you don't have a film showing; it's the UK's biggest industry-based international festival.

MASOUD AMRALLA AL ALI: There are the top festivals, which are well known and very difficult to get your film into. And then there are many intimate, small festivals. What I can say is, find a festival that suits your film. If your film is about a certain topic or region, you should find a festival focused on that with a good reputation. There are 3,000–4,000 film festivals around the world, so it's very hard to find your own, unless at the beginning you already know which one you want to submit to. Everybody wants to get into the top four or five film festivals. Sometimes they'll be disappointed because those festivals have limits with regard to how many films they can select, and some filmmakers wait for ages to enter their films into those and then end up not making it into them. For the world premiere of the film, you have to select a very prestigious film festival as that can help with marketing the film. One of the most important elements that you need to look for in a festival is whether it has a market. If it does, you are in a better festival than one without a market. With a market, you can do a double job at the festival. You can showcase your film and then find distributors and make deals, promoting it on the business side too. The ideal festival also has a market.

BENEFITS OF ATTENDING FESTIVALS

You can't help but grasp that reaching out is the only way to get ahead and that people appreciate you taking the time – it will benefit your career. In the lists chapter I have included festivals and conferences I think are worth exploring and attending.

GRAINNE HUMPHREYS: Festivals are all about discovery. Creating and developing a buzz and energy around new talent is a key role for most festivals. For established talent, festivals represent a consolidation of their position; their work is shown with more and more frequency, leading to greater awareness within the industry and public at large. And, of course, the final phase is the retrospectives and lifetime achievement awards!! It's a very safe and nurturing community – festivals celebrate and support filmmakers. Also, audiences are more attuned to the more experimental work and are more engaged with the process of filmmaking, which provides a wonderful source of strength at the start of a filmmaker's career. You'll meet your filmmaking peers and your most supportive audiences, who will be your most valuable source of support as your career develops.

SARAH GAVRON: So many benefits to attending a festival – meeting other filmmakers who have become friends, mentors and advisors; expanding my sense of what cinema is.

ASIF KAPADIA: By making shorts I started getting invited to film festivals. My interest was in foreign-language films, world cinema and the great filmmakers from around the world. It was while at a short-film festival that I realised I'm an international filmmaker. It was only by travelling with my films that I discovered that this was my place – the space I wanted to inhabit. It doesn't matter if your work doesn't go down well at home, if you are turned down by the British festivals, as I was, because my films were accepted at international festivals, where they won prizes. It was an interesting lesson, that you don't have to be restricted to your home market, where you live. I wanted to be an international filmmaker. I met my first producer, Bertrand Faivre, at a film festival in France. He saw *The Sheep Thief*, liked it and said, 'If you have an idea for a feature, come and talk to me.' So I got in touch once I had a script. Bertrand produced my first two feature films, *The Warrior* and *Far North*. Had I not gone to Brest, a short-film festival in the west of France, to see how it played to a French audience, none of that might have happened. The truth is that, at the time, not many UK producers were that excited by the idea of my wanting to make my debut feature in India.

MASOUD AMRALLA AL ALI: Festivals play an enormous role in a filmmaker's career. There are two types of films – films that are mainstream for the box office, and artistic films. Artistic films normally find themselves in festivals. The entire industry looks to festivals and their selections, so they can pick their films. Winning an award in a prestigious film festival gives a film an extra mile so it can survive and reach more audience members. It also means it can reach more industry people and distributors, giving it a life. Festivals play a huge role for independent filmmakers in getting their films out to audience members and building their careers, as well as helping the industry to find new talent.

MANJINDER VIRK: Festivals are a fantastic way to celebrate film and meet other enthusiastic filmmakers. Most festivals are run by people who love film.

315

SALLY EL HOSAINI: Festivals are an amazing showcase and way to connect with audiences, although I don't like the competition element. For me, this has been crucial. *My Brother The Devil* did well at over 40 festivals around the world. Having the film travel internationally has really helped my career. And so has winning awards. Which I feel conflicted about because I don't like that element. I've sat on a couple of festival juries recently, and I realise how arbitrary they are. It's a cliché to say it, but all the films that are nominated are winners. When you see behind the curtain and see how juries select films you realise that it's all so subjective. Film is subjective and that's what's beautiful about the medium. What somebody connects with, another person hates. How can you ever have winners and losers? Surely trying to reach consensus is detrimental to our film culture. And yet at the same time it really helps filmmakers to get the recognition and attention that awards bring. It's such a competitive industry that you've got to take what you can, but you do feel a bit dirty doing it.

SUSAN JACOBSON: There are many reasons people go to festivals: 1) to see films, 2) to work, 3) your film is in the festival and you are there to support it. I have been to festivals for work and never seen the inside of a cinema, although I managed to have some productive meetings and sell my film. I have been to festivals with my films and made fantastic contacts and spurned meetings. If you are going to see films, festivals are fantastic for opening you up to other forms of filmmaking and alternate voices and ideas.

ARAB NASSER & TARZAN NASSER: Our experience proved that if we can make short films of good quality they will take us to international festivals like Cannes. It was as if we had made a feature film! We understand the difference from a marketing and production perspective but our short-film experience has been great in bringing us to the point where we're on the door step of making our first long, 'novelist' film! The short film had been part of more than 30 festivals worldwide including the Cannes Film Festival. This created momentum for us and has had impact as we are now making a feature.

MUSTAPHA KSEIBATI: It's a small industry and getting to know the players is key. Festivals are a fantastic place to build profile, get representation and meet your peers.

GLENN MONTGOMERY: I find Cannes terrifying. It's very exciting to be there. That kind of networking, though, I'm terrible at it – I normally end up hiding in a corner. But the Cannes-effect has had a lot of impact, just to be able to say I've had a film screened there. The thing about Cannes is that it's very easy to get lost in the show and not get a lot out of it. The main focus is on directors and actors, so writers can find themselves being a little invisible. People are less interested in the writers. So try and organise meetings before you go. At smaller festivals you naturally end up talking to people but with the bigger festivals be strategic. Find out who's going and who it would benefit you the most to arrange meetings with beforehand.

MIRANDA BOWEN: The benefits of attending a festival have been a bit of visibility. A few phone calls. A chance to meet other filmmakers. A lot of free drinks and some fun.

TINA GHARAVI: I have been known to hide in hotel rooms during festivals, writing. They are important and valuable for the right people but for me they are a necessary torture. I leave this to my producers now. If I come, it's to meet other filmmakers and to watch films. The business side to these things, especially the idea of networking, leaves me cold. Saying that, some of the festivals have been delights (Sundance being one), where the festival goes out of its way to nurture the filmmaker.

REBECCA DALY: The best thing at festivals is seeing the audience reaction to your film. To experience that is both terrifying and brilliant. You learn so much through it. It's exhilarating; you get so much from hearing directly from them. I also love meeting other filmmakers, as what we do is quite isolating. You don't typically work with another director when you're working so it's good to meet others 'of your own kind'. Obviously, if your film is selected by a prestigious festival that's a great start. That was definitely my experience with *The Other Side of Sleep* and Cannes.

ROB BROWN: A good thing about making films is you get invited to international film festivals. I got to visit places in the world I haven't visited before. It keeps my enthusiasm for what I do burning, and it keeps you aware of films that are being made. It sounds silly but it's important to know if your new film idea is as original as you think it is or whether it has already been made by someone else. Festivals are a reward for your hard work when they are screening your film and hosting you. Seeing lots of films can remind you why you put yourself through the more difficult aspects of the job.

STEPHEN FINGLETON: Seeing your work with an audience of strangers on the big screen is what the festival experience is all about. They are the ultimate critics, simultaneously far smarter than you gave them credit for, yet also blind to what you thought was obvious. Get them in the palm of your hand. And, as a writer, networking is useful for getting people on your level to read your script – usually other writers or directors. But it all really comes down to the work. My career hasn't been boosted by film festivals at all, but I am friends with many people I've met on the circuit.

DESTINY EKARAGHA: When I was first starting out, I sent my short film *Tight Jeans* to every film festival that I could think of. It didn't matter what the theme of the film festival was, I sent it regardless and I went broke because of it. Don't do that! Sending films off to film festivals can prove expensive so I suggest that you really research the festival first. If your film is a rom-com, it may not be the best idea to send it to a film festival that usually takes sci-fi. Do as much research as you can – it may end up saving you money. Once a festival accepts your film, enjoy it! I love film festivals. An actual audience gets to see your film, and the alcohol and food are usually free. Win!

PHIL ILSON: A busy industry festival means that there will be people around that you want to meet, and the bar after the screening is essential for this. Many festivals have industry programmes, so it's a good thing to sign up for these in advance as it's where you'll meet your fellow filmmakers and future collaborators. A festival with a good public audience can also be great, as you can meet with your audience.

CURES FOR POST-FESTIVAL/ CONFERENCE BLUES

This has been one of my most popular blogs – how to stave off the post-anything blues. Going to a course, seminar or festival can get you fired up and reinvigorated. After all that time with other filmmakers talking passionately about the craft and new opportunities, you couldn't not feel inspired. I take a notebook to draw on in the weeks that follow. I also schedule a morning purely reaching out to everyone I met: it keeps up the momentum and deflects the doldrums. This is a window of opportunity, so capitalise.

•••

ROCLIFFE NOTES on...
KILLING THOSE BLUES

- Whenever someone gives you a business card, write down which event you met them at. You only need to meet someone once to 'know' them, said Mitch Hurwitz at the New York TV Festival!

- Carry a notebook, write things down. You'll forget as there's so much to absorb. List production companies, channels, all speaker references.

- Write down ten things you learned. Reading these through after the festival will re-inspire you.

- Write to all the peers you met. Send them links to your website or YouTube clips or any online info about you. Follow them on Twitter.

- Follow every speaker on Twitter. Tweet them how fab they were or what you liked or learned from their talk or work.

- Go to pitching sessions (always try to take part in one), write to the people on the panel (via their companies) and thank them. Ask what else they are looking for and what the best way to send them pitches is.

- Look at the festival programme and which companies support it. If it lists production companies, seek out who is at the festival and learn about their submissions process. Write and ask them how to submit if it's not apparent.

- Enlist your agent by sending them a list of who you met, requesting advice on how to best follow this up, asking if they can help.

- Drop the festival contact a line to say 'thank you' for the opportunity. Festivals love longevity, building relationships with people they featured early in their careers. Many offer a staggered payment scheme so you can book your tickets in advance.

- After a table read, send your actors a note. They are as keen to connect with you as you are with them.

- Contact the directors of the short films, webisodes or first-time features you've seen to see if they are interested in reading your work! Collaborate to accelerate.

....

ON AMERICA

Hollywood exists to make money – it's SHOW + BUSINESS and don't be fooled into believing you are awesome – everything is 'awesome'. It's a business, not just an art form – they invest with a view to making a profit. Everyone is looking for the right project and, from what I understand, all you need to do is write a good script or make a good film. Their viewpoint is that it can come from any quarter. What impressed me most about New York and LA is that everyone seems on their game and prepped. People generally seem incredibly supportive and open.

EDWARD BAKER-DULY: The industry as a whole is huge in the States. It's what makes it feel more 'legitimate' than anywhere else I've worked. There's always something going on: casting, workshops, post-production, voiceover, the list is endless. It justifies my whole rationale of coming to New York to seek out more opportunities, because above all that is an actor's lifeline. Unlike anywhere else I've worked, there's a 'hustle' mentality here and so much is dependent on who you know and who will give you an introduction. However, there's also huge generosity here when recognising talent, where it seems everyone wants a part in everyone's success because, even if the job doesn't land this time, the network has been established. Even though there are no guarantees, for those who have talent and ability and determination, there will always be a next time here because the process is ever ongoing.

CLAIRE WILSON: I went to film school in Vancouver so was trained in a sense in the North American system. Straight out of class I had some interest by a big film exec but I was green around the ears and didn't realise I should have jumped on it. I was also broke and had to go back to London.

MICHAEL KUHN: The first thing to note is that people in the UK often think that we're in some battle with Hollywood, though we're so far below the horizon that we're not even noticed by Hollywood in general. In reality, we're not in a war with Hollywood – they do their thing and we do our thing. The second thing is that, actually, all of my life spent in Hollywood I found the people extremely friendly and helpful. You could imagine that they didn't really think about us being international or anything like that. And the third thing to remember is that, unlike the rest of the filmmakers in Europe, we are competing for the same talent pool as the Americans. We have the disadvantage that we don't have the whole studio system to support the fight for key talent. We have to make do with subsidies and tax breaks and loads of other things that Americans don't have to deal with in such depth. I do think that one of the things we'll always suffer from here is not having enough ambition. There's absolutely no reason why you can't put on a big film here. There are plenty of examples of people from the UK who have achieved on a massive scale.

KIRSTEN SHERIDAN: I am living in LA. I came here specifically to get into the TV business because in Ireland there's one TV station with two shows. In America, there are 20 different networks and cable channels you can go to. It is a business over here. You feel that they need writers, need content. The reason I want to do TV is because the quality of the product is much stronger.

SAUL DIBB: I've never made a film in America. I've had meetings there. It's a funny place. You have a meeting, everyone is very upbeat, positive and they love your work. Then you leave the meeting and you've no idea how it actually went. Because no one will ever say a bad thing. One of the really great things about it is that there isn't a feeling of it being a 'boy's club' or being closed off, as there is in the UK. People will have meetings with you that you wouldn't expect to – they are so open to where a good idea can come from. They approach it with the viewpoint that no one knows which filmmaker is going to make the film that really, really works. My experience has been having meetings with the people you want to talk to and not minions. It feels very accessible.

JAMES DORMER: My experience of working in the American system as such is a bit odd. My first time was working on a movie, being flown out to LA for script meetings – not with Americans, though: it was with an English producer and German company. Then I worked on the TV show *Strike Back*, which is a co-production between Sky and Cinemax (part of HBO). I can only say good things about the notes we've had from HBO; they've been intelligent, intelligible and sensible, apart from notes about putting in more sex. It's understandable, though, as it's one of the MOs of the channel.

SUSIE CONKLIN: A typical American series will be written by a team of writers, led by the show-runner – the head writer who often originated the idea. They meet together over months to flesh out the series, from story and character arcs to the individual beats of each episode. It's a collective activity in which all the writers contribute ideas and debate their merit. Who writes what episode is determined later and it's the show-runner's job to lead that team and supervise the writing process. The buck stops with them. Early in my script-editing career I was lucky enough to spend time in the writers' room on *ER*, led by the acclaimed writer John Wells. I discovered that the great advantage of team writing is the rigour of the storylining. When you are making 20–24 episodes of something it's absolutely essential, but even on shorter runs, which are becoming more common in the US, the quality of that approach shows. But it's an expensive model because the writer must be paid for their total contribution to the show, not just their individual episodes. The British industry isn't geared up for that – at least not yet. There are hybrid show-runners cropping up in UK drama now, but until the writers are active contributors to the whole series I think it's mainly focused around the head writer having more creative control of the show.

MOIRA BUFFINI: I am such a sucker – I find it so glamorous. I fly over first class and I'm a complete pushover and can't believe my life has taken me here. But it's much more of an industry and less friendly than in the UK. The pressure is tremendous. There's quite a harsh working environment and, despite first appearances, it's quite small. There's much more of a film terminology in Los Angeles; a language I am learning and determined to acquire. As the budgets grow, so does the pressure, and I don't think anyone who works in LA would disagree. There's a lot of paranoia there and you have to be careful not to let it rub off on you. I have a family in the UK so I would never want to live there. It can be quite brutal and there are still people waiting tables after 20 years, after they've gone out to make it and haven't. The tales we hear are about those who get really lucky. I would say to anyone contemplating moving to the US, if you are absolutely burning and determined then go, but I have no advice on what you do when you get there, as that isn't what I did.

HOPE DICKSON LEACH: I went to film school in New York, worked as Todd Solondz's assistant for nine months, and prior to that did an internship in LA with Mario Kassar's production company. I've worked at Sundance and am still working with an LA-based producer on one project and co-writing with a US writer on another project. I went to the States as it seemed to me that the system there was about getting out and doing things for yourself. Though independent film looks a lot different now than it did in the 1990s when I fell in love with Jim Jarmusch et al, there's still a sense that if you want to make a film, you fight to make it and you *can* get it made. There's yet another new generation of really exciting indie filmmakers in the States at the moment, and the new technology serves to not only make your film, but to get it seen. The system is changing every year and filmmakers over there are finding ways to help shape the future of distribution and exhibition just as much as production. They are curating work, forming collectives, crowdfunding their way into existence. It's an exciting time.

SALLY EL HOSAINI: It's a business with a capital B. I've got representation out there and I've been to LA a few times over the last few years. I'd say that there, more than anywhere, you are reminded that it's a hard-nosed business. Artists can get trampled on and forgotten, and they very often are. There are really good people working out there too, though, who are trying to do really interesting films. The trick is trying to connect with the good guys. There's a reason why it's the epicentre of filmmaking in the world. There's quantity, but not quality. I remember the epiphany I had when I realised that the 'Writer's Store' was an actual shop and not just a website. For filmmakers, there's a lot to learn from the American model. Especially if you want to make films internationally – as I do. Go there when there's a reason to go there. Don't just go there to try to 'break in'. You meet so many people in LA who move there to do that. They are small fish in a very big ocean. I've met many waiters and waitresses trying to 'break in'. It's soul-destroying and most abandon their dreams.

KEVIN CECIL: In America the pitch is everything. There's a certain type of British writer who takes pride in not explaining things, being good on the page but being terrible in meetings or not going to them. You can't get away with that in America, unless you're a genius. You must be able to communicate and pitch your story. The good thing about being in a partnership is there are two of you so you don't get so freaked out in meetings. If one of you dries up, the other one can step in. It helps to prepare for your pitch and treat it as a performance. There are things I like more about the American system and things that I prefer about the British one. We have more variety of output. British broadcasters are able to experiment more and there's less fear of failure as the stakes aren't quite so high as in America. But there's a real professionalism about the American system and they have amazing resources.

LAWRENCE COCHRAN: The reality is that we don't have the money of the Americans, so we choose to make smaller series and to make a larger variety of them. For example, if we spent the money on *House of Cards* that Netflix now have, we would make two or three series per year. There's lots to admire about American stuff, but we see the best of it, and a small amount of our Press make it the best of what we're proud of at the BBC. However, the quality of the content is high and there are certain things that the Americans and the Danish and the Swedish get away with that we can't. We hold ourselves up to much higher standards because it's our lives being reflected, whereas something set in America or Sweden shows a foreign and exciting world. And that's part of the allure with them, and that will always be the case.

RICHARD COOKSON: My pet hate is when new writers respond to the question of 'What TV do you like?' by listing a string of American box sets and/or claiming not to watch any British drama. It's fine to have US TV and films as influences. But there are two important things to remember about the American shows: firstly, we only see the very best over here – *Breaking Bad* and *True Detective* are not the average. Secondly, while the people you meet in the industry are keenly aware of the big US shows, the box-set market isn't actually that widespread in this country. Those fantastic American shows are important, but they are niche – consumed by TV types and fans of culture, but not by the general population – and it's useful to keep that perspective.

KERRY APPLEYARD: In Canada, in terms of the creative process, it's writing rooms and show-runners. There's still a very definite place and need for creative producers, but the show-runner leads the creative vision for a show, supported and guided by the producer. Writers brainstorm, break and discuss the creative all together, whereas in the UK, for the most part, the writers work largely independently and are guided by notes from the producer.

BEN STEPHENSON: America has a very different commercial model, which means they require long series. Their financial models on network and cable require them to have long series in order to make their massive investments back. A series with 13–24 parts doesn't happen because of creative demands; it happens because of commercial demands. Over here, we have slightly more latitude to make shorter runs and the money is less high-stakes. In America, if a show has been commissioned for 24 episodes and after two episodes nobody watches it and they pull it, they've pulled millions of dollars' worth of cash. Here, if something doesn't work after two episodes, you can't pull a 24-part series because that would be most of the budget. If you look at something like *Game of Thrones*, the cost of that is probably five times the BBC2 drama budget. The point of the BBC is to offer range and programmes for everyone. If we made only 24-part series, we'd probably make about six a year. This would be lovely for some audiences, but not for other audiences. They are two very different models but we shouldn't worry about it.

ALEXANDRA BOYD: When I'm asked what advice I would give to someone wanting to work in Hollywood I will always ask: can you drive a car and can you do an impeccable American accent? During my ten years working in Los Angeles I had a great time but rarely worked in my own voice. There's a misconception that they are throwing parts in TV series and films out of the windows along Sunset Boulevard for English actors. Hugh Laurie and Damian Lewis have a lot to answer for! News flash: not so! There are lots of (American) actors in LA too! Contrary to what some people think – that Los Angeles is full of fakes and insincere people – I have to say that, while I was there, I got to know some of the most talented, focused, creative and driven individuals I have ever met. You have to be the same. But you're British so you will join the end of the queue of Americans who don't have to change the way they speak. Having trained at RADA and worked at the National doesn't cut it. *Coronation Street* or *Holby City*? No one cares. Unless you are a recognisable face on a successful show they have seen in the US, then you have to grow sharp elbows and work harder than the natives to get ahead. There's lots of work in LA but lots more people going for it. And PS, in the same way English actors think that US HBO series are so well written, they all think that BBC and UK drama and film are the BEST thing and wish they could work here. Ironic. I was very lucky, I got to live in a sunny place and work with some wonderful people at the top of the film industry. I learned a lot from them. But just like here in London, I still had to find a way to pay my rent and put gas in the car to drive the vast distances to get to auditions.

NETWORKING

There's an ancient phrase that I feel applies to meeting people – no man is your friend, no man is your enemy, every man is your teacher. I have always known that without the contacts I've made I wouldn't have a career today, but I had to deliver on the goods. There's a clear division between going out and learning about what people do and 'networking the room for the sake of extending your contact list'. Everyone knows when they've been 'networked' and it's awkward and uncomfortable. Instead, see it as forging relationships by talking to people, seeing movies, interacting and seeking opportunities. There's no point networking if you have nothing to show for yourself. The aim is to get your script into the right hands. In the early days, when you haven't got an agent or a champion, you are the only one who can sell yourself. Find out who is buying what, watch the schedules. It can be as much about listening intelligently to what established people have to say.

Go to TV and film festivals, Q&As. BBC Writersroom runs great seminars where you can meet people and chat. It's a bonding experience. Festivals and conferences abroad are great too. Don't be afraid to ask questions. Arm yourself with a list of four questions. Send a nice email and ask them to give you 15 minutes for advice over a coffee. We all know how important it is to foster and help rising talent – it's called giving back! You need to network wisely, finding a balance and not compromising your writing.

Gareth Edwards told me a story about a rich guy who gives up everything to be a writer in LA. He has 120 meetings and, when asked how he's getting on, he says he's a huge hit. The person asks him what job offers he's had and he says, 'Nothing, but I've had 120 meetings.' It's not very important if you're not doing the writing. Most of writing is writing, not networking, but if you haven't got an agent, you need to get your work out there and that involves meeting people. Every person you meet carries with them the opportunity for you to learn something.

WENDY MITCHELL: It's important to mention that, when you reach out to people, you should be thinking about what the person is doing at that time: are they promoting a film or show, are they in production, is it Oscar or BAFTA night? Chances are they will be completely consumed by that or staying up late.

CHRISTIAN MANLEY: I always used to feel like I was bothering industry people with unsolicited scripts; like I was Annoying New Writer Guy. Having been introduced to a good few more through BAFTA Rocliffe, I've learned that producers/commissioners are always open to looking at new material, if you approach them in the right way. These meetings are a bit like first dates – you have to sound confident and positive without being arrogant and pushy. It was really useful to meet some commissioners through BAFTA Rocliffe. Overwhelmingly their advice was to write what you love, not what you think they want to read. As someone whose voice is naturally set to 'weird', it gave me the confidence to continue writing what makes me laugh.

SASKIA SCHUSTER: Having a sense of being part of an industry is helpful. Comedy is collaborative, and it's also a business. Frustrating as it is for writers to have to compromise editorially, having a sense of the industry beyond the actual script process might hopefully help to mitigate some of those frustrations, and perhaps instil an understanding of why some notes are given. On the other hand they could make the frustration worse; some of those talks are pretty deadly. But making contacts from all walks of the industry and seizing every opportunity can't hurt.

AMIT KUMAR: My feature basically happened because of a networking party. I was hiding behind a potted plant and an Indian producer I knew came over and said, 'Hey, how are you? What's happening with your project?' I told him that we still had a gap and he said, 'We'll do it.' Actually, that triggered off them coming on board. I thought about it and I realised, if I hadn't been there behind that potted plant, my film wouldn't have been made. Now I think networking is important. If I get invited to a screening, even if I've seen the film before, I go and say, 'Yes, I've seen it, but I wanted to meet up with you.' I'm realising the importance of it and trying to somehow get round to doing it. It's not easy – it's just that the longer you've been in the business, the more people you know. There's a slightly greater chance that you know somebody who will introduce you to someone else.

●●●

ROCLIFFE NOTES on...

NETWORKING

- Have a strategy or game plan. Start with who you know – can they introduce you to anyone else? No one is obliged to make introductions for you and they may feel that that would be abusing another friendship. Don't have the expectation that anyone owes you anything, because they don't.

- The internet is your best friend. In fact, it's filled with friends and has lots about writing, written by writers, so get online. Network without even leaving your bed – write a blog, tweet, Facebook – get your name about online, be witty, proffer answers to people's questions. Get chatting – be plucky, get talking!

- Film events are also great for meeting with producers/directors who may be looking for a particular type of script. Ask them what they are looking for. Attend film, TV or writers' conferences – if you want an excuse to talk to the people sitting next to you, ask them what they've seen or are looking forward to seeing or where did they hear of this event?

- Volunteer to work at a film festival or event or organisation – it's a great way to get the inside track on what's going on and meet other people.

- Don't bombard people when approaching them or pitch at them. At the initial meeting, tell them why you wanted to meet them and ask if they would have a coffee with you at a time and location convenient to them.

- When meeting people, know your script and sum it up in one line, not twenty. Don't use this as an excuse to bombard the person with long, rambling pitches. Give them enough to want to read the script, not spoil it.

- Be clear about what you want from a meeting – is it representation, feedback, advice, introductions, or to solicit someone to work with you? Have a clear objective.

- Before meeting, do your homework. Watch some of the projects they've worked on. With every event or meeting you go to, you need to prepare yourself.

- Make a list of questions to ask: how did you get into this business? Who helped you most when you started out? What would you do differently now? What attracts you to a project? Most people are more comfortable talking about what they know, so get them to talk about their experiences. And don't forget to breathe as you ask questions.

- Be more than one screenplay. Maximise your portfolio by having a body of work, each of which you can sum up in a line.

- Have business cards with your email, mobile number, Twitter handle, etc., and carry them with you. A chance encounter with an exec or producer can change your life.

- When you meet someone, follow up in writing within a few days so you can't be forgotten. The worst that can happen is that they don't respond.

- Once you've bonded with someone, you can ask them to mentor you – a good mentor can teach you so much just by sharing their experiences. They don't necessarily give you script notes but can guide you.

•••

WRITERS AND DIRECTORS ON NETWORKING

Every writer and director may have started out by getting a meeting with a producer or development exec, but they had to follow up with a compelling script or cracking short film that the prospect couldn't take their eyes off. Charm may get your script read once, or your film watched, but it's your work that will get you more work and seal the deal – if your work is genuinely good.

SARAH GAVRON: In my experience it won't get you the gig as a director – your work will – but it *will* help. Following leads is always worth doing. The people you meet in this industry, through networking, often spark ideas or bring you ideas. Forming creative relationships is so important.

REBECCA DALY: The industry in Ireland is small and most of my career is based here. My opinion is that the work should speak for itself. Obviously you have to make connections with people, as you have to get your film into the right hands. I'm not a big networker, though.

I identify people I'd like to work with based on whether they do interesting work and their approach to their work.

LUCY CLARKE: I'm rubbish at networking so, no, I have no advice! It's hard to go to events, go to the pub with producers, etc., when you have two small kids and a husband who works abroad a lot. And a mortal fear of Twitter.

GARETH EDWARDS: When I was trying to get a job, I went round and trailed a lot of people and talked to them to get an understanding of what was going on, rather than making sure people knew who I was. It's more important to learn to learn than to network. It's much more important to watch and listen to programmes and find out what's going on in the comedy world. Whenever I go to something network-y, I grieve for my self-respect afterwards. It's better to be judged by what you've done than who you've chatted to. I appreciate, too, that this is easy for me to say as someone who is established.

SIMON HEATH: Networking isn't very important. Good writing speaks for itself.

DESTINY EKARAGHA: I'm not the best when it comes to networking. The temptation to just stand in one corner nodding and smiling can be huge sometimes. Don't do that! Talk to as many people as you can and really listen to what they're saying. Can they help you get your film made? For example, if you're there as a writer and you get talking to another writer that's good. Meeting like-minded people isn't a bad thing but remember that you are there to work. As a writer, ideally you should be looking for directors and producers; you should be looking for the team that will help to get your film made. Collect business cards and stay in contact with all the wonderful people that you've met. Also, this goes without saying but, although the drink is usually free, that's no reason to get drunk. This is a working environment, so pace yourself. Eat the canapés instead.

KATE LEYS: I'm terrible at parties. So I don't go to very many and I catch up with people over coffee or food instead.

MALCOLM CAMPBELL: I'm not great at networking, never have been. If you are not established, it's useful. It's also important to learn how to talk about your ideas and your writing style. Not just for meetings. There are more and more writers' rooms cropping up and you spend a lot of time talking about character arcs and hooks, pretty much every stage of the development process. You can't get away with being the introverted, tortured writer in those scenarios. You have to be able to pitch and defend your ideas, but be prepared to let them go. Rooms can be pretty unforgiving. The best ones work when you have a mix of writers who listen, who aren't precious, and who will contribute knowing their suggestions might be thrown out, because, ultimately, it's about the show, not your ego.

KIRSTEN SHERIDAN: I used to think networking was simply absolute arse kissing. I really did. I used to think it was the horrible adjectives that you associate with networking. That's what I thought it was and I used to cringe at the thought of it. Now that I've got a bit older, there's an element of that, but I don't think that's the element people like. People do recoil from that, even when they're on the receiving end. Networking now to me is simply about personality and, if you can be yourself within that, that's the only currency you have. If you're trying to be someone else and you keep speaking with someone else's voice (like if you're being too polite), people will smell it a mile away. I don't think of networking as a bad thing now at all, but you have to be very careful that what you're presenting is yourself, however that may be.

KEVIN CECIL: I like people and it's nice to work with people and then even become friends with them, but I've never been that hot at introducing myself to strangers. I've never been part of a private members' club. I joined BAFTA but that doesn't mean you can go hassle the stars. More important than networking is probably being

335

civil to those you meet along the way. My advice would be to have respect for the people around you and everyone you meet, because some of these people will end up becoming famous and successful.

MIRANDA BOWEN: I've never really done it! Not even sure how you would go about it. I personally feel an inherent horror at the idea of standing around with a warm glass of Pinot Grigio, a garish grin plastered across my face, trying to make small talk with people that could potentially wield a lot of power over my career. I am probably quite archaic in my approach, especially in a world where networking and social media are the order of the day, and I'm sure it works very well for a lot of people, but I feel that the work is what speaks loudest. No matter how good you are at networking, it's not going to make you a better writer or director. It may give you more opportunities, but ultimately the buck stops with the work.

SUSAN JACOBSON: Networking is important. Everyone moans about how they 'hate networking' but it just takes practice. And when you understand that everyone in the room is doing it, it's not so bad and can actually be quite fun.

DAVID SIMPATICO: I try to remember that I have something the other person wants: talent. It's important to remind yourself of that when you start to talk yourself into imminent disaster in the five minutes before going into the room. I try to know about the people I'm meeting, the work they've done, and the writers they like. I try to stop talking once I start. I always accept coffee, when offered. I try to find a common ground. Sometimes my unfettered opinions get me into trouble, but more often than not I find I am able to maintain an adult business conversation when the need arises. Though I do find myself sitting perched on the tops of couches by the end of meetings.

JON CROKER: It's horrific – like being a teenager all over again where you'd think you were at the wrong party and that everyone else in the room was more successful at life than you. Fortunately, God invented smartphones so now you can pretend you have to write an important email when there's nobody to talk to.

DANNY BROCKLEHURST: It's not something I feel comfortable doing but I can do it. It should feel organic. You naturally click with some people and others you will never feel right about. In the end, you should only work with people you feel are on your wavelength and those whose notes you respond well to. One thing I've learned is that if you don't like them to begin with it will only get worse, and any time I've not trusted someone I've gone on to work with it's come back to haunt me.

SETTING UP A TABLE READ

Writing can be a very solitary thing as so much of what we do exists solely in our heads. So, when we write, it's important that we capture all the dimensions of our imaginary characters in the written word and get what's inside our minds onto the page. One of the best ways to see if we have achieved this is to listen to other people read our work aloud. It gives a distance and a value to each voice, in a way that reading it aloud by yourself cannot. For a writer, it's really important to hear how the reading sounds.

For many a wordsmith, the first time their script comes alive is magical. It's also a very, very useful tool. Intimate table reads give an understanding of how the script is working. It's easy to tell if the characters have come alive. Did it make sense? Are too many characters saying the same thing? Getting feedback from actors is also helpful and can feed into the development process. I recommend that a writer or writer-director not take part in the reading, but instead listen and make notes.

I would always recommend doing a table read before casting the script. It doesn't matter if the script is a short, feature, sitcom or

TV drama, hearing the work read aloud will be of enormous value and undoubtedly improve the script.

....

ROCLIFFE NOTES on...

SETTING UP A TABLE READ

- Use the first table read as a development tool rather than a selling tool. Think of it as a spring clean – and would you invite people to watch you clean up? Probably not, but you can ask people to help you out. I would advise keeping the first reading very simple – actors, writer, director and producer and one or two trusted writer friends.

- Casting actors can seem like the most daunting task to begin with, so start with who you know. Do you know any actors? Do your friends know any actors? Ask the actors you know if they know other actors. You can also advertise for actors on Shooting People and PCR, or call drama schools and ring agents, giving them a cast breakdown. Be honest with actors and agents that this is a table reading to help with the development of the script and you would like the feedback of the actors. I would advise you not to promise anyone a role yet, as it's very early days. What if that role gets cut? That said, be appreciative of what an actor is bringing to the reading.

- Divide up the roles in advance and send the script to the performers so they know what roles they are reading. Assign a strong actor the role of reading the narration – they will drive the energy. Ask them to read it in a normal voice, without affectation, but to keep the energy up. Don't worry about casting people who don't physically fit the roles; instead, cast an actor who can bring out the personality and emotional depth.

- Send the script by email to each actor with a list of the parts they are playing. Rocliffe recommends using no more than 6–8 actors including the narrator – who only reads the stage directions/action, etc., and scene changes. If there's a clear protagonist and a clear antagonist then assign one actor each of these roles. Use two male and two female actors, younger and older, and assign each of the roles accordingly – older female, younger female and double up.

- Find a quiet, well-lit room. Pubs with music don't tend to work; however, many central pubs have quiet space and will give you the room. Make the location central for everyone, not just central to you. Give clear instructions as to the time and place and ask them to come 15 minutes early. Organise the reading at least four days in advance and confirm details before the day. You can use your home as long as it has room to accommodate everyone.

- Make sure to provide water, coffee and tea, as reading can be thirsty work. I would also suggest sweets of some kind – chocolate dries up the throat but boiled sweets can help lubricate the voice. Also supply highlighter and pencil/pens.

- Print out single or double-sided copies for the actors and bind them with ACCO clips so the pages will stay together. You will need a copy of the script for each of the actors reading and one for yourself. You can email these to them in advance, but don't expect actors to print their own copies and have to share. There's no need to print off pricey copies for anyone other than the writer, director and producers.

- For the first ever table read, the script should be read aloud by actors in a single sitting, i.e. without interruption. Don't stop to give notes or acting pointers during the reading. Make notes throughout. Be polite, not bossy – they are there to help you.

- Should you wish to record the reading, always ask the actors in advance if you can do so. This should only be used for your purposes to listen again. Don't distribute this recording as a selling tool.

- Discuss the script with the actors. Ask them what their thoughts are on the characters. They may feel a character is too thin, needs more backstory; were the goals, needs, wants of each character clear enough? Does each character have an arc or disappear? Do they feel the characters are thought through enough or under or overwritten? Write down all the notes you get. Thank the actors in person and then send a follow-up thank you in writing (by email). In the email, invite them to share with you any thoughts that have occurred to them since.

- Write up your notes that evening or the next morning while they are still fresh and make revisions immediately while you are still fired up.

FILMMAKERS ON WRITERS' GROUPS

What can I say? There would be no book, no BAFTA Rocliffe, if, in 2000, a group of people hadn't gathered above a pub in Islington, London and started to read and discuss the work of new writers. Nine people turned up to the first meeting (mostly friends of mine), but I kept it going. Three weeks later 30 people turned up, and then 40, and it grew. Soon directors and producers joined in.

STEPHEN FINGLETON: Form writing groups with your peers. When I was starting out I was a vociferous reader and many of my friends in the industry today come from the connections we formed through reading each other's work.

JOSH APPIGNANESI: I have writer friends whose work I love to read, even just to give notes or whatever.

NOTES ON DIFFERENT WRITERS' GROUPS

Eoin Rogers is an Irish writer who has won awards in international competitions such as Story Pros, the PAGE Awards, and the JDIFF pitching contest. He is also a story consultant for brands such as Unilever and Nokia. He studied at the New York Film Academy. I first met him when working on a short film by Oscar nominee Ruairi Robinson. Eoin is a keen supporter of writers' groups wherever he goes. Eoin gave me his thoughts on the different formats he's tried:

In New York City, I responded to an ad to join a group. There were two rounds of interviews (this is New York, after all!), so I had high expectations of the quality of the writers. Unfortunately, they seemed more interested in talking than writing. Their format involved members emailing their feature or pilot scripts beforehand to the group, and then we would meet and discuss every fortnight. This format is ideal if everyone is relatively experienced and dedicated. But that wasn't the case here and I found that people didn't take the time to read the full script, didn't show up because it wasn't their script that round, or else that new drafts of old scripts were simply being revisited by the group again and again (which shows how much they needed new members, stymied unfortunately by their high application criteria). There was a lot of navel-gazing. I left that group pretty fast.

In Dublin, there were two groups meeting once a month, which used a space provided by the Irish Writers Guild. In my beginner's enthusiasm I joined both and it made for an interesting comparison. They had the same format. Every month, two to three members of maybe six regulars would each bring a short script, some scenes, a pitch, or ten pages of a feature. We would then read the work quietly to ourselves and then we would go around the room for feedback. This approach means more people get their work read more often. Not having to prepare notes beforehand meant that more people showed up, but the notes would often be first impressions only and not very thorough. This format did not suit features as they could only be read in a piecemeal fashion. Instead, members would offer to read each other's feature scripts outside of the group for individual feedback. The first of these two groups was a beginners' group that unfortunately had a single disruptive personality who drove at least one sensitive writer away. The other group had a great balance of backgrounds, genres and gender. Like most groups, after a year or two, some of the writers became too busy to attend and fresh blood was needed. This changed the dynamic again. Both groups had maybe 8–14 members, with 5–10 attending at any one meeting. If ten attended, it could take too long to go around for everyone's feedback and we wouldn't cover more than one or two people's works.

A London group that I still attend has yet another format. They invite actors and perform table readings. The work is emailed to the actors beforehand and handed out as hard copies to them on the day. This group has maybe 30–50 members with 10–25 showing up at any one time. It's invaluable to hear your dialogue brought to life by actors and how they choose to interpret your words, for both good and bad (sometimes these are cold readings). Narration is read by an actor (best for the writer to be making notes). Genres like horror or action can be tricky because they're heavy on narration, which is never supposed to be heard, and long action scenes can seem interminable if badly written. This type of group really suits very developed work, especially where the writer wants to polish dialogue. I should mention that the founder is a no-nonsense chairperson and sets the tone by assuming that professionals need unflinchingly honest critiques and not pats on the back. So this format isn't for rough drafts – as I have learned to my cost! One downside to a very large group is a risk of herd mentality. Even if the chair tries to pick only those whose hands are raised, people can end up chiming in together and reinforcing one another's opinions so that a minority with alternative opinions refrain from commenting

(I know this because people often come to you afterwards). Also, sometimes the actors outnumber the writers, which skewers the type of feedback you get (not good or bad, just different). Like any notes, you have to weigh the experience of the reader, where they are coming from and not be swayed unless there's a general consensus (and sometimes not even then). Directors and guest speakers occasionally attend this group.

When I was living in the west of Ireland and in Kent, three small but long-running groups I joined had the same format, but were very different in terms of suitability for me personally. I write genre screenplays for cinema and TV. Most writers know narrative and I appreciate that all opinions are equally, if subjectively, valid as your first potential audience members. But in my experience, writers' groups with too many arty poets, 'serious' drama novelists, hobbyist housewives and dabbling retirees will struggle to give feedback on horror, sci-fi or fantasy scripts. And, equally, I am often at a loss when it comes to giving great insight into their haikus, prose and flash fiction. When I was starting off, I loved the range of age and different dramatic forms in groups. But now I only want to work with long-form storytellers, ideally screenwriters or playwrights. It's simply more efficient in terms of my time and theirs. Call me a snob, but there it is.

Overall, the different formats of writers' groups depend on where you are with your writing (join the most experienced group you can) and the (hopefully professional) approach of its members and (ideally ego-less) chairperson. Generosity of notes and openness to criticism is key. There's always someone further along the career path than you, and you can always be that person to someone else.

SETTING UP A WRITERS' GROUP

Before the BAFTA Rocliffe New Writing Forums became the showcase they are today, they started with a posting on Shooting People as simply the 'Rocliffe New Writing Forum'. I was searching for work and material to perform and finding it a very solitary task. I wanted to meet other writers and actors. My goal was to bring people together to read, discuss scripts and work collectively. I found the networking afterwards just as enlightening as the read-through.

It opened doors to an underground network of filmmakers and opportunities that I didn't know existed. Everyone was hungry for information, fresh material, a network and a safe haven for feedback. We grew to 100 people – all squished together above a pub in Islington – so I started a booking system. We kept it casual but structured and it grew with feedback. In 2001, I asked some amazing execs to come along and share their thoughts on the scripts. Our first guest was Ollie Madden followed by Ed King, Nik Powell and Michael Kuhn. Their insight and understanding of how the industry worked was so useful – this was new to us. Suddenly this world seemed accessible.

These days Rocliffe is run in partnership with BAFTA and is a very polished event, but its heart and soul still retain the spirit of that pub in Islington. The forums have a wonderful energy to them – they validate your opinion, open your mind to how the industry thinks and are a shared common experience. It's encouraging to hear other people's work and give them feedback. For us all, it's an opportunity to get away from the solitude of working alone – which is exactly what writing can be. More than a decade after their inception the fundamental structure remains the same – a ten-page extract is performed by actors after a few hours' rehearsal with a seasoned director. An industry guest gives feedback about the projects to each writer. The evening is rounded off with networking and mingling in the bar.

Sharing opportunities and interacting is essential. So is the feedback you give and receive. I can think of no better way to achieve this than by setting up your own script-reading group by distributing scripts, reading them and giving fellow writers feedback. I had no idea what a commitment Rocliffe would become (it's probably been my longest relationship) but it's a great buzz getting people together and seeing them make connections.

••

ROCLIFFE NOTES on...
SETTING UP A WRITERS' GROUP

- Set realistic goals of meeting once a month on a particular night. Be consistent. Early weekday nights suit most people, e.g. Tuesdays or Wednesdays. People ask about running them weekly or every two weeks but, from first-hand experience, enthusiasm tends to burn down and people will drop out. It's a huge undertaking and commitment.

- Invite a specific number of participants – 6–10 people keeps things tidy. This allows for dropouts (life happens), but also everyone gets a fair crack at receiving feedback. Appoint a different leader each time who is responsible for organising that particular meeting.

- Ask writers you know but also widen the net to include others you don't. Put a posting on Shooting People, tweet using the hashtag 'scriptchat', ask the Writers' Guild and BBC Writersroom to RT to their mailing lists, Facebook and other social media outlets to attract other writers.

- Let the group decide etiquette and goals and be clear about these from day one. Group dynamics can be extremely powerful. Everyone should know how to give and receive feedback and what is acceptable and what isn't – the last thing you want is to kill someone's creativity and confidence.

- Do you read the script in advance or on the night? Focus on one or two scripts each meeting? You should rotate who gets their material read. There has to be give and take. Different people should have turns at getting feedback and giving feedback. Everyone should have an opportunity. Create a timetable and rules.

- Reading scripts on the night will restrict your time. Decide on the structure of the evening – how much time will be given to each script and how much time each person should spend giving feedback. I would recommend no more than four minutes of airtime per person or, if a general discussion, keep it to 30–40 minutes per script per evening.

- Use the writers' group to create goals and deadlines such as deciding everyone will write a five-minute short film which will be circulated in advance or read on the night and given feedback, or a one-page treatment for a film or TV idea. Graduate to feature films.

- Set targets so everyone knows when they have to circulate a script and when they need to have read it by. Use the meeting to share knowledge about competitions and schemes.

- Venue is crucial. Pubs and coffee shops will be up for the business you will bring them. Try a local museum café. In London I recommend the British Library or the British Museum cafés. Keep it centrally located and not just central to you. Avoid using people's houses as it's better to be on neutral territory.

- After the meeting, whoever is the leader should send out an email to everyone who attended so they can keep in touch. You shouldn't be afraid to go out once in a while and a writers' group is a great focus point for a writer.

••

WRITING A BLOG

Write a blog! It can be about any subject or topic that interests you and can be easily set up using something like Blogspot or Tumblr. Stick to a pattern – weekly, fortnightly or monthly – and then tell people about it. Encourage others to comment. Don't let your blog get in the way of your script writing. It should complement your work, not distract you from it. Follow other blogs: Stephen Fry, Lucy V Hay, Ben Blaine's blog on Shooting People.

My first blog in 2011 documented my training to run ten kilometres for a charity for Libya. It was a testament to my utter dislike of running, while raising awareness of what was going on in Libya. My second blog led to this book, as I recognised the need and desire for information on writing, directing and producing. Blogs can be great attention pads.

Kayleigh Llewellyn, now a rising star in the world of comedy writing, writes the blog sensation 'My So Called Life in a Box', which had 120,000 hits in its first week and averages about a 1,000 hits per day. I therefore couldn't think of anyone better to write this section of the book.

KAYLEIGH LLEWELLYN: I wanted an opportunity to establish my voice as a comedy writer, and a blog seemed like a quick and accessible way of doing that. You're not waiting around hoping that a broadcaster will produce one of your shows. Instead you can just be creative in the exact way you choose, when you choose to do it, and launch it for public consumption – which is so refreshing compared to the rest of the world of writing. The blog has landed me work writing for *Glamour* magazine, and as a regular panellist on *Not The One Show* for London Live. A book agent also approached me and I am currently developing the blog as a book.

Although it hasn't directly contributed to my work as a writer of TV comedy as of yet, it has definitely raised my profile – which is always useful. Also, working on the blog daily is just a really beneficial way of constantly honing my craft. It also helps that various influential people within the industry are able to read it and get an instant feel for my comic style, without having to meet me or a read a lengthy 30-page script.

In general, if something is well written and interesting, there's always going to be a place for it in the market. There are two things, I think, that led to the success of my specific blog. The first is it focuses on the woes of working within the customer service sector, which is something that people all over the world can relate to, and therefore gives it a mass appeal. The second is that, by the time I began writing the blog, I'd already been documenting my experiences at work for six years, which meant that I had a huge wealth of material to plunder. I launched the blog with around 200 posts already featured, and have continued to update it around 3–5 times per week since then – so there was loads for people to sink their teeth into from the start, and a reason for them to keep checking back regularly. If you launch your blog with just one post, on the other hand, and then perhaps only update it once or twice a month, it may be harder to capture people's interest and keep them returning, which of course is what you need to boost your hit rates.

EXERCISES TO ENERGISE YOUR SCRIPTS AND KILL WRITER'S BLOCK

Finding yourself blocked creatively, unable to get into the writing flow or feeling stuck, can be a writer's nightmare. It's easy to lose focus and then question whether this is something you should be doing as a career. Some people call this writer's block.

When faced with a writing block, don't abandon writing. The one thing that separates those who succeed from those who fail is simply not giving up. Should none of these exercises work, put the script away and come back to it in a week or more. Never give up the dream – and if all else fails, take a new story, like a fairy tale, and give it a modern twist just to do something a bit different. Commit to a career, not a screenplay.

Sometimes it's simply our approach that hampers us: we've been so conditioned to think a certain way that, as adults, writing may seem like a chore. One of the best courses I attended for really learning to expand your mind creatively was the Writers' Gym. It really tackles creative blocks. Ellis Freeman is a superb teacher and writer and I can't praise the course highly enough.

MOIRA BUFFINI: I've had it twice, both times because of exhaustion. If you have that, you must not write until the exhaustion recedes. You have to let yourself off the hook. When you are working so much, you can just fall off the edge of the cliff. You haven't noticed that when you pour ideas and work out, out, out without putting anything back in that you will dry up. I have got better at spotting the signs and managing my workload.

SUSIE CONKLIN: I don't know any writer who doesn't get stuck at some point. In my case I tend to dance around a project a bit at the beginning. I'll delve into research, which I love to do, but I have to police myself and make sure I'm not putting off the actual writing. I think it's natural to feel a twinge of self-doubt at the start – am I an imposter to think I can do this? You need to find ways to shut that voice out. But sometimes you're blocked because of a specific problem and it's worth doing a little detective work – is it that you're unsure about the story, or a particular character? Have you been given notes that you don't understand? If you can pinpoint the area of difficulty, you can often work your way out of it, or ask for help. Sometimes I just need a conversation with my script editor or producer and the knot will untie itself.

PAULA MILNE: People have writer's block because they confuse the activity of writing with writing. In fact, above my desk is a sign: 'Don't confuse the activity of writing with writing.' Writing is thinking. Writing is walking around the local park spending half the day on just naming your characters and getting a purchase on them. Thinking what it's about, determining the tone and structure. It's only if you haven't done those things, if you haven't done the thinking and the groundwork, that you get the block.

....

ROCLIFFE NOTES on...
WRITER'S BLOCK

People often ask me what they can do to make their work fresher, more original, less predictable. There's honestly no magic formula to freeing up a script, but exercises help writers to think a little differently about how they are approaching an idea or thread. I can honestly say that, for me, these exercises make the work richer and deeper. I've learned them through reading and attending courses like the Writers' Gym and, over time, have adapted them to fit in with what I am doing on my own courses to alleviate the helplessness that new writers often feel. No one says writing is easy, but if you try these it can add a bit of fun to the process.

- Write a one-page outline of the story using the following format – 100 words or less on the beginning, 300 words for the middle and 100 words on the resolution. If this doesn't work for you, try using the 12 steps laid out in *The Writer's Journey* by Christopher Vogler.

- Change the protagonist and point of view of the story in the treatment. Telling a story from a different perspective or viewpoint can create a fresher outlook or original take on a familiar story. The power of a word, be it a pronoun or the gender, can remarkably change the landscape of the story.

- When reading it back, ask what you need to add or take away. It's great to see how the emotional interactions of the characters change, and also how you will have piqued the interest of a reader.

- Try to imagine what would happen if you did something different with each character after each act. What if they did this... what if they did that... what if a meteor landed... what if they reacted this way instead of the way they do... what if the murderer is actually a figment of his imagination? List a number of potential scenarios. Only allow yourself ten minutes to do this and incorporate these ideas into your script.

- Explore the backstory of the protagonist and antagonist before the script begins – it only needs to be one page, or ten minutes of writing. Now incorporate that into the script.

- Spend ten minutes writing what happens to the protagonist and antagonist when the script finishes. Have they changed much or enough?

- Write down any emotions your characters are experiencing in the script, and then write a minimum of five actions that convey that emotion. Emotional actions are great because they describe what the character is feeling or internalising. Think about how you can convey the emotion using the emotional state of the character and their point of view on what is happening, without ever telling the reader what the emotional state is or what has motivated it.

- List ten adjectives to describe the character traits of your protagonist; then, on the same page, list adjectives which are the complete opposite to create an antagonist or antagonistic forces. Do your characters adhere to these character traits and how do they influence the plot?

- Sometimes the mere thought of writing can be isolating so tweet out a #writingsprint to see if any others out there in the world want to write with you. There's no time limit or bad time to call it and it makes you feel less isolated.

- One of the great joys of writing is the time you can justifiably spend researching. You can watch documentaries, contact charities that deal with issues in your script, interview people, do a web search on the subject matter, watch similar films or films in that genre. Go do some research!

- Rewrite some scenes without dialogue. How much visual imagery or emotional action can you create without words? Can you use sound and colour to capture what is going on?

•••

CREATIVE AIDS

I keep a list of things to do to focus me, beyond caffeine and deactivating Facebook. I also play classical music and have my computer tell me when the hour is changing so I don't let the day run away with itself.

OL PARKER: There's a brilliant programme, which I'd recommend to anyone, called Freedom, which turns off the internet on your computer for a period of time. It's extraordinary. You work and write for ten minutes, and then you think, 'That's good; now I'll go on the internet,' but you can't, so you just go back to work. So I use that, but not as often as I should.

JULIETTE TOWHIDI: I use music. I find theme tracks for each project and play the same pieces over and over, so when I sit down in the morning it's like a Pavlov's dog reaction – it gets me into the world much quicker. Also, I use scene cards, and leave the actual writing till as late on in the process as possible. Planning is all, I believe. I know writers differ on this. But I can't start a script without knowing where and how I'm going to end it.

LUCY CLARKE: I draw up a list of five chores I need to do first thing in the morning, then once I've got those five mundane tasks done I find it easier to focus my head on writing. Also, writing down tasks that I need to do as soon as I think of them helps, otherwise they just swirl about in my head, getting in the way. I find it hard to compartmentalise my life when even my study ends up invaded by toys and laundry.

TINA GHARAVI: Listening to music for the scenes and playing it over and over. I also bring this music into rehearsals or readings with actors. I lock myself away for a concentrated period – an intense writing session for two weeks to write that first draft. At that time I block everything else out. I barely leave the room (and room service here is key). I immerse myself entirely.

KATE OGBORN: I'm a big fan of doing scene breakdowns, just as a way of tracking changes across the script. You literally take the script and break down each scene into a couple of sentences. I've used that in the past as a way of doing notes, so you can see from one draft to another how to move around scenes and what's changed. It's a tool that makes having those practical conversations easier.

REBECCA DALY: I do listen to music when I write, mostly classical/ instrumental; lyrics confuse me when I'm writing. Also I switch the music off every once in a while as, especially if it has a strong feeling, it can lend the writing a feeling that it doesn't actually have itself, which can be dangerous.

JAMES DORMER: Reading non-fiction or fiction, watching documentaries or programmes about that kind of thing for research purposes. That's where you tend to get the freshness and the things you couldn't make up, that give a reality to the story.

SALLY EL HOSAINI: I really love OmmWriter. It's free writing software that you can download. It makes writing on a computer a beautiful, creative experience. It has different backgrounds you can use, gentle acoustics to inspire you and the most satisfying clicks ever as you type. Or if silence is your thing you can disable all that stuff. I love it.

CLAIRE WILSON: I have Mac Freedom, an internet blocker which is my saving grace. A clear diary means a clear mind, so I try not to book anything in advance.

WHAT CAN THE DIGITAL AGE DO FOR WRITERS?

It's changed everything, from the way we make films to how we distribute them. Not only can you shoot a film on your phone, you can write one on it too!

DAVID FLYNN: The interesting thing that digital media has allowed, in a way which was never the case when I was entering the industry, is that there's no real excuse for not having done anything now. It's an easy way to start testing your ideas on an audience for real. Getting out there, using YouTube and all the different tools available and seeing what does and doesn't work is something that this generation can do, that nobody's been able to do in the same way in the past.

BEN STEPHENSON: The diversity of channels means that there's probably a greater range of drama. That's certainly more the case in America as there's more money there. Ultimately I think the thing that audiences want is good-quality drama, and that is inevitably going to come from relatively well-funded organisations. The method of then delivering it to the audience will depend on numerous factors. What's innovative about Netflix is the way that they distribute their programmes, not necessarily the programmes they make per se. It's all about a means of delivering it that's more convenient for audiences. I don't believe it fundamentally changes the types of dramas that are made.

STEPHEN FINGLETON: Vimeo Staff Picks is more important than winning a major award. If you want to break into Hollywood, online is really the only way. They couldn't give a rat's ass if you screened at the Berlinale – you want people to Google your name and have your best work ready. They don't have five minutes to email you for a password-protected link.

GARETH EDWARDS: I met an actor at an audition, and he said he'd done an online sitcom and I watched it and a project has grown out of that. It was very funny, made me laugh. I've made a few things out of watching things on YouTube and stuff like that.

IVANA MACKINNON: It allows people an audience they might not otherwise have – you can make a film and upload it and get feedback, which is amazing. You can also see where in the world people respond best to your style, which is important metadata. There are more opportunities to get things made, but equally the digital revolution has destroyed the supply chain so everything has to be made cheaper, and the micro-budget economy of filmmaking is a worrying and unsustainable development.

ANDREA CORNWELL: The digital medium has changed things; it has been partially responsible for a big shift in attitude towards filmmaking for the worse. What type of camera you use is really neither here nor there when it comes to telling a story, yet it's used to drive all kinds of major decisions about the number of weeks that you shoot and the level of budget that all departments get. It's really tough. A low-budget film when I started out was considered to be one that had cost about £2–3 million. Obviously, these days we've got publically funded schemes to make films for around £100,000 – that would have been a short-film budget when I started, not one for a feature film. That's a real problem, because while certain sorts of voices thrive in those very low-budget worlds, others very much don't. Unfortunately it's not a trend that is going to reverse.

SHANE ALLEN: It's accelerated the process because, years ago, you would wait for someone to do an Edinburgh show or you'd have to schlep to some dingy pub in Camden to see them. That was mostly stand-up focused because you know a lot of the programmes that followed were vehicles for stand-ups. Whereas now, with the internet, you've got people who don't want, or haven't got the nerve, to do stand-up. Writers don't tend to be the most confident people, and now there are ways for people to articulate and express themselves that don't involve the live comedy circuit, so you can make parody videos or animations or short pieces of sketch work, and that's a great way to get discovered because you can reach so many people, so quickly. Someone like Terry Mynott as a performer: he posted himself doing impressions on the internet and an agent got in touch with him, and then from there a producer worked with him to come up with the show *The Mimic*, which ended up on Channel 4 and is coming up for a second series. It's just a brilliant way to get access; you get instantly into a producer's inbox or a commissioner's inbox and it's all on merit. It opens doors in a kind of much more egalitarian way than the old-fashioned method of having to put on a show or write a whole script for somebody's in-tray, which may then sit there for a while.

UNDERSTANDING THE DIGITAL CONTENT LANDSCAPE

I believe writers and writer-directors today need to know how to use the digital content landscape to their advantage. There have never been as many opportunities for writers. If you think about it, 50 per cent of the internet is made of text. You can't ignore digital content. It's everywhere and, thanks to the internet, is more accessible than ever via sharing on websites, emails and on social media.

When I was younger I used to write short stories, enter competitions and then look at the *Writer's Annual Year Book* to see where I could send them. I had more rejection letters than anything else but it didn't deter me. I had to write. In college, we the journalism students ran a magazine-style radio show at lunchtimes. That's where I discovered things are scripted. One of my favourite things we did was record interesting news items, features and a TV and radio guide for the blind. I later worked for a national newspaper and then moved to Paris where I worked on English-language magazines that were handed out for free in the Metro. I was young and carefree with a day job, and so had plenty of scope to find my voice and my own style, learning the craft as I went along. It was great to see my name in print, even though I worked for free. Those opportunities still exist but today it's a very different landscape to the 1990s.

At the 2013 final of the MSN Short-Form Storytellers Challenge at the New York TV Festival, new creators submitted a two-minute pilot for a $75,000 commission, there were five finalists and everything from sketch-show to gadget-show formats. I learned that content draws clicks and that means marketing. More and more companies are looking for alternative ways to place their brands, particularly since ad blockers are costing millions in lost advertising revenue, so much so that Google has paid Adblock to put its adverts on the 'white list'.

The way we look at content, from the Netflix model of binge show watching, to six-part, two-minute web series, has changed. We can now click from phone, tablet and computer to TV. This is the age of transmedia – storytelling across a wide platform on many different outlets.

I don't believe it has ever been a more exciting time to be a writer and filmmaker. All these channels are looking for content, but one thing is for certain – the web is a writer's and performer's medium. You are able to make your work accessible more instantaneously and, if you get it right, it can be a great showcase.

• •

ROCLIFFE NOTES on...
DIFFERENT ONLINE CONTENT OUTLETS

It's never been cheaper to send things out into the world. We can email our scripts, make our submissions online, but there are other ways of getting our voice and our work out there:

- We Transfer It, Dropbox, Google Docs – all these are about sharing information.

- Virals and web series – these can be anything from fully developed 50-minute episodes to the preferred model of two minutes.

- Tweets – producers and executives are looking at tweets for comedy one-liners. It's a great way to show how clever and funny you can be within the parameters of 140 characters.

- Short films – drama has never looked so good.

- Blog posts – sharing an open opinion.

- Images – pictures are a powerful medium.

- Authonomy – posting books.

- Podcasts.

- Ebooks.

- Journalism – comments sections on news sites, contributor-led sites, etc.

- Tumblr.
- Instagram.
- Pinterest.

••

HAVING AN ONLINE PRESENCE

Social media is all about interaction and engagement so it's as much about recognising other people's comments as it is contributing your own points. For example, tweeting and retweeting people will make others take an interest and follow you back as a result. It is constantly changing so this info will be outdated soon.

Sharing helpful information is a good way to get yourself noticed and could be the means of an introduction to someone useful.

Get onto mailing lists. There are fantastic newsletters which list events, competitions, training, and general opportunities that you may not have known about! I recommend BAFTA, BFI, BBC Writersroom, Creative England, IFB, Skillset and BLAPS (Channel 4's online comedy vehicle) to start with. There are also some great regional ones, e.g. Film London, Northern Ireland Screen, Creative Scotland, Film Agency Wales. Every region wants to tell you what they are up to. Know what's going on in your neck of the woods!

You can build communities really quickly but, like everything worthwhile, it takes time and effort, so work on developing your network on one channel rather than building up profiles on five. It needs commitment and content on a regular basis:

- Twitter is forever evolving and is one of the best ways to hear about news and opportunities as well as an online resource. My favourite writing-related Twitter accounts to follow are:

@BAFTA
@bbcwritersroom
@TheWritersGuild
@SkillsetSSC
@Deadline
@BANG2Write
@HayleyMckenzie1

- There's also Euro Scriptchat on Twitter, monthly on a Sunday at 8 pm. Using the hashtag #scriptchat you can meet other writers online.

- All the regional agencies (Film London, Northern Ireland Screen, etc.) have mailing lists you can sign up to.

- You can write a blog.

- Facebook pages are great for keeping up with what's going on and there are loads of useful links and discussion topics. Have you 'liked' BAFTA's and Rocliffe's pages?

- Watch online masterclasses and then tweet, post, blog about them – there are thousands. Try BAFTA's Guru site – you can watch things lasting anything from 90 seconds to 30 minutes and it's free.

Protect your online reputation. Don't put people or an organisation down and don't be really rude about them. Social media sites are like standing on a mountain and stabbing a feather pillow on a windy day. You have no idea where those feathers will land. Only tweet or post what you would be happy shouting out in Oxford Circus. Avoid showing your anger about rejection or complaining about a production company, agents or editors. Keep that for discussions with your friends and family!

BEST ADVICE OUR CONTRIBUTORS WERE GIVEN

One of the greatest tools we have is our ability to ask for advice, so I asked our contributors what nuggets of wisdom they've picked up along the way.

ASIF KAPADIA: When I interviewed Ken Loach in 1997, a key moment for me was learning about his process of making films, specifically working with non-professional actors and the idea that non-professionals are suddenly expected to become method actors. He told me it was never going to happen! His view was that you should find people who are the character that you are looking for and be prepared to change the script to fit that person. The same for a great location – don't rebuild a location to fit your script, change the script to fit that great location. It's all about being flexible and making sure you use what is in front of you, rather than spending lots of money changing what you have. You may write something that climaxes in a cathedral but when you go to find the cathedral you may stumble across a beautiful tree. That tree is your cathedral, a natural one. So you change your script to fit with the tree and film there. You don't have to have lots of money to change things that are not key to the story. Know when to be flexible and when not;

know what is the crux of the idea behind why you want to make this film and keep that close to your heart, write it down on top of your computer, on your wall. Remember the reason you want to make this film, what is the something you are not going to compromise on and why. With *Senna* the thing I didn't want to compromise on was talking heads. I just knew that would have broken the spell. Everyone kept saying 'It's a documentary – just go and interview someone!' and that would have been much easier, but we chose the difficult route because I knew it would make it a more special film. Each film has to have that behind it.

MICHAEL KUHN: You should never, ever be convinced by someone else into doing a film that you don't believe in. That is the absolute definite worst thing that a producer, director, financier, creator, editor, actor, anyone can do. Don't do things that you don't believe in or know in your heart that you shouldn't be doing. It's very easy – it's one of the most common traps that people fall into.

CAT VILLIERS: Nothing is impossible – wise and challenging words given to me by the wonderful photographer Norman Parkinson, in my first career as a magazine editor.

BOB BALABAN: I was about to direct my first feature about 30 years ago. I asked Steven Spielberg for advice. He said, 'Wear comfortable shoes,' which was great because it happens to be true. Plus it also reduces directing to something extremely practical and understandable. Coming from the mouth of one of my favourite filmmakers, it suddenly made the whole mysterious process seem doable.

MIA BAYS: Be careful who you are nice to on the way up, as you'll meet them on the way down. And I love a quote from Rudyard Kipling on the creative process. I repeat it often: 'Drift. Wait. Obey.' That's exactly it, so succinct.

SUSIE CONKLIN: I script-edited for Paul Abbott on several projects and he told me that when he'd hit a wall on a particular script, he'd bring up a blank page and start typing hell-bent for leather on something that had popped into his head. It might be some new character that doesn't fit into what he's doing. Or just a scene that was intriguing him. It was great advice – things *do* pop into your head all the time when you're writing. And you tend to ignore them because you're focusing on the current script. But throwing these ideas out there can be really liberating. Sometimes they're the seed of a new story, and sometimes it simply serves to get you unstuck.

DAVID CHIKWE: I remember my mentor at Talkback, Sally Debonnaire, saying 'always gauge the temperature of the room as you enter it'. If you're entering a room, different people will have different agendas, different wants and needs; there will be a whole hierarchy and background that already exists before you come in. What you should do is get the temperature of the room first. I think that is very useful when you're pitching to agents, to commissioners, when you're meeting writers, when you're doing story conferences. In every situation, it's about what's going on in the space that I'm not aware of, and how I slot myself in.

ROBIN GUTCH: Let it go and move on. Lots of people told me that.

DANNY HUSTON: My father, John Huston, asked me what you do when you look from left to right and right to left. I thought about it and then gave up. 'You blink!' he said. 'That's a cut. Don't look at the nonsense in-between and concentrate on what you want to see.' This lesson has been extremely valuable. One can tell an amateur filmmaker because they're filming everything around them, like a tourist in a new city waving the camera around. My father was telling me that, as a filmmaker, we should break things down and choose what we want the audience to see – from the face of the statue, to full length, to the face again. Think about how you tell the story, what you choose to see, how you choose for the observer to see, how you investigate characters – that's the blink. It's the focal point of a cinematic eye.

SIMON HEATH: Producing is like grilling cheese on toast. You stand and watch it for an age and nothing happens. Turn your back for a second and it burns.

JOSH APPIGNANESI: Give up, you're not good enough. That one really got me motivated.

SASKIA SCHUSTER: Only work with people you respect.

SALLY EL HOSAINI: The American indie filmmaker Hal Hartley said, 'Work well, be happy.' I loved it because it reminded me to keep things simple, not to overcomplicate things, and to enjoy the work I was doing. It's hard to remember basic things when you're constantly hustling to get something made or to get a film moving. The film industry is a business and you really have to make things happen and to a certain extent be your own producer. If you're a creative person, like me, and the producing side of things isn't really your strength, you have to force yourself out of your comfort zone and into those areas to learn about the business. When you do that you feel so far away from why you wanted to make films in the first place. This advice reminded me to enjoy my work and that even the struggles are worth it. I feel incredibly privileged to do something that I am so passionate about. Work is my life; it's such simple advice, but it really meant a lot to me.

SHANE ALLEN: To work in a creative industry – be creative! In my early days as commissioner I didn't quite understand the job. I thought that you judged things and that you were the sort of arbiter of what was and wasn't funny, rather than being a catalyst for other people to be creative. Andrew Newman gave me a very helpful piece of advice – that anyone can sit and criticise or slag something off or say why it doesn't work. We're in a creative industry so we need to be the person making everyone step above and creatively be more ambitious. Be nurturing, constructive and encourage people rather than being some kind of voice of doom. That was good advice.

KERRY APPLEYARD: Don't be afraid to pitch in silly ideas. You never know what might work.

OL PARKER: There's a great Anne Lamott book called *Bird by Bird*. She tells the story of when she was a kid and her older brother had a school project on birds that he'd had the entire summer holiday to write. It's due the next day and the entire family are in the kitchen, and her brother is sitting at the table, surrounded by paper and books on birds, just weeping at the enormity of the task ahead. His dad sits down next to him, puts his arm around his shoulders and says, 'Just take it bird by bird, buddy, bird by bird.' That's saved my life many times. It's taught me to try not to think of things as a whole, to take each screenplay scene by scene. One page at a time, and try not to worry about the bigger picture.

JULIETTE TOWHIDI: 'You can't learn writing – you just have to do it, and keep doing it. It's like developing particular muscles. You need to exercise them constantly.' That was from French screenwriter Jean-Claude Carrière when, as a naïve, aspiring writer in my twenties, I rang and asked if I could be his assistant in the hope that some of the magic would rub off.

GUY HIBBERT: I was told by writer James Saunders to 'never be afraid to throw away your best lines and your best scenes'. You've got to get the whole right; you can't be too precious about your work. Keep throwing away and keep rewriting. Keep playing with it.

KEVIN CECIL: Richard Curtis said not to have two character names beginning with the same letter as it makes the script difficult to read. So we never do that. He also said you should have points of real emotion in your script. Obviously, it depends on your script, but we've found that pretty helpful.

KIRSTEN SHERIDAN: The best advice I've had, in a funny way, has come simply from watching my father, Jim Sheridan, on set. He's never given me advice, but watching how he is with actors and crew –

there's absolutely no act on his part. He never had to act the part of director. He is just as open, vulnerable and chaotic as the characters in the story. Being true to that is the most powerful place you can be. Whether you know the answers or not doesn't matter, whether you are 'in charge' doesn't matter, none of that stuff matters. It's just about whether you get to the heart of the story. That's something I learned by osmosis.

PAULA MILNE: Mine came from a painter and nothing to do with the screen. I wasn't taught screenwriting – I learned it. The painter said 'Have a talent for your talent'. He meant create the best arena for your work; as a painter, for example, that means getting your work seen and recognised. So have a talent for your talent, because you have to realise you're engaging with an industry. It's a brutal, tough industry, which is run by not necessarily stupid people, but people who have other concerns than you. You have to be clever and learn how to deal with the industry and recognise your mutual dependence. Whatever your talent is, have a talent for it.

KATE OGBORN: There are three things that people have said to me that really rang true. Tony Grisoni's 'If it feels like homework, don't do it', which is great but doesn't always work for producers, as quite a lot of the things that we do feel like maths homework, but we have to do them anyway. When I started at Revolution, heading up their TV slate, Andrew Eaton said that it was better to have one productive meeting than lots of time-wasting ones. Don't take a scattergun approach – find the person or project that you feel you could really make a difference to. Before I started *The Deep Blue Sea*, Paul Webster advised me that Terence could not compromise. It helped me realise that the filmmaker I was working with had a vision so precise that the notion of compromise was anathema to him. It's not him being difficult – it's that that's the only way he can work and you have to facilitate and support that. Otherwise, you waste time trying to make him work in a way that's completely unnatural.

KAYLEIGH LLEWELLEYN & MATTHEW BARRY: Your career is more than one script (thanks, Farah!). Write realistic dialogue. If you can write in the way that people actually talk, you will already be ahead of 90 per cent of your peers.

CLAIRE WILSON: I read an interview with David Mamet where he said that, if you want to be a writer, you have to 'write, write, write'. It doesn't get simpler than that.

LIZZIE BATES: I found John Yorke's book *Into the Woods* really helpful. He makes it clear why having conflict in every single scene is crucial, and how important it is to bring the audience into a scene in the middle of the action – they should join a scene late and leave early!

TONY COOKE: One producer I worked with always asked 'What would REALLY happen?', and sanity-checking the logic of plots, reactions and jokes is totally worth it. It's so easy to forgive wobbly logic for the sake of something funny, but it can weaken everything.

ANNE-MARIE DRAYCOTT & CHARITY TRIMM: Anne Gilchrist at Tidy Productions said something that remains in the forefront of our minds: 'Make sure your script starts with a bang!'

ADVICE FROM THE CONTRIBUTORS

Quite strange me adding something in here considering this book is filled with advice but, for my part, I have to say: don't give up; it's never too late to start – age doesn't matter unless you are cheese; don't commit to a screenplay, commit to a career; handle rejection with dignity – talent will out.

SIMON HEATH: This could also be a what not to do (like stalk our offices)! Persevere, but don't badger. Nobody likes to be bombarded with emails and calls.

SAUL DIBB: This is your chance to make your mark, so make the film you want to make – being sure to start with the knowledge that all the people behind you (financiers, producers, etc.) are on board for that. Persevere and be prepared to jump through a thousand hoops – and to go through each one successfully in order for the film to work. You have to have huge amounts of stamina, determination. What I do when I embark upon a project is write down what the essence of that project is. That way I can always come back and find my coordinates. The further you go in the filmmaking process, the easier it is to get steered away from what you originally intended to do. There are lots and lots of voices coming in and people with other agendas, trying to steer your film in one direction or another. What I find is, if I reduce in essence what it is I want to make, what I want it to be, how I want it to look, what the story I want to tell is, that is terribly useful to come back to as a compass point.

DAVID FREEDMAN: Love what you make, but never fall 'in love' with it. I made that mistake once. Never again.

CAT VILLIERS: Find your voice, your creative voice, and make yourself aware of the business as a whole. Take the time to look at how films are put together. Go to film festivals and understand that this is one of those rare industries which is both creative and business-led. Don't be afraid to break rules. If I hadn't gone and done something which everybody told me was impossible, I'd have never made my first film.

RICHARD COOKSON: Writing takes practice and creativity – so keep at it. Don't take the knock-backs personally, and remember that talent will shine through.

GRAINNE HUMPHREYS: Get the script into the best possible shape and work with the best people you can – enthusiasm and passion will get you meetings with many professionals. Finally, take your time before you premiere your film – once it's been screened, you can't take it back and start again.

368

LEE ARONSOHN: It's not too late to go to law school.

JULIETTE TOWHIDI: You have to be thin-skinned to write, then thick-skinned to survive the development process. You have to have a lot of patience, humility, an ability to listen, be a great collaborator, as well as having steely self-belief, the ability to spend hours on your own, and absolute obstinacy about your voice. You have to be utterly determined, because the system can destroy you if you're not. If that sounds contradictory it's because it is, which is why it's not a job suited to everyone. In my case, I also had to learn that things happen a lot more slowly than you hoped or anticipated. I would say, put in your 10,000 hours. There are no short cuts – just blips. Don't let producers or executives or money people put you off. They have the worldly power, but ultimately the medium belongs to us. Don't be afraid to take your time to get there. If you have talent, you also need to be dogged.

ARAB NASSER & TARZAN NASSER: It would be the same advice that we give ourselves; that art in general isn't something easy or simple. It also requires a lot of research, thinking and continuous study and being aware of what is going on. It's very important to be aware of what has been accomplished or achieved by movies before in order to be fresh with ideas. We try to create our own style, which takes longer to be discovered. Try not to think too much in terms of definition, titles and names such as 'movie producers' and the like, but think rather about the films that you will produce and the privilege of being a filmmaker.

SERENA BOWMAN: Seize any opportunity. Any work that you can get as a writer will help you hone vital skills and it's really difficult to get original work commissioned without proving yourself first. Also, get rid of any snobbery you have about writing, for example working on soaps; they are a way to hone your craft and get through the development process. I think it's very important to realise that you'll have to do a lot of hard work before you can achieve what you want to achieve.

IVANA MACKINNON: My essentials would be: find truth tellers, stay interested in things outside film, and therefore stay interesting, and try to speak in your own authentic voice, as that's what you really have to offer the world.

DESTINY EKARAGHA: The film industry can be a very hard one to function in. Sometimes it's feast, sometimes it's famine. Sometimes you're working, sometimes you're not. Sometimes it feels like the end of the world, sometimes it feels like you're on top of the world. It can be a real rollercoaster ride. My advice would be to savour every moment of it because, however we measure success, my hope is, when we get there, we'll look back on it all and laugh.

PAUL ANDREW WILLIAMS: Don't stop. The only way you'll fail is if you stop because, if you haven't stopped, there's always the possibility that you can succeed. That's a fact. It only can't be done when you stop. If you want to do anything you have to say 'I will do this no matter what it takes and I will keep going until it's done'. That works.

ANDREA CORNWELL: For writers, current knowledge is number one. If you are a writer, you should see as many films as you can, read as many screenplays as you can and be aware of what's currently in the pipeline. If you are pitching a re-versioned fairy tale or a Bible story, be aware how many of those are in circulation at the moment. There are always going to be times where you think you have a unique story, something very obscure, and unfortunately something similar will be in progress with another production company. That does happen and that's just bad luck. But there are also the trends that are subconsciously produced across the industry and you must be aware of them too. For directors it's kind of the same. It depends whether you're pitching yourself to be attached to other people's projects or if you're out selling your own work. That is certainly the most powerful place to be as a new director – somebody who is sitting on the material that people want. It's very difficult, although not impossible as a new director, to get attached to other people's

370

material unless you're one of the few super-hot commercial ones or you've made the short film of that year that everyone's excited about. Then people find themselves sitting behind major Hollywood studio productions off the back of one short film – that absolutely does happen because people always want to find the next hot thing and it's easier to take a gamble on somebody fresh. Be realistic, though – it doesn't happen very often and it tends to be people who've got a very specific niche. For example, they're coming out of the VFX world or comedy or something very specific.

KAYLEIGH LLEWELLEYN & MATTHEW BARRY: Don't be a diva. Be professional, reasonable and friendly – in short, behave in a way that will make people want to work with you. It goes a long way. Oh – and be good. If you want to be a writer – write. Stop talking about doing it and actually do it. Hard work beats talent when talent doesn't work hard.

KATE LEYS: Listen. And instead of saying 'of course, it's all about the story', read scripts, all the time.

LUCY CLARKE: Say yes to everything. It's terrifying at first, and you may fail, but you will learn and that's the important thing. Also, even the most rubbish jobs will somehow lead to other jobs, your network will grow, etc., and suddenly you're on stage accepting a BAFTA (I wish...).

SHANE ALLEN: Some people, naively thinking they've created a masterpiece, will demand a six-part series on BBC1 instead of aiming, more realistically, to do a pilot, a radio series, an online piece – something where they can learn their craft. You don't want to run too quickly. And you've got to be very, very passionate and very driven to go on that journey. Rejection is going to happen repeatedly; it happens to everyone and success comes from loads of talent and self-belief and a bit of luck. You've got to be in the right place at the right time with the right script.

FREQUENTLY ASKED QUESTIONS

I was really curious to know what people get asked the most. Having been hosting Q&As for more than 15 years, I'm always surprised by the diversity of the responses from audiences, but also how many of the same questions are raised again and again. The question I am asked the most is which one of my parents is Libyan. I guess it's because of my surname, Abushwesha (pronounced AH-BUSH-WESH-AH), sounds so Irish. So I asked the filmmakers contributing to this book what question – aside from 'Can you read my script? – they get asked the most.

ASIF KAPADIA: Each film that I am showing brings its own common questions or set questions. A lot of people don't realise I've made fiction films so it tends to be more surprise at the fact that I have made several drama films. I get asked by younger filmmakers how you survive when you make films, because that is a big problem.

MUSTAPHA KSEIBATI: Can I touch your hair?

BOB BALABAN: People are often interested in how such an unlikely sort as myself got started being an actor. I must represent some sort of living symbol of hope for accountants and lawyers and psychiatrists with thespian tendencies. I always tell them I always did everything I could to live my dream. And if I couldn't exactly live it I tried to position myself somewhere next to it.

ANDREA CORNWELL: If I'm on set then it's usually for more money!

JAMES DORMER: It's not really a question, but people always say, 'I've got a really good idea for a story – you should do this.' Everyone's interested in their own ideas – which is fair enough, as the same goes for me. Usually...

MICHAEL KUHN: Can I have a job? I say 'No!'

SHANE ALLEN: 'Can I send you something?' – I get that at every single social and industry event, which is fair enough because it's the gig! As a commissioner I also get asked 'What are you looking for at the minute, what is there room for?' And, actually, you can't be too prescriptive. There's no secret formula to commissioning; it's just driven by the ideas, really, and the best ones come out of nowhere.

PETER HARNESS: How do you become a writer? It's hard to answer that without looking like a prat. You write. If you want to be a writer, then you've got to commit to it. A lot of people say 'I'd really love to be a writer', and so would everyone else in the world. If you want to do that, give up your job, sit down and write.

PAUL ANDREW WILLIAMS: Will you read my script? I'm not saying no, but it might never happen. Every now and again I do. I don't have time to read my own stuff.

CATHERINE WILLIS: I get asked by people to be cast in their own production, or to put family members in, and that's awkward. With films, the biggest question we get about an actor being cast is 'Will they do it?' 'Will Tom Hardy do it?' And the simple answer is 'I don't know', but sometimes casting directors know or have a feeling, an instinct, whether they will or not. If an actor doesn't want to do it, they'll ask me what I said or did, and it's all the casting director's fault. I've been doing this a while so don't question my methods! I would say 'The script isn't there yet, but these guys have real potential'. That means more than you going in saying 'This is the best script ever'. Agents trust me because I've been doing it for so long.

CLAIRE WILSON: What have I seen of yours? Do you write the dialogue or the action? I wonder why people are so baffled by the role of a writer.

REBECCA DALY: 'Is it more difficult to be a female director than a male director?' 'Why are there so many female characters in your films?' Gender needs to be discussed and is definitely an issue. I wish the questions I got were more interesting and dealt more with the actual issue, though. I just think it runs deeper than these kinds of questions. I often think, 'Well, I've never been a male director so I wouldn't know.' I'd love to get to a place where no one asked me why I have so many female characters in a film, that it could be seen as not such an unusual choice.

DANNY BROCKLEHURST: Do I know anyone famous – yeah, I know Max Beesley.

LAWRENCE COCHRAN: I'm asked by my circle of friends why we're not making *Breaking Bad* or *The Wire*, and I get into heated debates about the BBC being for everyone, not just the people who like that type of show.

ROB BROWN: Is your director of photography, Justin Brown, your brother? (He isn't.)

LUCY CLARKE: How do you think of jokes? Tell us a joke (which I can't, as I never remember jokes, even when I only wrote them two hours ago – weird, I know).

RICHARD COOKSON: What is Steven Moffat really like? New writers usually ask about how to get their work seen or what we're looking for in new projects.

GLENN MONTGOMERY: When's your next film coming out? No one seems to grasp just how long it takes to complete a film. People tend to lose interest as three years go by and you're still waiting to go into production and people forget.

MANJINDER VIRK: Do I want to act, write or direct? To which I would answer that the three are compatible and that each informs the other.

SUSAN JACOBSON: How do you get the finance to make a film? It's always about money.

SALLY EL HOSAINI: I keep getting asked about being a 'female director'. I hate those questions. I'm so tired of it, but I understand it's because there haven't been a whole lot of women directing films. I've always chosen not to let my gender come into the equation. It doesn't affect what stories I want to tell, or how I want to tell them. Virginia Woolf said that a writer being androgynous would lead to true creative freedom. In that sense my ideal is to be an androgynous filmmaker.

MIRANDA BOWEN: How did you do it for the money?

JULIETTE TOWHIDI: 'Are you pleased with it?' upon submitting a draft, which is impossible to answer without sounding either smug or unprofessional.

LEADS AND LISTS

These lists are by no means comprehensive and definitive and, although all information is correct at the time of publication, you should check the individual websites for details of how to submit your work. Always research the approach policies for submitting scripts or approaching an agent/agency first – agents have different preferences/specialisations/remits. Send them what they ask for – nothing more and nothing less.

I see these lists as a way to get you started – for something more comprehensive look at the following publications and websites:

- The Writers' & Artists' Yearbook
- The Writers Guild of America
- Talent-Agencies Find The Best
- Agent Query
- Contacts

UK AGENTS WHO ACCEPT UNSOLICITED SUBMISSIONS

- Blake Friedmann (www.blakefriedmann.co.uk)
- Cecily Ware Literary Agents (www.cecilyware.com)
- Dench Arnold (www.dencharnold.com)
- JFL Agency (www.jflagency.com)

- Linda Seifert Management Agency (www.lindaseifert.com)
- Marjacq Scripts (www.marjacq.com)
- MBA Literary Agents (www.mbalit.co.uk)
- Micheline Steinberg Associates (www.steinplays.com)
- Rochelle Stevens and Company (www.rochellestevens.com)
- Sheil Land Associates (www.sheilland.com)
- The Lisa Richards Agency (www.lisarichards.ie)
- The Tennyson Agency (www.tenagy.co.uk)
- Valerie Hoskins Associates (www.vhassociates.co.uk)

UK AGENTS BY REFERRAL ONLY

These agents don't accept unsolicited material, only work based on recommendations or by invitation. Allow up to 12 weeks to hear back. You should say in the cover note who has recommended you.

- Berlin Associates (www.berlinassociates.com)
- Burkeman & Clarke (www.burkemanandclarke.com)
- Casarotto (www.casarotto.co.uk)
- Creative Artists Agency (www.caa.com)
- Curtis Brown (www.curtisbrown.co.uk)
- David Higham Associates (www.davidhigham.co.uk)
- Gemma Hirst Associates (www.gemmahirst.co.uk)
- Imagine Talent (www.imaginetalent.co.uk)
- Janet Fillingham Associates (www.janetfillingham.com)
- Kitson Management Ltd (www.kitsonmanagement.co.uk) – soon to be launching a new initiative called KM's New Dramatists' Club.
- Knight Hall Agency (www.knighthallagency.com)
- Peters Fraser and Dunlop (www.petersfraserdunlop.com)
- Sayle Screen (www.saylescreen.com)
- Smart Talent (www.smart-talent-kent.co.uk)

- The Agency (www.theagency.co.uk)
- The Writers' Company (www.writerscompany.co.uk)
- United Agents (www.unitedagents.co.uk)

US AGENTS WHO ACCEPT UNSOLICITED SUBMISSIONS

- Above the Line Agency (www.abovethelineagency.com)
- Abrams Artists Agency (www.abramsartists.com)
- Affinity Artists Agency (www.affinityartists.com)
- Allensworth Entertainment, Inc (www.allensworthentertainment.com)
- Alpern Group (www.alperngroup.com)
- Brogan Agency (www.thebroganagency.com)
- Filmtrix Agency (www.filmtrix.com)
- Suite A Management (no website)

US AGENTS BY REFERRAL ONLY

- Circle of Confusion (www.circleofconfusion.com)
- Creative Artists Agency (www.caa.com)
- Gersh Agency (www.gershagency.com)
- Innovative Artists (www.innovativeartists.com)
- International Creative Management Partners (www.icmtalent.com)
- Kerwin Agency (www.kerwinagency.com)
- Monteiro Rose Draven Agency (www.monteiro-rose.com)
- Original Artists (www.original-artists.com)
- Paradigm Talent Agency (www.paradigmagency.com)
- Rebel Entertainment Agency (www.reptalent.com)
- Verve Talent Agency (www.vervetla.com)
- William Morris Endeavor (www.wma.com)

LISTS OF THEATRES OPEN TO UNSOLICITED SUBMISSIONS

Most of these theatres have an unsolicited policy which means they have remits, submission processes, creative briefs and windows of opportunities. Check their websites carefully for details and deadlines. This list is by no means exhaustive but is just to get you started.

UK

- Arcola – www.arcolatheatre.com
- Bush Theatre – www.bushtheatre.co.uk
- Everyman Theatre – www.everymanplayhouse.com
- Finborough Theatre – www.finboroughtheatre.co.uk
- Hampstead Theatre – www.hampsteadtheatre.com
- Lyric Theatre Belfast – www.lyrictheatre.co.uk
- National Theatre – www.nationaltheatre.org.uk
- Old Red Lion – www.oldredliontheatre.co.uk
- Royal Court Theatre – www.royalcourttheatre.com
- Royal Exchange – www.royalexchange.co.uk
- Sherman Cymru – www.shermancymru.co.uk
- Soho Theatre – www.sohotheatre.com
- The Traverse Theatre – www.traverse.co.uk
- Theatre 503 – www.theatre503.com
- Tinderbox Belfast – www.tinderbox.org.uk
- West Yorkshire Playhouse – www.wyp.org.uk

Ireland

- Abbey Theatre – www.abbeytheatre.ie
- Druid Theatre – www.druid.ie
- Fishamble – www.fishamble.com

- New Theatre – www.thenewtheatre.com
- Scripts – Ireland's playwriting festival - www.scriptsireland.com
- Theatre Upstairs – www.theatreupstairs.ie

LIST OF SHOWCASES/INITIATIVES

- Academy Nicholl Fellowships in Screenwriting
- BFI London Film Festival – First Film Competition
- BlueCat Screenplay Competition
- Carl Foreman Award
- Catalyst funding and mentoring scheme
- Coming Up – Channel 4
- Douglas Hickox Award
- IFB/JDIFF Untitled
- iFeatures initiative
- Microwave film scheme
- Northern Ireland New Talent Focus
- Page International Screenwriting Awards
- Red Planet Prize
- Sitcom Trials
- Wellcome Trust and BFI Screenwriting Fellowship in association with Film4

LIST OF FESTIVALS, CONFERENCES AND TALENT CAMPUSES

Most of these festivals run talent campuses, for which you need to apply well in advance.

- Austin Film Festival & Screenwriting Conference
- Berlin Talent Campus
- BFI
- Binger Institute

- Doha Screenwriting Institute
- Dubai International Film Festival
- Equinoxe
- Galway Film Fleadh
- Guardian Edinburgh International TV Festival
- ICA Lab
- Jameson Dublin International Film Festival
- LOCO
- London Screenwriting Festival
- Mediterranean Film Institute Script 2 Film Workshops
- New York TV Festival
- Sundance Labs
- Torino Film Lab

LIST OF COURSES – UK AND IRELAND ONLY

The following is a selective list of organisations that run both long and short courses.

- City Academy
- Euroscript
- Filmbase
- London Film Academy
- London Film School
- Met Film School
- NFTS
- Professional Writing Academy
- Pulse College
- Raindance
- Royal Conservatoire of Scotland

- Screen Academy Scotland
- Skribita
- Storylining
- The Two Phils
- Writers' Gym – Ellis Freeman

LIST OF SCRIPT CRAFT GURUS

Creative Essentials provide accessible, comprehensive and affordable how-to guides on a range of subjects, written by experts in their field. They include case studies and in-depth analysis, practical advice, interviews with key creatives and resource guides to funding bodies, distribution outlets, available courses, and come complete with DVDs packed with additional material ranging from shorts and extracts, to templates, spreadsheets, sample contracts, release forms, checklists and more. They aim to provide a one-stop solution for experts and beginners alike, for experienced and aspiring writers, directors, filmmakers, teachers and students.

Here are some other contributor recommendations:

- Aristotle – *Poetics*
- Blake Snyder – *Save the Cat* (book and seminars)
- Charlie Harris – *Complete Screenwriting Course: Teach Yourself (Teach Yourself: Writing)*
- Christopher Vogler – *The Writer's Journey: Mythic Structure for Writers*
- Craig Batty – *Screenplays: How to Write and Sell Them*
- David Trottier – *The Screenwriter's Bible*
- Jeff Bollow – *FAST Screenplay* (online system)
- Jeffrey Schechter – *My Story Can Beat Up Your Story* (also developed TotallyWrite software and seminars, and the advanced screenwriting structuring application, Contour)

- John Truby – *The Anatomy of Story, Great Screenwriting* (DVD/ Video/MP3 audio seminar course), *Blockbuster* (story software)
- John Yorke – *Into the Woods: How Stories Work and Why We Tell Them*
- Joseph Campbell – *The Hero with a Thousand Faces*
- Julie Gray – *Just Effing Entertain Me*, Tel Aviv Writer's Salon, The Red Slipper Writer's Room
- Karl Iglesias – *Writing for Emotional Impact*
- Kate Leys – Feature-film script editor. Teaches masterclasses and workshops at various places during the year including the London Film School and Binger Institute.
- Konstantin Stanislavski – *An Actor Prepares, Building a Character, Creating a Role*
- Lajos Egri – *The Art of Dramatic Writing*
- Linda Seger – *Making a Good Script Great*
- Lucy V Hay – various books on writing
- Marilyn Horowitz – *How to Write a Screenplay in 10 Weeks, The Four Magic Questions of Screenwriting* (books and seminars)
- Michael Hauge – *Writing Screenplays That Sell*
- Phil Parker – The Writers' Factory (courses in the UK)
- Pilar Alessandra – *The Coffee Break Screenwriter, On the Page* DVD, classes and script consultation
- Robert McKee – *STORY* (book and seminar)
- Ronald Tobias – *20 Master Plots*
- Syd Field – *The Foundations of Screenwriting, Screenplay, The Screenwriter's Handbook, Four Screenplays*
- William C Martell – *The Secrets of Action Screenwriting* (17 Blue-Books & Audio Courses)
- William Goldman – *Adventures in the Screen Trade, Which Lie Did I Tell?: More Adventures in the Screen Trade*
- Yves Lavandier – *Writing Drama*